Logics of Disintegration

Logics of Disintegration

Post-structuralist Thought and the Claims of Critical Theory

---◆---

PETER DEWS

VERSO

London · New York

First published by Verso 1987
Second impression 1988
© Peter Dews 1987

Verso
UK: 6 Meard Street, London W1V 3HR
USA: 29 West 35th Street, New York, NY 10001 2291

Verso is the imprint of New Left Books

British Library Cataloguing in Publication Data

Dews, Peter
    Logics of disintegration: post-structuralist thought
    and the claims of critical theory.
    1. Structuralism (Literary analysis)
    I. Title
    801′.95   PN98.S7

* **US Library of Congress Cataloging in Publication Data**

Dews, Peter
    Logics of disintegration.

    Bibliography: p.
    Includes index.
    1. Structuralism.   2. Frankfurt school of sociology.
    3. Philosophy, French—20th century.   I. Title.
B841.4.D49   1987   149′.96   87–21623

ISBN 0-86091-105-5
ISBN 0-86091-813-0 (pbk.)

Typeset by Boldface Typesetters, London EC1
Printed and bound in Great Britain by
Biddles Ltd, Guildford and King's Lynn

For my mother and father

Contents

Preface and Acknowledgements

The origins of this book date back a long way, to my first encounter with post-structuralism as a postgraduate student at the University of Essex in the mid 1970s. At the time, I was struck by the power of inventiveness of post-structuralist thinking, while simultaneously being disturbed by an awareness that many of its implications ran counter to my most deeply held political convictions. Over the year, I have tried to work through this tension theoretically, in the belief that the logic of disintegration can ultimately be resisted on logical grounds.

I would like to thank the following friends and colleagues for having commented on sections of the manuscript at various stages of its development: Perry Anderson, Jay Bernstein, Paul Davies, Tony Manser, Francis Mulhern, Peter Osborne, David Pugmire, Jonathan Rée, Hugh Tomlinson and David Wood. I would also like to thank those students – some of whom are now friends – who attended my classes on Continental philosophy in the Extra-Mural Department of London University between 1982 and 1986, and in collaboration with whom many of the themes of this book were initially argued through. I have fond memories of our lively discussions, both inside and outside the classroom. Georgie Born, Andrew Bowie, Barrie Selwyn and Julian Roberts have helped me a great deal through their friendship and encouragement. Colin Dibben assisted with last-minute proof reading. And finally, I owe thanks which I can scarcely begin to express to Ruby Briggs, for all her advice and solidarity over many years.

Parts of chapter 4 first appeared in *Diacritics*, Fall 1984, under the title 'The Letter and the Line: Discourse and its Other in Lyotard'. I am grateful to the Johns Hopkins University Press for permission to reprint this material. Chapter 5 is a slightly altered version of an essay which first appeared in *New Left Review* 144, March-April 1984, under the title 'Power and Subjectivity in Foucault'.

Wherever possible, reference has been made to accessible English editions of texts which first appeared in other languages, but I have frequently revised the translations or provided my own.

Peter Dews
Cambridge
July 1987

Introduction

Over the past two decades the style of French thought known as
post-structuralism has exercised an extraordinary influence over
intellectual life in the English-speaking world. Post-structuralist
strategies and forms of analysis, oriented towards the dismantling
of stable conceptions of meaning, subjectivity and identity, have
become central to the theoretical armoury, and in some cases have
brought about the transformation, of a wide variety of disciplines
in the humanities and social studies. In the field of literary
criticism, the procedures of deconstruction pioneered in the work
of Jacques Derrida have sparked off wide-ranging debates on the
nature of literature, its relation to other forms of textuality, and –
beyond this – on the fundamental philosophical issues of language
and interpretation. In the domain of social theory and the history
of thought, the writings of Michel Foucault have been a major
stimulus, encouraging new perspectives on the relation between
political, administrative and epistemological structures, while
Jacques Lacan's reformulation of psychoanalysis has contributed
to developments in areas such as film and cultural theory, and has
provided the focus of debates on gender construction in contemporary feminism. More recently, the work of Jean-François Lyotard has become widely known as a significant intervention in the
current discussion of modernity and postmodernity, a discussion
which brings many of the regional analyses of post-structuralism
to bear on the task of a more general characterization of the
present age. Furthermore, it is not merely in the English-speaking
world that the French thought of the 1960s has exercised this
power. The recent history of Italian philosophy and social theory,

for example, has been marked by a constant critical reference to French paradigms, while in Germany post-structuralist interpretations of native thinkers such as Nietzsche and Heidegger have become an increasingly influential component of the dominant intellectual mood. Indeed, throughout the advanced capitalist world – and beyond – post-structuralism has achieved far more than a merely academic diffusion and has helped to shape a broader political and cultural climate.

But whatever the continuing vitality of post-structuralist modes of thought outside the borders of their country of origin, post-structuralism can no longer be considered a living force in France itself. In retrospect, a shift of philosophical outlook as radical as that represented by the rise of structuralism in the early 1960s, can now be seen to have begun in the mid 1970s, when the ephemeral *Nouveaux Philosophes* appeared on the intellectual scene. For, despite its superficial and journalistic tenor, the *Nouvelle Philosophie*, with its insistence on the political primacy of human rights, its calls for a revival of metaphysical thinking, and its explicit espousal of the religious, did function to break down a number of taboos which had constrained French thought over the previous decade and a half. From the late 1970s onwards it became possible to pose *philosophical* questions about the foundations of ethics, the nature of political principles, and the universal status of legal rights, in a manner which would have been unthinkable during the heady years of 'anti-humanist' and 'post-philosophical' experimentation. However, unlike the transition from 'phenomenology' to 'structuralism', the decline of post-structuralism has not been brought about by the emergence of a relatively cohesive new philosophical outlook. Rather, the undermining of the dogmatic avant-garde consciousness of post-structuralism has made possible a fragmentation and pluralization of philosophical activity in France. In some cases there has been a return to a more explicit Heideggerian allegiance, combined with an intensification of interest in figures connected to the Heideggerian tradition, such as Levinas and Blanchot, often as a means of access to religious and ethical questions. In others, there has been a revival of phenomenological and hermeneutic themes; for example, a re-evaluation of Merleau-Ponty, and of thinkers such as Paul Ricoeur, whose work – much of it produced during the 1960s and 1970s – was formerly unjustly marginalized by the predominance of structuralism and post-structuralism. There has also been a significant revival of political philosophy in France, exemplified by the recent work of Claude Lefort,[1] with new appropriations of the distinctive Tocquevillian tradition of French liberalism, more sociologically and historically oriented than its Anglo-Saxon counterpart. Finally, there has been a vigorous opening out of French thought towards alternative intellectual traditions, in particular a new sympathy for the procedures and concerns of analytical philosophy, and an interest in contemporary German debates in the areas of aesthetics, hermeneutics and Critical Theory.

If one were to attempt, however, despite this pluralization, to identify one development which would symbolize the distinctiveness of the French philosophical scene in the 1980s, compared with the entire preceding period since the Second World War, then the obvious choice would be the upsurge of interest in Kant, a thinker who had been out of fashion in France for over fifty years, since the Hegel renaissance of the 1930s. What this turn towards Kant indicates is an appreciation that the Nietzschean assault on a repressive reason itself depends on a dogmatic conception of the relation between knowledge and pre-cognitive interests, that an unqualified hostility to the universal in the domain of ethics and politics has a profoundly menacing – as well as an emancipatory – aspect, and that a wilful self-restriction of analysis to the fragmentary and the perspectival renders impossible any coherent understanding of our own historical and cultural situation. Kant's virtue, in the eyes of contemporary French philosophers, is to have definitively unmasked the claims of totalizing metaphysics (for which read: the Hegelian and Marxist traditions), without undermining the objectivity of moral principles, and without ruling out entirely the use of totalizing concepts, which are attributed a specific *regulative* status. More generally, the need to transcend a reductive relativism towards a more universal standpoint, particularly in the domain of ethics and right, is now no longer seriously at issue among French philosophers: such universality is seen as an indispensable brake on potentially coercive claims to self-realization, whether Hegelian, Marxist or Nietzschean in origin. The real focus of debate is rather the *status* to be attributed to this universality: whether it derives from an experience of the transcendent,[2] whether it can be grounded through transcendental reflection in a manner close to that of Kant himself,[3] or whether – as argued by thinkers influenced by Foucault – it can be understood in a more historicist mode, as a central component of *our* tradition.[4]

Unfortunately, as is characteristic of major shifts of intellectual orientation, where a polemical attitude tends to predominate, particularly among the rising generation, it can scarcely be said that the modes of French thought of the 1980s have formed a balanced evaluation of the strengths and weaknesses of their immediate predecessors. Just as structuralism and post-structuralism masked the complexities of the phenomenology of Sartre and Merleau-Ponty, by attacking a parodied conception of the subject as fully self-grounding and self-transparent to which neither had adhered, so the new sympathies for enlightenment and modernity have tended to obliterate the strengths of the post-structuralist interrogation of philosophical reason. A clear example of this distortion of perspective can be found in the work of Luc Ferry and Alain Renaut, two of the most active of the younger generation of philosophers, who have attempted a comprehensive evaluation of what they term '*La Pensée 68*'[5]. For despite the validity of Ferry and Renaut's highlighting of the political dangers and incoherences of a thoroughgoing anti-humanism, the force of the thought of Marx, Freud and Nietzsche can scarcely be sidestepped by the elementary move of pointing out the self-undermining character of the determinism supposedly implied by the 'hermeneutics of suspicion', by countering genealogy with simple asseverations of the autonomy of textual meaning, or by appealing to a Popperian epistemology which is still a novelty in France.[6] Similarly, the currently popular theme of the revival of the autonomy of philosophy, its escape from an irresponsible Nietzschean vandalism, seems curiously out of step with the intense self-questioning of philosophy which is continuing elsewhere, and which post-structuralism, amongst other intellectual currents, has helped to inspire. The valid recognition of the need to draw on the conceptual resources of the philosophical tradition, and a foreshortening of perspective which conflates structuralism and post-structuralism, has produced a curious restoration climate, in which the need is felt to protect philosophy from a supposedly diminishing relation to the human sciences.[7]

Given these unbalanced reactions, it might appear that more sustained and considered critical attention has been paid to the strengths and weaknesses of post-structuralist thought *outside* France. Certainly, in the English-speaking world there has been an intense and widespread debate around the issues raised by post-structuralism, and a great deal of penetrating and sophisticated commentary has been produced. However, because – up until recently, at least – post-structuralist thought has been predominantly taken up by literary and cultural critics, rather than by philosophers, certain characteristic limitations have marked the reception and evaluation of post-structuralism. Most obviously, writers whose prime concern is with the application of post-structuralist theory, and whose predominant expertise is in the field of literature and literary and cultural history, have often tended to exaggerate the novelty of post-structuralist positions, sometimes to an almost apocalyptic extent. The avant-garde consciousness of post-structuralism, what Habermas describes as the sense of 'invading unknown territory, exposing [oneself] to the dangers of sudden, shocking encounters, conquering an as yet unoccupied future',[8] has been taken at face value, with little attempt being made to enquire into possible philosophical antecedents of the positions discussed or adopted, or into their relations to other contemporary philosophical currents. It is for this reason that, in the first chapter of this study, I have chosen to devote so much attention to a debate in the history of philosophy – namely that between Fichte and Schelling – which at first sight may appear remote from contemporary concerns. For the reception of Derrida's work, perhaps more than that of any other recent French thinker, has been marked by an astonishingly casual and unquestioning acceptance of certain extremely condensed – not to say sloganistic – characterizations of the history of Western thought, as if this history could be dismissed through its reduction to a set of perfunctory dualisms. At the very least, I hope to have shown that the strategy of Derrida's critique of transcendental philosophy, and the problems which this strategy raises, are not entirely unprecedented, and that the assumption – central to the whole pattern of post-structuralist thinking – that the concept of the subject implies an immobile, self-identical, and constitutive centre of experience seriously underplays the complexity and subtlety of the ways in which subjectivity has been explored within the Western philosophical tradition.

The second major limitation of the Anglo-Saxon reception of post-structuralist thought has been a continuing lack of clarity about the political consequences of its characteristic positions. Again, one could argue, this failure is the result of a predominant concern with application amongst those thinkers in the English-speaking world who have taken up the devices and approaches of post-structuralism. For while there has often been a *de facto* alliance between the intellectual Left and recent French theory, with post-structuralism providing tools of analysis which have been widely applied, there has sometimes been little attempt to think through the ultimate compatibility of progressive political commitments with the dissolution of the subject, or a totalizing suspicion of the concept of truth. In this respect, however, the debate over the political content of post-structuralism has frequently not been much advanced by those critics, whether from the Left or from the Right, who are more sensitive to its social implications. From a conservative, humanist position – for example – Gerald Graff has had many perceptive things to say about the ethos of post-structuralism, about its continuity with modes of thought – such as romanticism – with which it takes itself to have broken, and about its fundamental complicity with the 'real ''avant-garde'' [of] advanced capitalism, with its built-in need to destroy all vestiges of tradition, all orthodox ideologies, all continuous and stable forms of reality in order to stimulate higher levels of consumption.'[9] Similar arguments have, of course, also been made from the Left – for example by Terry Eagleton.[10] Yet one often has the impression that such criticism ultimately relies on a moral appeal, leaving the central contentions of post-structuralism, which are powerful and complex, untackled and undefeated on their own terrain. It is not sufficient to point to the ultimate passivity, or even the politically disastrous implications, of a mode of thought which prides itself precisely on a reckless integrity and consistency, and which is therefore willing to brave all consequences. Rather, it must be shown that, for all its posture of radicality, post-structuralist thought is itself bound to certain vulnerable and unquestioned assumptions. The fundamental issue here, of course, is the sense in which a philosophical position which assumes the foundations of the classical forms of critique to be necessarily and oppressively identitarian can itself continue to perform a critical function. Can post-structuralism dismiss the claims of critical theory (in the sense of its titles) while continuing to satisfy these claims (in the sense of its demands)?

The present book has been written as a contribution to the exploration of this question, in a climate where internal developments within the mainstream of English-speaking philosophy have led to post-structuralism finally ceasing to be an almost exclusively literary preserve, and to greater possibilities of interchange between different philosophical traditions. Its approach is to establish a set of contrasts and *rapprochements*, both between the work of four prominent post-structuralist thinkers, and between the themes of post-structuralism as a whole and the treatment of similar issues to be found within the work of the Frankfurt School. This tradition has been taken as the pole of comparison because, as the recent upsurge of interest in post-structuralism among contemporary Critical Theorists suggests,[11] there are striking convergences between the Frankfurt interpretation of Marxism and post-structuralist thought. Yet for all its suspicion of the complicity between philosophy and domination, and its awareness of the repressive functioning of classical conceptions of truth and reason, Critical Theory never abandons the aim of an integrated understanding of the dynamics of modernity. While grounded in Marx and the 'hermeneutics of suspicion', it also seeks to retain the indispensable heritage of classical German philosophy. In the light of this synthesis, as I hope to demonstrate, the relations between post-structuralist positions can be read as revealing an unstable process of compensation, in pursuit of an understanding whose possibility has in fact already been ruled out on a priori grounds.

In conclusion, a few words should perhaps be said about the temporal and thematic confines of the present work. For reasons which will by now have begun to become clear, the cut-off point for extended discussion in this study is the late 1970s, for by this time post-structuralism can be said to have already dissolved as a cohesive set of attitudes in France. It is clear that major works of Foucault's last period, in their concern with problems of individuality and ethical conduct, with the relation between freedom and truth, and with the self-interpreting and self-constituting activity of the subject, have broken with many of the Nietzschean assumptions which were central to his thought throughout the major part of his career.[12] Similarly, it can be argued that Lyotard's two books dating from 1979, *Just Gaming* and *The Postmodern Condition*, are transitional works, already introducing Kantian themes, and revealing a new respect for the rationality of debate and dialogue, if not for consensus. Fascinating as these transformations and reconciliations in the work of Foucault and Lyotard are, it would be inappropriate to include discussion of them – even if there were space – within a work whose aim is to explore the nature of an earlier, supposedly 'post-philosophical' phase. I have, however, made some brief remarks about these developments, as well as pointing out some similar – less acknowledged – discrepancies in Jacques Derrida's evolution. Finally, some explanation should perhaps be given for the omission of any extended discussion of the work of Gilles Deleuze. Deleuze is unique among post-structuralist thinkers for the constancy with which his thought has been guided by certain fundamental Nietzschean assumptions. However, having decided that it was feasible to discuss only one version of the direct Nietzscheanism which reached the peak of its influence during the 1970s, I have chosen to concentrate on the work of Jean-François Lyotard. This is not only because – in contrast with Deleuze and Guattari's *Anti-Oedipus* – this phase of Lyotard's thought is still comparatively little known in the English-speaking world, and throws a different light on his later concern with 'postmodernity', but also because, in its instructive engagements with Merleau-Ponty and Lacan, and its own internal development, it illustrates in an exemplary way the motivation, dynamic, and difficulties of the philosophy of desire.

1

Jacques Derrida:
The Transcendental and Difference

Although 'post-structuralism' is the term most commonly employed in the English-speaking world to refer to those philosophical currents which succeeded the enthusiasm for formalist and objectivist modes of thought which typified the early and mid 1960s in France, this designation cannot be understood in a strictly chronological sense. For long before structuralism became, albeit briefly, the dominant intellectual fashion, its oversights and limitations had already been pinpointed by thinkers whose work would be later included under the rubric of post-structuralism. In his seminars of the mid 1950s, for example, Lacan had already criticized the deterministic tendency of Lévi-Strauss's thought, which led to the transformation of social structure into a kind of 'para-animal formation' or machine, and consequently to an inability to account for the eccentric position of the speaking subject.[1] Similarly, Michel Foucault's *Madness and Civilization*, published in 1961, was informed by a sensitivity to the repressive functioning of the modern human sciences, which preceded the vogue for the human sciences launched by Lévi-Strauss's work in anthropology, and in particular by the publication of *The Savage Mind* in 1962, whose final chapter emblematically demolished Jean-Paul Sartre's philosophy of history. At the same time, however, both Foucault and Lacan were, in their different ways, profoundly influenced by structuralism. Lacan's conception of a 'symbolic order' which constitutes the primary unconscious determinants of human speech and action was directly derived from Lévi-Strauss's theory of society as a complex of signifying systems, while Foucault's work of the later

1

1960s attempted to apply, in the domain of the history of knowledge, the conception of structures independent of – and determining – human consciousness.

A further level of complexity is introduced into these relations by the fact that Nietzsche's influence, which seems typical of the post-structuralism of the 1970s, was felt *before* the structuralist wave of the sixties. The clearest example of this is perhaps Deleuze's *Nietzsche and Philosophy*, dating from 1962, which outlines an anti-dialectical strategy, based upon a philosophy of forces, which was to be central to some of the major texts of the following decade, including Deleuze's own *Anti-Oedipus*. But Foucault, too, has stressed that it was a reading of Nietzsche, rather than Saussure or Lévi-Strauss, which enabled him to break with 'historicism and Hegelianism', and the rationalist teleology of phenomenological approaches to the history of science, during the 1950s.[2] From this standpoint, the turn towards structuralism in the work of thinkers such as Deleuze and Foucault can be seen as a kind of temporary expedient, an alternative means of achieving their anti-historicist and anti-subjectivist goals, which could in turn be discarded when the intellectual mood began to turn against what came to be seen as the restricting claims of objectivity. The sudden irruption of a paean to Nietzsche, in the midst of the strict, dispassionate analyses of *The Order of Things*, is undoubtedly the most striking symptom of this tense and complex relationship between pre-structuralism, structuralism, and post-structuralism.[3]

Nevertheless, the chronological implications of the last of these terms cannot be entirely discounted. For although post-structuralism can be shown to be 'older' than structuralism itself in France, it was not until the late 1960s that the possibility of a theoretical advance beyond structuralism began to dawn upon public consciousness. Up until this point, even projects as diverse as those of Foucault and Lacan, and as subversive of Lévi-Strauss's original intentions, could be included under the generic title of structuralism, the common denominator of hostility towards phenomenology, and a new precision of attention paid to the immanent relations constituting symbolic or discursive systems, being sufficient to obscure any deeper theoretical discrepancies.[4] Furthermore, such was the implicit equation of philosophical activity with a phenomenology of the Sartrian type, that Lévi-Strauss's proclamation of the redundancy of the concept of the subject seemed to herald the end of philosophy – considered as a speculative, narcissistic and unscientific mode of discourse – altogether. The theme of a positivist supersession of philosophy was in the air, and, in their different ways – Lacan as psychoanalyst, Foucault as historian of cultural formations, even Althusser as theoretician of theoretical practice – the leading French thinkers of the early and middle 1960s tended to present their work as being not simply anti-phenomenological, but as something other than philosophy in the traditional sense, as convergent – if not identical – with science.

In this respect, the structuralist vogue can in part be seen as a turning away from German philosophical models towards the major *native* philosophical tradition of the twentieth century, that of positivism. Behind the figure of Lévi-Strauss, it often seems to be Durkheim who is providing the fundamental assumptions for the theoretical enterprises of the middle sixties.[5] For it was Durkheim who, long before Lévi-Strauss, abandoned the philosophy in which he had been trained out of dissatisfaction with its literary and unscientific character, its empty dialectical ingenuity, yet remained committed to the resolution of philosophical problems with social-scientific means. Furthermore, a number of distinctive features of Durkheim's programme can be seen to have left their stamp on the structuralist work of the sixties. One can note, firstly, a resolute objectivism, combined with the conviction that systems of collective representations form an ontologically autonomous level of reality, a conviction which distinguishes this tradition from the type of reductionist positivism more familiar in the English-speaking world – philosophically, an attempt is made to steer between empiricism and Kantianism, by treating categorial structures not as immutable features of the human mind, but as embedded in social contexts; secondly, a stress on the priority of social and symbolic systems over the individual, who acts under their constraint, and on the fact that the operation of these systems is unconscious, determining the individual in ways of which he or she cannot be aware; and lastly, a critique of introspection as a mode of knowledge, and a belief that philosophical speculation depends upon unwarranted extrapolation from the experience of the individual. Traces of this constellation of attitudes appear in the work of figures such as Foucault, Althusser and Barthes during the 1960s, with a persistence suggesting deeper cultural roots than the work of Lévi-Strauss. One significant contrast with Durkheim, however, can be observed in the fact that, whereas Durkheim was willing to engage in discussion of his own epistemological standpoint, even if the outcome of such engagements was not entirely satisfactory, structuralism in general repudiated any epistemological enquiry, or reflexive interrogation of its own assumptions, undoubtedly in large part because it was believed that any such enquiry could only be conducted within the terms of a philosophy of consciousness and the subject.

In 1967, however, the philosopher Jacques Derrida published a cluster of works – *Speech and Phenomena*, *Writing and Difference*, and *Of Grammatology* – which marked the first major break with this structuralist consensus, and rapidly secured their author a leading position in French intellectual life. In contrast to the majority of his contemporaries, who – as we have seen – accepted some kind of *rapprochement* with structuralism, Derrida had refused, from his first essays of the late 1950s onwards, to accept the 'self-evidence' of the methodological precepts on which structuralism relied. From the beginning he insisted that the structuralist human sciences, far from being capable of supplanting philosophy, were based upon philosophical, indeed metaphysical, assumptions which demanded interrogation, and in doing so he restored the rights of philosophical thought – or at least of some successor to philosophy – to challenge the role and status of the sciences, rather than being obliged to approximate to this status.[6] In retrospect, Derrida has spoken of his 'solitude', and of his 'oblique, deviant, sometimes directly critical relationship' to the dominant theoretical modes of the 1958-68 period, during which he established the bases of his own position.[7] This is not to suggest, of course, that Derrida was the first thinker to develop a philosophical critique of structuralism: from the very beginning the structuralist advance had been challenged by writers of the calibre of Sartre, Merleau-Ponty, Lefebvre and Ricoeur. Yet, for all their frequent acuity, these critiques went largely unheeded, since their refusal to abandon entirely the concept of the subject, and their recourse to 'pre-structuralist' philosophical resources – Hegelian and existentialist versions of Marxism, phenomenology, hermeneutics – could be dismissed as theoretically regressive. It was not until the early 1980s, when the political perils of 'anti-humanism' had become unmistakably apparent, that any significant revaluation of the traditions represented by these thinkers began.

Derrida and Husserlian Phenomenology

Derrida's success, in the intellectual climate of the late 1960s, was based upon an ingenious double theoretical movement, which is central to all his work. He began as a phenomenologist, centrally influenced by Husserl, and his major philosophical debts are clearly to precisely those thinkers – Hegel, Husserl and Heidegger – whose authority structuralism was taken to have undermined. This affiliation to the tradition of German Idealism allowed Derrida to develop a powerful critique of the limitations of an ahistorical formalism and positivism. Yet, at the same time, Derrida turns many of the insights of the structuralist critique of meaning and of the subject against the tradition to which he belongs, thereby creating the impression of a break even more radical than that of structuralism with phenomenology and the philosophy of consciousness.

Given the frequency of relativistic appropriations of Derrida, particularly in the English-speaking world, it is important for an understanding of the overall structure of Derrida's thought to note that his critique of structuralism, and of associated positions, is heavily reliant upon a reactivation of the *anti-relativist* impulse of Husserl's phenomenology. One of the driving forces of Husserl's thought is a reaction to the climate of intellectual crisis which pervaded the years around the turn of the century, a crisis which the very success of the nineteenth century in extending empirical science into the human domain – in the form of psychology, anthropology, historiography – had largely contributed. For if all human beliefs, as these disciplines suggested, could be explained as the effects of natural, psychological or historical causes, it no longer seemed possible for any particular set of beliefs, whether religious, scientific or philosophical, to claim a privileged objectivity or veracity. The nascent 'human sciences' themselves appeared to lead towards a self-cancelling scepticism and relativism.[8]

Husserl's solution to this problem relies on two fundamental contentions: that even those theories which suggest an external conditioning of consciousness must ultimately be based upon data which are presented to consciousness, and that, in all such experience it is possible to distinguish *what* is presented from *the fact that* it is presented, the essential from the empirical. Thus, whatever the causes of experience and belief discovered by scientific investigation, such discoveries cannot affect the intrinsic meaning of phenomena, as these are initially revealed to consciousness. This meaning can be revealed by suspending the ontological and theoretical commitments of the 'natural attitude', up to and including the very belief in a world independent of consciousness – an operation which Husserl terms the 'transcendental *epoche*' or 'reduction'. In this way, not only will historical or psychological relativism be circumvented, the unprejudiced description of the essential structures of experience will constitute a new, rigorously scientific philosophy which will place the empirical sciences themselves on an apodictic basis, while at the same time – a theme which becomes ever more urgent in Husserl's later writings – preventing the 'objectivist' impetus of the sciences from leading to a culturally disastrous obliteration of awareness of the constituting role of subjectivity.

In the earliest of his published essays, 'Genesis and Structure in Husserl's Phenomenology', Derrida already shows an awareness of the parallels between Husserl's intellectual situation and his own, and is also evidently sympathetic to the general orientation of Husserl's solution. In a series of scarcely veiled references to contemporary theoretical developments, Derrida vigorously denies that the 'methodological fecundity' of the concepts of structure and genesis in the natural and human sciences would entitle us to dispense with the question of the foundations of objectivity posed by Husserl. He staunchly defends the priority of phenomenological over empirical enquiry, arguing that, 'The most naive employment of the notion of genesis, and above all the notion of structure, presupposes at least a rigorous delimitation of prior regions, and this elucidation of the meaning of each regional structure can only be based on a phenomenological critique. The latter is always first *by right* . . . '[9] A similar attitude is expressed in Derrida's article of 1963 on Levinas, 'Violence and Metaphysics', where he argues, against Lévi-Strauss, that the 'connaturality of discourse and violence' is not to be empirically demonstrated, that 'here historical or ethnosociological information can only confirm or support, by way of example, the eidetic-transcendental evidence'.[10] Furthermore, this parrying of what is seen as a self-contradictory relativism is also central to Derrida's review of *Madness and Civilization*, and hence to the highly symptomatic contrast between Foucauldian and Derridean modes of analysis. For what Derrida objects to in Foucault is the attempt to define the meaning of the Cartesian *cogito* in terms of a determinate historical structure, the failure to grasp that the *cogito* has a transcendental status, as the 'zero point where determinate meaning and non-meaning join in their common origin'.[11]

However, the passages where Derrida's affiliation to Husserl on this point are perhaps most unmistakably evident are to be found in *Of Grammatology*. Thus, in his discussion of 'Linguistics and Grammatology', Derrida argues that, although Hjelmslev's work must be admired as the most radical development of the Saussurian tradition, in its 'bracketing' of the substance of expression, of the distinction between speech and writing, nevertheless Hjelmslev fails to pose the question of the 'condition of all linguistic systems'. For Derrida, this question can only be posed through a reduction to a level of experience which is distinct from the empirical and factual experience from which Hjelmslev wishes to make linguistic theory independent: 'The parenthesizing of regions of experience or of the totality of natural experience must discover a field of transcendental experience. This experience is only accessible in so far as, after having, like Hjelmslev, isolated the specificity of the linguistic system and excluded all the extrinsic sciences and metaphysical speculations, one asks the question of the transcendental origin of the system itself, as a system of the objects of a science and, correlatively, of the theoretical system which studies it: here of the objective and "deductive" system which glossematics wishes to be. Without that, the decisive progress accomplished by a formalism respectful of the originality of its object, of "the immanent system of its objects", is plagued by a scientific objectivism, that is to say by another unperceived or unconfessed metaphysics.'[12] It should be noted that the basic structure of this argument, in which the question of the meaning of objectivity is considered *de jure* prior to any objective enquiry, is by no means merely a feature of Derrida's early work, a temporary residue of his phenomenological formation. For, as late as *Positions*, Derrida stresses that 'what I first learned about this critique [of historicism] from Husserl . . . seems to me to be valid in its argumentative schema'.[13]

However, this endorsement of Husserl is only a stage of Derrida's argument. Although he accepts the *relative* validity of the transcendental standpoint, over against what he would consider to be a naive objectivism or relativism, Derrida has also been fascinated, since the beginning of his career, by what he has termed the 'un-thought out axiomatics of Husserlian phenomenology'.[14] This problem is already powerfully raised in Derrida's first major text, the 'Introduction' to his translation of Husserl's late essay on 'The Origin of Geometry', a text whose problems – Derrida has emphasized – 'have continued to organize the work I have subsequently attempted in connection with philosophical, literary and even non-discursive corpora, most notably that of pictorial works.'[15] 'The Origin of Geometry' is such a significant point of departure for Derrida because it represents one of the most strenuous of the late Husserl's attempts to think the historical dimension of the constitution of objectivity. As Husserl's work progressed he became increasingly conscious of the inadequacy of the 'static' transcendental analyses of the period up to the first volume of *Ideas* (1913). In his later, 'genetic' phenomenology Husserl's attention shifts from the 'modes of givenness' (*Gegebenheitsweisen*) of objects, to the manner in which strata of objectivity themselves are built up, to how the cultural level – for example – emerges from the psychological level, and this in turn from the body and from nature. Yet this very concern also entails a realization that more fundamental levels of experience cannot be direct objects of description, but must rather be made the focus of a '*Rückfrage*', a questioning back which seeks to uncover rather than merely to describe. Furthermore, this questioning necessarily acquires a historical dimension, since cultural and scientific traditions can only be constituted over time. However, while probing ever deeper into these historically sedimented levels of experience, in an effort to uncover the genesis of reason and objectivity *within* history, Husserl is always concerned to avoid any tilt towards historical relativism. In his later works he can be seen as striving to maintain a delicate balance between fidelity to the concrete complexity of the historical and life-worlds, and the universality and rational perspicuity which are essential to the transcendental status of his project.[16]

From such a standpoint, Derrida's 'Introduction' to 'The Origin of Geometry' can be seen as concerned with the point at which this balance begins to break down under the pressure which Husserl places upon it. For Derrida, this is the point at which Husserl becomes conscious that language, and more specifically writing, is a necessary condition for the stabilization and communication, within a cultural tradition, of the ideal objects of geometrical science. Given that we are obliged to assume the factual existence of a first geometer, the focus of Husserl's enquiry becomes: 'How does geometrical ideality (just like that of all sciences) proceed from its primary intrapersonal origin, where it is a structure within the conscious space of the first inventor's soul, to its ideal objectivity?'[17] In Husserl's view, the first – albeit preliminary – stage in this transition to objectivity takes place in the medium of linguistic intersubjectivity: 'In the contact of reciprocal linguistic understanding, the original production and the production of one subject can be *actively* understood by others . . . In the unity of the community of communication among several persons the repeatedly produced structure becomes an object of consciousness, not as a likeness, but as the one structure common to all.'[18]

However, even actual communication between the inventor and fellow scientists is not sufficient to establish the objectivity of geometrical knowledge, for what is still lacking is 'the persisting existence of the ideal objects even during periods in which the inventor and his fellows are no longer wakefully so related or even no longer alive.'[19] It is at this point that the importance of writing, which Husserl describes as 'communication become virtual', becomes apparent: for it is only through the detachment from any *actual* subjectivity which writing makes possible that the objectivity and communicability of scientific knowledge can be finally secured.

In Derrida's view, however, this account of the dependence of objectivity, and hence truth, on embodiment in a linguistic medium introduces a startling twist into the sequence of phenomenological reductions. For what this account entails is that 'Speech is no longer simply the expression (*Äusserung*) of what, without it, would *already* be an object, caught again in its primordial purity: speech *constitutes* the object and is a concrete juridical condition of truth. The paradox is that, without the apparent fall back into language and thereby into history, a fall which would alienate the ideal purity of sense, sense would remain an empirical formation imprisoned as fact in a psychological subjectivity – *in the inventor's head*. Historical incarnation sets free the transcendental, instead of binding it. This last notion, the transcendental, must then be rethought.'[20] This paradox is only intensified by Husserl's realization that – in its permanency and its independence of any actual subjectivity – writing must be considered as the *telos* of speech as 'the highest possibility of all constitution'. For inseparable from this independence is the possibility of the forgetfulness and even destruction of that meaning which it was the very purpose of writing to conserve. As Derrida suggests, 'The silence of prehistoric arcana and buried civilizations, the entombment of lost intentions and guarded secrets, and the illegibility of the lapidary inscription disclose the transcendental sense of death as what unites these things to the absolute privilege of intentionality in the very instance of its failure.'[21] The possibility of the appearance of truth, in other words, is coextensive with the possibility of its disappearance: in its quest for foundational certitude, transcendental phenomenology reaches a point at which it begins to undermine the very project which set it in motion.

As is well known, this insight into paradoxical status of writing, as both instituter and underminer of truth and meaning, will form the basis for a series of analyses of philosophical and literary texts which can be said to constitute the core of Derrida's achievement. In Derrida's view, within the Western philosophical tradition, writing, with its intrinsic dangers of loss, dispersal, and potentially endless delay of meaning, has been systematically subordinated to speech, which is privileged as a medium which tends towards the erasure of its own externality. The experience of hearing oneself speak (*s'entendre parler*), in which the vehicle of meaning is produced from within the speaker's body, and is perceived in the very instant of its production, appears to secure the immediate return of intended meaning to the intending consciousness in a closed and secure circle of immanence. However, for Derrida, this security is an illusion. All language is 'writing', in the sense that the possibilities of both meaning and of the non-recuperation of meaning are intrinsic to it. But if this is the case, then philosophy considered as a mode of discourse oriented toward a definitive capture of a meaning or truth, will tend to be checked and contradicted by its dependence on a medium whose dangers it must believe it possible to transcend. It is this structure of self-undermining which Derrida reveals in his readings of texts by thinkers as diverse as Plato, Rousseau, Hegel and Saussure. In all these cases, the relegation of writing to the status of an inferior substitute for the spoken word is thwarted by inadvertent and surreptitious admissions of its indispensability. It is the activity of uncovering such systematic incoherences within a text, rather than striving to reveal a unified meaning, which Derrida refers to as 'deconstruction'.

The significance of the speech/writing opposition on which deconstruction initially focussed extends far beyond the specific domain of language, for in Derrida's view it reveals in a particularly striking manner a structure of opposition which is characteristic of the Western philosophical tradition as a whole. Western metaphysics relies upon a series of oppositions – between mind and body, the intelligible and the sensible, culture and nature, male and female – in which one pole is elevated above the other, but can only be so prioritized through denegations of its dependence on its contrary, which generate a fundamental incoherence. Furthermore, if the repression of language as writing, the belief that language can ultimately be transcended in a direct apprehension of what Derrida terms the 'transcendental signified', is the condition of possibility of these oppositions, then the means of escape from this metaphysical incoherence can only be a new way of thinking about language. Derrida tries to open up such a new mode of thought through the introduction of a series of terms of art, of which the most common and influential has been '*différance*'. Through the use of this term Derrida suggests the impossibility of closing off the differing and deferral of meaning in language, a suggestion in which the potential endlessness of the Husserlian *Rückfrage*, the striving to recover an original sense, combines with Saussure's insight into the differential structure of language, according to which the meaning of each term depends on its contrast with all others. For Derrida the movement of *différance*, language as writing, undermines the interpretive aim of grasping the coherent and unitary meaning of a text, of revealing its definitive truth.

Deconstruction, Hermeneutics and the Transcendental

Although Derrida's account of language as 'writing' and '*différance*' has had a remarkable impact, particularly in the United States, where it can justly be said to have revolutionized literary criticism, and although it has been greeted as opening up unprecedented perspectives on meaning, interpretation, and indeed the fundamental nature of Western philosophy, it can be argued that *some* of what are taken to be novel Derridean arguments are in fact less original than they seem, when seen against the background of the hermeneutic tradition. It is too often assumed that the only alternative to deconstruction is a naive objectivism. However, from the very moment that modern hermeneutic thought emerged, when – in the work of Schleiermacher – the activity of understanding as such became the object of concern, rather than the appropriate means of interpreting specific texts, insights which directly anticipate the supposed discoveries of post-structuralism can be found. Schleiermacher, for example, is fully aware of the primacy of language in all interpretive activity, and cannot be accused of anticipating the ultimate erasure of language before the 'transcendental signified'. In his *Hermeneutik* he argues that, 'The only thing which is presupposed in hermeneutics is language, and everything to be discovered, which includes the other subjective and objective presuppositions, must be discovered out of language.'[22] Furthermore, once this primacy of language – which tended to be played down by later representatives of the tradition such as Dilthey – has been accepted, then many apparently 'Derridean' conclusions follow. For example, Schleiermacher presents the argument, which Derrida develops through a radicalization of Saussure, that the diacritical structure of language leads to endless deferral: 'Language is infinite because every element is determinable in a particular way through the rest.'[23] Furthermore this same structure can also be discerned in the relations between texts, so that interpretation is impossible without the recognition of an 'intertextuality', in which the meaning of a text is modulated by other contiguous texts, and the meaning of these in turn by further texts, in a process which has no determinable boundaries. Finally, as a result of these insights, Schleiermacher fully accepts that interpretation is an endless activity: 'The task posed in this way is an infinite one, since it is an infinity of the past and the future which we wish to perceive in the moment of speech.'[24]

Despite many inflections and shifts of emphasis – Dilthey, for example, can be seen as retreating in certain respects towards a more psychologistic and objectivistic account of interpretation – philosophical hermeneutics has preserved these insights up to the present day. This can be seen clearly from the work of Gadamer, whose thought presents numerous parallels to that of Derrida. For Gadamer, too, Western philosophy, since the time of the Greeks, has been involved in a struggle against language, in a denial of the intimate relation of language and thought: 'From the earliest times onward the Greek philosophers fought against the seduction and confusion of thought in the ''onoma'', and held instead to the ideality constantly achieved in language.'[25] Gadamer, however, believes that there are currents within the Western philosophical tradition which run against this tendency, and considers his task to be a break with the 'forgetfulness of language' through a linking up with these traditions. Like Derrida he portrays interpretation not as a matter of penetrating to an ultimate, objectifiable truth, but rather of being caught up in an endless 'happening of meaning' which transcends the distinction between subject and object. In fact, in many presentations of Derrida's thought, there appears to be little to distinguish the play of *différance* from Gadamer's account of the 'endlessness of meaning'.

In contrast to the imprecision of some of his followers, Derrida himself is extremely careful to demarcate his thought from even the most radical of hermeneutic positions, drawing a number of crucial distinctions. For however insistently Gadamer and other post-Heideggerian hermeneutic thinkers may emphasize the 'fundamental unclosability of the horizon of meaning',[26] nevertheless the view is maintained that interpretation must take place *within* an horizon, in other words must be guided by what Gadamer terms 'transcendental expectations of meaning' – expectations which are essential conditions of hermeneutic activity – and by an anticipation of coherence which is implicit in the ideal of truth. Derrida, however, repudiates this assumption of an inevitable orientation towards meaning, which he takes to be connected with the belief that the endlessness of interpretation is due to an inexhaustible semantic wealth of the text. Thus, in 'The Double Session', he argues that 'summation is impossible, without however being exceeded by the infinite richness of a content of sense or meaning; the perspective functions as far as the eye can see, without having the depth of an horizon before which or into which we will never have ceased to advance.'[27] In contrast to the hermeneutic position, Derrida's view is not that meaning is *inexhaustible*, but rather that any specification of meaning can only function as a self-defeating attempt to stabilize and restrain what he terms the 'dissemination' of the text. Meaning is not retrieved from apparent unmeaning, but rather consists in the repression of unmeaning. As Derrida states: 'If one cannot summarize dissemination, seminal differance, in its conceptual tenor, this is because the force and the form of its disruption *burst* the semantic horizon.'[28] A stress on multiple, or even infinite, meanings, still attempts to evade this rupture.

Although this opposition between Derrida and the post-Heideggerian hermeneutic tradition may appear a comparatively minor matter, compared with the gulf which separates both from positions which insist upon the primacy of intention in the determination of meaning, or upon objectivity as an interpretive ideal, it nevertheless has profound implications for our evaluation of Derrida's work, since it points towards assumptions which lie at the very heart of his philosophical enterprise. Perhaps the best means of tracking down these assumptions is to return to Derrida's own starting point – the working-through and eventual break with the phenomenology of Husserl. For Derrida, of course, is far from being the first philosopher to develop a major critique of Husserl. Much of European philosophy in the twentieth century has been haunted by Husserl's conception of a 'transcendental reduction' – even if as something to be resisted – so that a comparison of Derrida's founding deconstruction of Husserl with other critical strategies may provide an insight into the distinctiveness of Derrida's approach. In developing such a comparison, one can well begin from the work of Theodor Adorno, whose suitability derives from a number of factors. Firstly, Adorno's philosophy is marked by a lifelong engagement with Husserl's thought. His doctoral dissertation, written in 1924 at the age of 21, was a critical discussion of Husserl, and during the 1930s Adorno once again returned to work intensively on Husserlian phenomenology, the result being one of his major philosophical texts – *Zur Metakritik der Erkenntnistheorie*.[29] Furthermore, like Derrida, Adorno's attitude to Husserl is always tempered by a deep respect for his integrity and consistency, a respect which transcends theoretical disagreements. And finally, the philosophical position from which Adorno detects the inconsistencies in Husserl bears numerous resemblances to that of Derrida. A contrast of the manners in which 'negative dialectics' and deconstruction approach Husserl's transcendentalism may therefore help to highlight the deep structure of Derrida's thought.

At first sight, both Adorno and Derrida appear to focus on the same difficulty in Husserl's phenomenology, insofar as both are concerned to locate the points at which the immanence of transcendental consciousness begins to fracture. As we have seen, Derrida locates this breakdown at the point at which language and, in particular, writing is acknowledged as an essential condition of transcendental constitution. Although Adorno does not focus specifically on language, his analysis in *Zur Metakritik der Erkenntnistheorie* appears to lead in the same direction. Thus, in the first chapter of the book, 'Critique of logical absolutism', he argues that Husserl's defence of the pure validity of logical laws against any psychologistic contamination results in a contradictory attempt to sever logic from any determinate – and this means external, contingent – content of thought. In the same way, Husserl's conception of meanings as 'ideal unities', separable in principle from the specific experiences in which they are discovered, must be interpreted as a striving to escape from a dependence on facticity which Husserl himself implicitly admits, when he argues that the grasping of an 'essence' through imaginary variation must take some factual example as its point of departure. Furthermore, Husserl's insistence that the grasping of such an essence can take place in an instant of vision denies the temporality of consciousness, the interweaving of presence and absence which conceptual thought entails, and which for Adorno is inseparable from individual conscious life: 'Yet one can meaningfully speak of categorial activity only when the immediate is related to the past and the future, memory and expectation. As soon as consciousness does not abide by the pure concept-free "This here", but rather forms any concept however primitive, then it brings into play knowledge of non-present moments which are not "here", not intuitive and not absolutely singular, but distilled from some other. Always more belongs to the "proper sense" of an act than its proper sense, the canon of Husserl's method.'[30] This critique of 'proper sense', and of the primacy of the 'living present' will also be central to Derrida's account of Husserl.

However, despite these convergences, Adorno reaches conclusions markedly different from those of Derrida, insofar as his discovery of the antinomies of Husserl's phenomenology leads him to question the very concept of the transcendental, and therefore the notion of a pure subjectivity. From the beginning of his career, as his 1931 inaugural lecture on 'The Actuality of Philosophy' makes clear, Adorno had argued that the transcendental *moment* of subjectivity should not be hypostatized into a 'transcendental subject', abstracted from and considered as constituting the empirical individual. For Adorno 'the subject of givenness is not transcendental, ahistorically identical, but takes on forms which change historically, and which can be understood in historical terms.'[31] Furthermore, for Adorno, this rejection of transcendental purity is part of a more general attack on philosophical primacy: philosophy itself, obliged to abandon its traditional claim to 'grasp the totality of the real through the power of thought', can no longer legislate for empirical knowledge, but is rather caught up in a relation of reciprocal dependence with it: 'Philosophy will only be able to derive material fullness and concretion of problems from the state of the individual sciences at a specific time. But this does not entitle her to raise herself above the individual sciences, to take its "results" as ready-made and meditate over them at a secure distance.'[32] For Adorno, the distinction between science and philosophy does not consist in the level of abstraction or generality, but rather in the fact that 'the individual science accepts its discoveries, at least its last and deepest discoveries, as indissoluble and resting in themselves, whereas philosophy already grasps the first discovery which it encounters as a sign whose task it is to decipher. In short: the idea of science is research, that of philosophy is interpretation.'[33]

We are already sufficiently familiar with Derrida's sympathy for the 'argumentative schema' of Husserl's critique of historicism, and his general endorsement of the *de jure* priority of transcendental over empirical enquiry, to anticipate that he would by no means agree with these Adornian conclusions. Indeed, the assumption that he would not can – in an indirect way – be tested. For although Derrida has never directly engaged with the thought of Adorno, he has criticized an account of Husserl which moves towards similar conclusions – that of Merleau-Ponty. Merleau-Ponty, of course, did not approach Husserl from within an alternative dialectical tradition, but rather sought to stretch and extended Husserl's thought, through sympathetic interpretation, in the directions which he required. Nevertheless, his account converges with that of Adorno, in so far as both are concerned to uncover the reef of facticity on which any transcendental enquiry must run aground, and – in consequence – to define a new relationship between philosophy and the sciences. In his essays on 'The Philosopher and Sociology', and on 'Phenomenology and the Human Sciences', Merleau-Ponty suggests that Husserl himself, towards the end of his career, began to appreciate the limitations of his conception of 'essential insight' (*Wesensschau*). Particularly impressed by a reading of Lévy-Bruhl's *La mythologie primitive*, Husserl wrote a letter to the author in which, according to Merleau-Ponty, 'he seems to admit that the philosopher could not possibly have immediate access to the universal by reflection alone – that he is in no position to do without anthropological experience or to construct what constitutes the meaning of other experiences and civilizations by a purely imaginary variation of his own experiences.'[34] Furthermore, Merleau-Ponty finds confirmation of this shift in Husserl's position, to an acceptance that 'the eidetic of history cannot dispense with factual investigation',[35] and therefore of a collaboration between *Forschung* and *Deutung* similar to that evoked by Adorno, in precisely the same passage which is so crucial to Derrida – the discussion of language in 'The Origin of Geometry'. 'Husserl', Merleau-Ponty writes, 'will only be bringing the movement of all his previous thought to completion when he writes in a posthumous fragment that transitory inner phenomena are brought to ideal existences by becoming incarnate in language. Ideal existence, which at the beginning of Husserl's thought was to have been the foundation for the possibility of language, is now the most characteristic possibility *of* language.'[36]

Significantly, however, in his 'Introduction' to 'The Origin of Geometry', Derrida is explicitly hostile to this attempt to soften the line between the empirical and the transcendental. He suggests that Merleau-Ponty mistakenly attributes to the earlier Husserl the view that the empirical specificity of any possible history or culture could be deduced from an essence determined by a process of imaginary variation. However, Derrida argues, this was never Husserl's expectation: phenomenology does not claim to predict a priori the plenitude of the empirical world, but only to specify the essential structures of any possible history, society or culture. For Derrida, to admit that empirical facts could have any status other than that of examples for the procedure of imaginary variation 'contradicts the very premiss of phenomenology', which is that 'essential insight *de jure* precedes every material historical investigation, and has no need of facts as such to reveal to the historian the a priori sense of his activity and objects.'[37] Furthermore, in Derrida's view, the comparison of societies and cultures would be impossible unless guided by a priori insight into the sense of these objects: 'In order to attain this sense of every civilization or every experience, I will first have to reduce what there is of my own (in the factual sense of course) in the civilization and experience from which I start. Once that sense of the experience or civilization in general has been made clear, I could legitimately try to determine the *difference* between the various facts of civilization and experience.'[38] In general, Derrida contends, in opposition to Merleau-Ponty's thesis of a *historicization* of phenomenology, that to the very extent that Husserl in his later work increasingly makes history an explicit object of enquiry, his phenomenology is able to liberate itself from history, rather than being unwittingly subject to it: 'We could then be tempted by an interpretation diametrically opposed to that of Merleau-Ponty, and maintain that Husserl, far from opening the phenomenological parentheses to historical factuality under all its forms, leaves history more than ever *outside* them.'[39]

The very forcefulness, almost vehemence, of this opposition to Merleau-Ponty and – by extension – to Adorno, seems to intensify the difficulties of accounting for Derrida's position. For, as we have seen, from the 'Introduction' onwards, the thematic of writing in Derrida's work appears to be connected with the fracturing of the immanence of transcendental consciousness, its exposure to its repressed 'outside'. As Derrida writes, 'since, in order to escape wordliness, sense *must* first *be able* to be set down in the world and be deposited in sensible spatiotemporality, it must put its pure intentional ideality, i.e. its truth-sense, in danger.'[40] Furthermore, the concept of writing is connected to a series of concerns which also have their parallels in the work of Derrida's French predecessor and his German counterpart, most notably a repudiation of foundationalism in philosophy, a conception of language as the very fabric of meaning rather than its incidental clothing, and a desire to challenge and break down the rigid, dualistic hierarchies of metaphysical thought. Given these similarities, based in the common conviction that philosophical consciousness cannot, even by the most strenuous act of reflection, retrieve itself from dispersal and establish a pure self-coincidence, the problem becomes one of explaining why Derrida remains so determined to prevent any contamination between the empirical and the transcendental.

In fact, the beginnings of an answer to this question can already be found in the concluding pages of the 'Introduction' to 'The Origin of Geometry', where Derrida discusses the function of 'Ideas', in the Kantian sense of concepts of that which can never appear in experience, in Husserl's thought. Husserl fully appreciates that transcendent objects, everything which belongs to nature and to the world, can never be adequately given to phenomenological consciousness: their being is given only in the form of a continuing harmonious flow of experience. However, Husserl argues, we are obliged to *assume* the coherence of an infinite totality of experience which can never be given to a finite consciousness, since 'in the phenomenological sphere, there are no contingencies, no mere matter-of-fact connections (*Faktizitäten*); all is essentially and definitely motivated.'[41] The 'Idea' of a completed givenness is therefore essential to the structure of experience. (This posture of infinite anticipation is the complement of the *Rückfrage* which underpins 'The Origin of Geometry'.) However, whereas for Adorno, 'the infinite was the paradoxical shape in which absolute and, in its sovereignty, open thought took control of what is not exhausted in thought, and which blocks its absoluteness',[42] Derrida does not treat the Husserlian Idea as a means of blocking the intrusion of facticity. Rather, Husserl's admission of essentially inadequate givenness into a philosophy *founded* on self-evidence, 'the grasping of an entity with the consciousness of its original being-there-itself (*selbst-da*)',[43] is taken as revealing not that the transcendental project itself is inherently suspect, but rather that 'since this alterity of the absolute origin structurally appears in *my Living Present* and since it can appear and be recognized only in the primordiality of something like *my Living Present*', then 'Difference would be transcendental'.[44] In other words, for Derrida the permanent evidential gap within phenomenology itself, which *appears* to be the result of the intrusion of facticity and historicity, is the effect of a transcendental structure more fundamental than that of consciousness.

This pattern of argument is repeated in Derrida's classic analysis of Husserl's theory of the sign, *Speech and Phenomena*. Here Derrida suggests that Husserl's attempt to erase the 'external' and 'indicative' functions of language through a series of reductions which culminate in a self-addressed inner speech, is condemned to failure. There is no domain of 'phenomenological silence', of intuitive self-presence prior to the representational, and therefore divisive, function of language. But once the necessity of a medium of representation has been admitted, the structure of repetition, the connection to past and future, which is essential to the representational capacity of language, undermines the immediacy of self-presence. Furthermore, Derrida argues, Husserl himself is pushed towards this conclusion by the immanent logic of his phenomenology of internal time consciousness. For, to the extent that Husserl himself admits that present consciousness is inseparable from protention and retention, modes of awareness which are *neither* the representation of absence *nor* the intuition of presence, then the immediacy of self-presence, upon which his conceptions of evidence and truth depend, is revealed as illusion.

However, Derrida's response to this collapse of Husserl's philosophical project is *not*, like that of Adorno or Merleau-Ponty, to move 'downstream' towards an account of subjectivity as emerging from and entwined with the natural and historical world, but rather to move 'upstream', in a quest for the ground of transcendental consciousness itself. In his 'Introduction' to 'The Origin of Geometry', as we have seen, Derrida speaks of difference as 'transcendental', indeed he speaks of a 'primordial and pure consciousness of difference'. By the time of *Speech and Phenomena*, however, Derrida has realized that this is an incoherent formulation. Instead, he begins to speak of a difference, or '*différance*', which would be a 'primordial nonself-presence'.[45] For if presence and self-presence are essentially conditioned by the structures of time and writing, which cannot be reduced to presence, then the 'movement of differance is not something which occurs to a transcendental subject. It is what produces it.'[46] *Différance* appears to be – in a non-historical sense – 'older' than presence and the transcendental reduction, which now acquires the status of a 'scene, a theater stage'.[47]

Derrida and German Idealism

At first sight, this is a startling and rather puzzling move, generating many of the paradoxes which are such a characteristic feature of Derrida's work. In order to clarify what is at stake here, therefore, it may be useful to refer to an earlier episode in the history of modern philosophy, where the question of the limit-ations of transcendental consciousness, and the problem of what might lie 'beyond' such a consciousness were similarly at issue. The episode which I have in mind – one which is a crucial turning point in the development of German Idealism, and which is there-fore of exemplary relevance to subsequent philosophy – is the transition from Fichte's *Wissenschaftslehre* to the younger Schelling's philosophy of identity.

Fichte's *Science of Knowledge* can best be understood as an attempt to render Kant's critical philosophy consistent, by making its implicit assumptions theoretically explicit. In Fichte's view, Kant had made a crucial advance in philosophy in showing that self-consciousness, the 'transcendental unity of apperception', is the condition of all empirical consciousness, that it is the formal unity of the self which requires the procedures of categorial synthesis which transform the manifold of intuition into a coherent, objective world. However, Fichte considers that Kant's theory also remains insufficiently developed, insofar as Kant merely accepts the categories 'ready-made' from the traditional classification of forms of judgement, and insofar as he continues to speak as though our immediate awareness of particulars is generated by a 'thing-in-itself' outside all experience. For Fichte, the task of philosophy is to provide an answer to the question: 'What is the source of the system of presentations which are accompanied by the feeling of necessity, and of this feeling of necessity itself?' And since this system of presentations is what we mean by experience, philosophy must therefore 'furnish the ground of all experience'.[48] However, a philosophical position which simply accepts the duality of thought and intuition is unable to provide such a ground. Fichte's fundamental aim, therefore, is to transform the scope of the concept of self-consciousness intro-duced by Kant. Rather than being merely the highest condition of the synthesis of thought and intuition, the transcendental unity of apperception will now become the principle of the difference of thought and intuition. Fichte proposes to reveal the entire struc-ture of experience, in both form and content, as the unfolding of the activity of an absolute self.[49]

The nature of self-consciousness therefore becomes Fichte's fundamental concern, and indeed in a far more intensive manner than in any previous philosopher, since for Fichte it must provide the fully perspicuous point of origin of all knowledge, the matrix of all form and all content. However, by virtue of the centrality of this concern, Fichte becomes aware of the incoherence of the modern, post-Cartesian theory of the self. Fundamentally, this theory is based on the concept of reflection: selfhood, which means self-consciousness, consists in a relation in which the subject turns back on itself and grasps its own identity with itself, in which the object is the reflection of the subject, rather than something *other than* the subject. Despite its long historical currency, which has lasted up to the present day, this theory is fraught with intractable difficulties. The relation of reflection is intended to provide an account of what it is to be a self, yet in the very activity of reflection the self is already presupposed; for if the subject of the act of reflection were not already the self, then the object-self of which it comes to have knowledge could not be identical with it. Furthermore, unless the subject-self is already in some sense acquainted with itself, then it cannot *recognize* the object as itself: there is nothing *inherent* in a reflected image which reveals to the onlooker that it is his or her *own* image, and the subject cannot appeal to any third term for knowledge of identity of the two poles, since this would involve an infinite regress.[50]

Fichte's solution to these difficulties is to abandon the reflection model, and to develop a theory of the self as *positing* itself. Through this move, Fichte attempts to avoid the contradictory implication that a subject-self pre-exists the process of reflection; both the relation and the consciousness of the identity of the related elements must be conceived of as emerging simultaneously. This is what the term 'positing' is intended to imply. It denotes an activity in which something emerges absolutely, and, in emerging, enters into a relation with knowledge. Thus, Fichte argues that we must conceive of the self as positing itself, not in the sense that the self is the object posited, but rather in the sense that the self is nothing other than this *act* of positing. The fusion of activity and passivity in this unique process is suggested by Fichte through the use of the term 'intellectual intuition'. Kant had speculated on the possibility of such a mode of awareness, but had argued that it could not be available to a finite, discursive consciousness: human knowledge can only be based upon the assembly of conceptual and intuitive elements which derive from distinct sources. However, Fichte argues that Kant's own 'transcendental unity of apperception' is itself such a mode of awareness, since our consciousness of our own selfhood is both immediate and non-sensory. Yet it is important to note that the existence of the self as transcendental point of origin cannot be demonstrated theoretically, for here the very possibility of theory, of experience and the knowledge of experience, is in question. In a manner which is not fortuitously anticipatory of Husserl, Fichte is obliged to abandon argumentation in favour of an appeal to a distinctive mode of experience, to a self-evidence which is metaphorically expressed as *vision*: 'We cannot prove from concepts that this power of intellectual intuition exists, nor evolve from them what it may be. Everyone must discover it immediately in himself, or he will never make its acquaintance. The demand to have it proved for one by reasoning is vastly more extraordinary than would be the demand of a person born blind to have it explained to him what colours are without his needing to see.'[51]

Although Schelling's earliest philosophical writings are to a large extent a response to, and commentary on, Fichte's *Wissenschaftslehre*, and although, even in later years, he never ceased to acknowledge his debt to Fichte, from the beginning it is possible to detect a different emphasis and a divergence of approach.[52] Unlike Fichte, who is engaged in a reflection on the absolute conditions of consciousness, and who insists that these conditions must be implicit *within* consciousness, Schelling argues that the non-self-sufficiency of finite knowledge legitimates the *concept* of the absolute, and develops an analysis of what is implicit in this concept. Furthermore, self-consciousness is necessarily conditioned by its opposition to objective consciousness, and therefore cannot itself play the role of the unconditioned or the absolute. 'Self-consciousness', Schelling writes, 'is no free act of the immutable, but an enforced striving of the mutable I, which, conditioned by the not-I, struggles to save its identity and to find itself again in the onward-rushing stream of change (or do you really feel free in your self-consciousness?).'[53] Like Fichte, Schelling argues that in order for us to know anything at all, in order for the regress of explanation to be brought to a halt, there must be an absolute point on which all knowledge depends. Yet, unlike Fichte, he also contends that nothing which appears in consciousness – not even the self – can be absolute, and is therefore obliged to seek for a ground of consciousness itself, although it was not until 1801 that this divergence of approach became an open disagreement. In his 1827 Munich lectures 'On the History of Modern Philosophy', Schelling recounted his break from Fichte in the following manner: 'However, it immediately appeared that the external world is of course only there *for* me, insofar as I am also simultaneously there for myself and conscious of myself (this goes without saying), but that also conversely, insofar as I am there for myself, am conscious of myself, with the utterance of the I am, I also find the world – there – in being, thus that in no case can the already conscious I produce the world. However, nothing prevents us from returning from this I now conscious of itself in me to a moment when it was not conscious of itself – to assume a region beyond the now *present* consciousness, and an activity which comes into consciousness not in itself, but through its result.'[54]

Fundamentally, Schelling's critique of Fichte can also be seen as directed against the residual structure of reflection in Fichte's own thought. As we have seen, Fichte's philosophy consists in a struggle to overcome the incoherence of the reflection theory of self-consciousness, yet – at the time same – he insists that philosophy must begin from something which is known with immediate certainty, and – in line with the central tradition of post-Cartesian philosophy – finds this certainty in the self. However, Schelling objects that to begin from any kind of self-knowledge is to fall below the level of the absolute: the dualism of knower and known, as Fichte himself made clear, cannot generate, but presupposes, their identity. In Schelling's view, even the formula 'intellectual intuition', as Fichte employs it, betrays this duality. Furthermore, to the extent that Fichte begins from knowing, even in the unique form of the primordial self-positing of the self, he remains one side of the opposition of knowing and being which must itself be cancelled in the absolute. Up until 1801, with the publication of the 'Exposition of my System of Philosophy', there remains an ambiguity on this score in Schelling's work. He continues to speak of an 'absolute I', even though he draws a sharp distinction between this I and the 'subject', to the extent that his friend Hölderlin believed him to have strayed on to a Fichtean path. Nevertheless, it is clear that Schelling was always resistant to subjective idealism, that the basic tendency of his thought is to break out of the immanence of transcendental consciousness towards an encompassing unity, rather than to reflect critically on the conditions of knowledge.[55]

This basic tendency of Schelling's philosophy, in contrast to that of Fichte, is clearly revealed at the beginning of the essay, 'Of the I as Principle of Philosophy'. For whereas Fichte's primary concern is to preserve the possibility of human freedom against the temptations of dogmatism, to prevent the assimilation of the subject by the object by showing that objectivity is merely a condition of possibility of self-consciousness, itself posited by the absolute subject, Schelling's concern is with the circularity of any attempt to derive subject from object *or* object from subject. Since the subject is conditioned by its relation to the object (and to this extent – Schelling suggests – is itself an object), no less than the object is conditioned by its relation to subjectivity, neither can provide that absolute starting-point which it is the task of philosophy to seek. For Schelling, in other words, both subject and object are split by their relation to their opposite. No stability can be found within the subject-object relation itself, but only by transcending this relation, towards absolute identity. It is for this reason that Schelling can write that it is the very concepts of subject and object which are the 'guarantors' of the absolute.[56]

It is difficult to ignore the echoes of this Schellingian procedure in Derrida's fundamental philosophical strategy. For Derrida, too, the difficulty of metaphysics consists in the fact that it begins from one of a pair of opposites which is treated as a founding term, even though it is in fact intrinsically bisected by its other. This is why Derrida insists, for example, that idealism cannot be defeated by counterposing a materialism, but – ultimately – only by going beyond the duality. Thus he argues that, 'At the point at which the concept of *différance* . . . intervenes all these metaphysical oppositions (signifier/signified; sensible/intelligible; writing/speech; *parole/langue*; diachrony/synchrony; space/time; passivity/activity; etc.) . . . become non-pertinent.'[57] Consequently, like Schelling, Derrida is only able to characterize what he terms '*différance*', 'arche-writing', or the 'trace', through a sequence of fundamental negations, arguing in *Of Grammatology*, for example, that the trace is 'origin of all repetition, origin of ideality, . . . is no more ideal than real, no more intelligible than sensible, no more transparent signification than an opaque energy, and *no concept of metaphysics can describe it*.'[58] Furthermore, in the same work, Derrida himself seems to hint at the similarity of his procedure to that of Schelling, insofar as he describes it as one of moving 'beyond', rather than falling short of, transcendental criticism, to the level of what he explicitly terms an 'ultra-transcendental text'.[59] Derrida also stresses that this ultra-transcendental text 'will so closely resemble the pre-critical text as to be indistinguishable from it',[60] thereby showing himself to be sensitive to the possibility of accusations of metaphysical dogmatism, of the kind which Fichte levelled against Schelling. However he believes that the beyond can be barred from returning to the within, and thus that the standpoint of finite consciousness can be transcended, by what he terms a 'track in the text'. But this track can only be the mark of speculation: Derrida, in other words, is offering us a philosophy of *différance* as the absolute.

Différance and the Regress of Reflection

There are, of course, some immediate objections which could be made to this drawing of parallels between Schelling's critique of Fichte and Derrida's critique of Husserl. In his early writings, Schelling's aim is to discover 'the unconditional in human knowledge'. Following directly in the steps of Fichte, he argues that 'if there is any genuine knowledge at all, there must be knowledge which I do not reach by way of some other knowledge, but through which alone all other knowledge is knowledge . . . If we know anything at all, we must be sure of at least one item of knowledge which we cannot reach through some other and which contains the real ground of all our knowledge.'[61] By contrast, Derrida's work has been centrally – and highly influentially – concerned with the repudiation of all notions of ground and origin. For Derrida, to seek for such an origin, is to seek an impossible escape from the differential movement of language, towards the 'transcendental signified'. In the more popular appropriations of Derrida, this argument has been understood as providing licence for more or less facile versions of relativism, of the kind which – as we have seen – Derrida himself always set his face against.

In fact, on closer inspection, Derrida's attitude to the problem of origins is far more complex than such appropriations would give one to suspect. Certainly, he challenges the idea that *différance* or the trace could be considered as an origin, but *only* insofar as he considers the concept of origin, in its philosophical function, to be inseparable from that of presence. In fact, Derrida engages in a characteristic double manoeuvre. He frequently describes *différance* or the trace as 'older' or 'more originary' than presence and identity, but then goes on to stress that an origin of presence which cannot itself be made present can no longer be considered as an origin – it might, perhaps, have been more accurate to say: can no longer perform the *epistemological function* of an origin. Thus, in *Of Grammatology*, Derrida writes: 'There cannot be a science of differance itself in its operation, as it is impossible to have a science of the origin of presence itself, that is to say of a certain nonorigin.'[62]

In this respect, however, Derrida's position runs strictly parallel to that of Schelling. For Schelling, too, repeatedly denies that the absolute I can be objectified, can be made *present*. Thus in his early essay, 'Of the I as Principle of Philosophy', Schelling argues that 'the unconditional can lie neither in a thing as such, nor in anything that can become a thing, that is, not in the subject.

It can lie only in that which cannot become a thing at all; that is, if there is an absolute *I*, it can lie only in the absolute *I*. Thus, for the time being, the absolute *I* is ascertained as *that which can never become an object at all*.'[63] (It is important to bear in mind that, despite his Fichtean vocabulary, in this essay Schelling already understands the absolute I not as subject, but simply as absolute identity.) Given this concept of the absolute, we might well expect Schelling's theoretical activity to be accompanied, like that of Derrida, by an inseparable reflection on the conditions of meaning of its own discourse. Since the finitude and discursivity of thought renders it *in principle* incapable of attaining the absolute, an unclosable gap opens up between the *claim* of philosophy and its possible performance. If the absolute is unknowable, then the task of philosophy becomes nothing other than the explication of this unknowability itself. In a similar manner, Derrida is concerned with the unthinkability of *différance*, with the incessant attempt to turn back language against itself, and with the necessary failure of that attempt. Furthermore, the restless character of the work of both Derrida and Schelling ('the Proteus of German Idealism') can be seen not as a manifestation of arbitrariness or inconsistency, but rather as a logical consequence of their point of departure: it is only through the repeated development and the repeated collapse, of *Systementwürfe*, philosophical strategies and terminologies, that the nature of philosophy's 'impossible' object can be obliquely indicated.[64]

Despite the plausibility of these philosophical parallels, which are not intended to obliterate the major differences between romanticism and late modernism, but merely to suggest that Derrida's project cannot be presented – as it has been by some of his less critical admirers – as *unprecedented* in the history of philosophy, it could be contended that there is one crucial point of divergence between Derrida's thought and the thought of Schelling. The work of the early Schelling culminates, at the point of his explicit break with Fichte, in an *Identitätsphilosophie*, a theory of absolute identity, into which the oppositions which structure finite experience collapse. Derrida, however, is the consistent enemy of identity, the thinker of uncancellable difference. Yet even this contrast is more complex than it appears at first sight. For, in Derrida's work, *différance* cannot be defined through its oppositional relation to identity, since it is considered to be the 'nonoriginary origin' of presence and identity, and as such cannot be *dependent* upon them for its determination. But, if *différance* does not stand in opposition to presence and identity, then neither can it differ from them. However, if it were to be maintained that *différance* differs from identity, then by this very token it can *not* differ absolutely, since all determinate differences are internal to *différance*. Absolute difference, in other words, which is what Derrida must understand by a *différance* which is the 'possibility of conceptuality', and thus of determination, necessarily collapses into absolute identity.[65]

It should be noted that Derrida himself is not unaware of this relation. In *Speech and Phenomena*, for example, he explicitly equates '*différance* within auto-affection' with the 'identity of identity and non-identity'; while in 'The Double Session', in connection with his analysis of the 'hymen' in Mallarmé, he speaks of the abolition of 'the difference between difference and nondifference'.[66] Furthermore, this awareness is not restricted to occasional, comparatively casual remarks, but is explicitly theorized by Derrida. In his programmatic essay on '*Différance*', he develops the theme of *différance* as the same: 'philosophy lives in and from *différance*, thereby blinding itself to the same which is not the identical. The same is precisely *différance* (with an 'a') as the deviant and equivocal passage from one differing thing to another, from one term of the opposition to another. One could thus take up all the oppositional couples on which philosophy is constructed and from which our discourse lives, in order to observe not the effacement of the opposition, but the announcement of a necessity such that one of the terms appears as the *différance* of the other, as the other "differed" in the economy of the same . . . '[67] It is clear that what Derrida means here by the 'same' is the non-numerical identity of the unconditioned. However, this very recognition on Derrida's part now raises a further series of problems. For, in the majority of his work, Derrida bases his analyses on the concept of absolute difference: of an essential *logical priority* of non-identity over identity.

The observation of this discrepancy between Derrida's own philosophical awareness, and the pervasive *emphasis* of his thought – an emphasis which has been crucial to its appeal – leads us back to the problem from which we began: that of the distinction between hermeneutic conceptions of the endlessness of interpretation and Derrida's own account of the 'dissemination' of the text. This is because Derrida's portrayal of interpretation as the attempt to enclose the play of the text within the identity of a meaning, and his belief that any such attempt is a counter-violence enacted against the 'effective violence of disseminating writing', is crucially dependent upon the concept of absolute difference, which is in turn – as we have seen – an *interpretation*, which Derrida himself acknowledges to be one-sided, of the standpoint attained through a break-out from transcendental consciousness. It is arguable that the point at which structuralism, in its French guise, most crucially influences Derrida's thought, is precisely in this interpretation. For it was one of the commonplaces of French interpretations of Saussure, that – within a linguistic system – the differential relations are logically prior to, and determine, the identity of the terms, that meaning is wholly a function of oppositions. As Derrida himself argues in 'The Ends of Man', structuralism made possible a 'reduction of meaning', in contrast to and beyond the phenomenological 'reduction *to* meaning'.[68] However, it is apparent that this structuralist position runs counter to Derrida's own more or less explicit awareness of the 'identity of identity and non-identity' – the impossibility of prioritizing one over the other.

In fact, even prior to its Derridean radicalization, the assumption central to much of French structuralism, and – for the most part – unquestioned by both its defenders and its detractors, that meaning can be generated by the differential relation between linguistic elements alone, can be seen to be incoherent. For, since these elements are not *natural* unities, their very identification depends upon the attribution of a meaning to them. It is only those differences which are experienced as *semantically* relevant by the speakers of a language which enter into the structure of *langue*. Thus, although structuralism was correct to argue that differentiality is a *condition* of meaning, it cannot be seen as the sole determinant of meaning since the structure of differences can itself only be semantically discriminated. The identity of meaning is no less a condition of difference, in other words, than difference is a condition of identity.[69] However, although this argument leads us towards the conclusion that identity and difference are not opposed to each other in the manner they have often been conceived to be, it does not oblige us to adopt a philosophy of the absolute, of the identity of identity and non-identity. Rather, the relation between identity and difference must be seen as mediated by the peculiar lack of self-identity of the speaking subject, which thereby becomes an indispensable third term. The reciprocal relation between meaning and structure is secured by an interpreting and meaning-transforming subject which seeks to understand itself, to coincide with itself, through language, although this coincidence can never be complete. Once this circularity, and the role of the subject within it, is accepted, however, the success of

Derrida's attempts to escape from this circle, or rather to disintegrate it, seems to require further scrutiny.

Once again, these implications can perhaps best be drawn out by returning to the problems of the reflection theory of consciousness, which – in its Husserlian form – is one of Derrida's major foils. We have already seen how, beginning with Fichte, this theory is convicted of a vicious circularity, insofar as it is obliged to presuppose the very selfhood which it sets out to explain. Another way of developing the same criticism, however, would be to expose more directly the infinite regress in which reflection theory becomes embroiled. By the later 1790s Fichte had become explicitly aware of this regress, and explains it very effectively in his *Versuch einer neuen Darstellung der Wissenschaftslehre*: 'You are conscious of yourself, you say; thus you necessarily distinguish your *thinking* I from the I which is *thought* in its thinking. But in order for you to do this, that which thinks in this thinking must be the object of a higher thinking, in order to be an object of consciousness; and you immediately obtain a new *subject*, which is once more conscious of that which was formerly self-consciousness. But I now argue again as before; and once we have begun to proceed in accordance with this law, you can nowhere show me a place where we should stop; we will continue to infinity, needing for each consciousness a new consciousness, whose object the former is, and thus we will never be able to reach the point of assuming an actual consciousness.'[70] However, Fichte continues, there *is* consciousness ('*Nun aber ist doch Bewusstsein*'), which entails that there must be a consciousness which is simultaneously and immediately consciousness of itself. We must conclude that: ' . . . there is a consciousness in which the subjective and the objective are in no way to be separated, but are absolutely one and the same. It is such a consciousness which we require in order to explain consciousness at all.'[71] As we have seen, Schelling does not dissent from the implication of this analysis, that consciousness is inexplicable, except on the basis of a pre-reflexive, pre-predicative unity. Schelling's disagreement, rather, hinges on the crucial fact that, for Fichte, this unity can still only be conceived as a form of consciousness: a position which permits the fissure of reflection to reappear within absolute identity.

If we now turn once more to Derrida's work, it becomes clear that the account of the 'movement of the signifier' which blocks the possibility of any interpretive closure, is strictly analogous to Fichte's account of the endless regress of reflection. For Derrida no term or text is the bearer of a self-evident meaning. This meaning must be instituted through a further term or text, and the meaning of this in turn by a further term or text, in a process which Derrida names the 'logic of supplementarity'. For Derrida, in the encounter with language, 'You are indefinitely referred to a concatenation without basis, without end, and the indefinitely articulated retreat of the forbidden beginning as well as of hermeneutic archaeology, eschatology or teleology.'[72] But, at this point, Fichte's argument can be turned against Derrida. For, just as the regress of reflection renders the phenomenon of consciousness inexplicable, so – on Derrida's account – there could never be an emergence of meaning: there would be nothing but an unstoppable mediation of signs by other signs. The majority of Derrida's interpreters have, of course, resisted this implication of his position: Derrida is portrayed as merely suggesting that meaning is far more insecure, elusive, undecidable than philosophers had previously imagined.[73] Yet the logical consequence of his argument is not the volatilization of meaning, but its destruction.

Our discussion of post-Kantian idealism has provided us with the means to detect the crucial flaw in Derrida's position. True to his Husserlian background, Derrida thinks of identity in terms of presence and self-presence, but then discovers that such self-presence is always already fractured by difference. 'Auto-affection', Derrida writes in *Speech and Phenomena*, 'is not a modality of experience characterizing a being which would already be itself (*autos*). It produces the same as relation to oneself within the difference from oneself, the same as the non-identical.'[74] However, as we have seen, the same cannot be conceived as the *product* of difference – for this is precisely the erroneous assumption of reflection theory. Yet, lacking any conception of a pre-reflexive identity – Fichte's 'immediate consciousness in which subject and object are simply one' – Derrida is obliged to assume a priority of non-identity, with the consequences for his account of meaning which we have just observed. Derrida has failed to appreciate, in other words, that we cannot interpret the same as the non-identical without also interpreting the non-identical as the same – as the reflexive splitting of a pre-reflexive unity. It is only within the field of tension between an identity which cannot be represented, and a representation which can never be that of identity, that the phenomenon of meaning can be accounted for – as we shall shortly also learn from Lacan.

It is interesting to note, in this context, that both Fichte and Schelling were fully aware of the 'Derridean' consequences of the sacrifice of non-relational identity. Towards the end of the second book of Fichte's *The Vocation of Man*, the meditating self spells out the consequences of its realization that the originating unity of consciousness is itself merely a thought, a fiction (*Erdichtung*): 'There is nowhere anything lasting, neither outside me, nor within me, but only incessant change. I nowhere know of any being, not even my own. There is no being. *I myself* know nothing and am nothing. There are only *images*: they are the only thing which exists, and they know of themselves in the manner of images . . . I myself am only one of these images; indeed, I am not even this, but only a confused image of images. All reality is transformed into a wondrous dream, without a life which is dreamed about, and without a spirit which dreams; into dream which coheres in a dream of itself.'[75] Similarly, Schelling remarks that without an absolute I 'all existence, all reality' would be 'dispersed constantly, lost ceaselessly', and that knowledge would be 'an eternal round of propositions, each dissolving into its opposite, a chaos in which no element can crystallize.'[76] Although both Fichte and Schelling argue that this conclusion must be ruled out, since it contradicts basic features of knowledge and self-knowledge, it would be difficult to find more powerful evocations of what Derrida understands by 'dissemination'.

Meaning and the Self

It should not be assumed, however, that the only means of escaping the difficulties of Derrida's position, in which dissemination 'overshoots the mark' – as it were – and results in an abolition of meaning which Derrida himself could not have seriously intended, is to return to some version of absolute idealism. It is true that in Fichte and Schelling, and in a rather different sense in Hegel, the structures of reality as a whole are interpreted as the mediations and transitional points in the unfolding of an implicit identity towards fully conscious self-coincidence – although Hegel is the only member of the trio who believes that this coincidence can be articulated theoretically. But the concept of a pre-reflexive identity can be retrieved from this speculative framework. This is made clear by the hermeneutic and post-Husserlian phenomenological traditions, which retain the key notion of a pre-reflexive self-acquaintance, but abandon the claim that the structure of the world is simply the structure of subjectivity, by distinguishing between the subject – which is *not* understood as self-present –

the language in which this subject is caught up, and the world which language interprets. In this way it is possible to overcome the difficulties generated by Derrida's conviction that our only choice is between a view of the subject as an immobile centre, a core of self-certainty, or the acceptance that there is no subject at all, except as an 'effect' of the play of the text.

In order to illustrate the characteristic features of this type of position, it may be useful to return once more to the thought of Merleau-Ponty. As we have already remarked, Merleau-Ponty was no less concerned with the limits of the transcendental perspective than is Derrida, yet there is a sharp difference of opinion between them over the interpretation of Husserl and, consequently, over the appropriate means of escape. Furthermore, Merleau-Ponty's critique of Husserl pushes him towards insights which converge with those of the hermeneutic tradition, and towards a challenging of many features of the traditional philosophical understanding of language which are also a target of Derrida's. A consideration of Merleau-Ponty's philosophy of language may therefore help to show how a 'downstream' move from transcendental consciousness can be connected with the theme of pre-reflexive identity.

The first feature of Merleau-Ponty's position which should be noted in this context is that he does not believe any more than Derrida in the possibility of a 'transcendental signified', an objectifiable meaning in principle separable from language, and directly available to consciousness. For Merleau-Ponty it is an 'objectivist illusion' to believe that 'the expressive act in its normal or fundamental form consists, given a signification, in the construction of a system of signs such that, for each element of the signified, there corresponds a signifying element – in other words in representation.'[77] Accordingly, there can be no self-present subject prior to language, who employs language merely as the vehicle of already conscious signifying intentions. However, Merleau-Ponty does not conclude from this that there must be a 'movement of the signifier', independent of the subject, which generates both subject and meaning as an effect. He clearly perceives that without some conception of a subject which expresses and comprehends meaning through language, and therefore provides a point of departure and return, we would become trapped in an infinite regress: 'Signs do not simply evoke other signs for us and so on endlessly.'[78]

Merleau-Ponty's central problem therefore, one which is bequeathed to him by the difficulties of Husserlian phenomenology, is how to think of subjectivity, of intention, of expression and comprehension, in a manner which escapes the failings of the philosophy of reflection. From a Derridean standpoint, Merleau-Ponty's response to this problem might appear to be contaminated by the same illusion which Derrida detects in the assumption of a domain of 'phenomenological silence', of pure pre-linguistic seeing, in Husserl. For Merleau-Ponty writes: 'It is the error of semantic philosophies to close up language as if it only spoke of itself: it lives only from silence; everything which we cast towards others has germinated in this great, silent landscape which never leaves us.'[79] Yet, to assume that Merleau-Ponty could be indicted in this way is to overlook the distinction which has been central to our examination of Derrida's critique of the metaphysics of identity and presence. For much of Merleau-Ponty's work is an attempt to explore precisely that domain of pre-reflexive self-awareness which is also important for Fichte and Schelling. However, equipped with the refined phenomenological tools inherited from Husserl, Merleau-Ponty is able to explore this awareness through a deepening of the description of empirical consciousness, rather than through an abstraction from it.

Thus, in 'The Prose of the World', Merleau-Ponty writes that 'there is indeed an interior language, a signifying intention which animates linguistic events and, at each moment, makes language a system capable of its own self-recovery and self-confirmation.'[80] There must, in other words, be a form of hermeneutic circle, in which an anticipation of meaning is confirmed. Although Merleau-Ponty, in the same text, stresses the fragility and contingency of language, he also perceives that there would be no meaning, without a return from this disseminative dispersal: 'We must find in history itself, with all its disorder, that which nevertheless makes possible the phenomenon of communication and meaning.'[81] This conception should not be taken as implying that the circle of a self-confirming immanence – which is Derrida's major target – has not been broken open, that we are now merely faced with the immanence of a hermeneutically mediated, rather than transcendental, consciousness. Rather, the disruption of identity and the recovery of identity are simply two moments of the same process. We cannot speak of a final adequation of intention and expression, but only of a perpetual interplay of adequation and inadequation. The movement which Derrida attributes to the 'play of *différance*' itself, is rather the movement in which – in an incessantly repeated gesture, since the gap can never be finally closed – the speaking subject attempts to render explicit what is implicit, and in so doing continually surprises itself. Similarly, in the case of interpretation, there must be an anticipation of meaning which is *both* confirmed and disappointed. The distinction between this position and that of Derrida can perhaps best be summarized by recalling that, for Derrida, the collapse of the transcendental signified entails the 'absence of a centre or origin',[82] allowing no thought of a subject which is no longer an origin, but a *focus* which is never fully present to itself. By contrast, for Merleau-Ponty, 'that which permits us to centre our existence is also that which prevents us from centering it absolutely'.[83]

The Politics of Deconstruction

Although Derrida's basic philosophical moves cannot be considered unprecedented in the history of Western thought, much of the success of his work has undoubtedly been due to its posture of strenuous radicality, to its apparent undermining of the central props of our entire intellectual tradition. But, precisely because of the extremity of this challenge, a complex and ambivalent relationship has grown up between deconstruction and other, more explicitly political forms of radicalism. On the one hand, deconstruction seems to go beyond a 'left' critique which remains dependent on supposedly 'metaphysical' assumptions; on the other hand, the deconstruction of philosophical reason has been accused in turn of undermining the possibility of rational opposition to existing institutions, and therefore of accommodating – even if indirectly – to the *status quo*. Furthermore, this tension and ambiguity are not simply a matter of the reception of Derrida's thought, but are already present in Derrida himself. In many passages, particularly of his earlier writings, the erosion of the metaphysics of presence is presented in a rhetoric of liberation, most famously at the close of his essay on 'Structure, Sign and Play in the Human Sciences', where Derrida contrasts a 'sad, negative, nostalgic guilty, Rousseauist facet of the thinking of freeplay' with what he terms 'Nietzschean *affirmation* – the joyous affirmation of the freeplay of the world and without truth, without origin, offered to an active interpretation.'[84] This liberation is thought predominantly in terms of an anti-hermeneutic approach to texts, of a Nietzschean 'active forgetfulness', a release from the longing for an impossible truth. However, from the early 1970s onwards, Derrida makes more persistent – and undoubtedly sincere – attempts to link the theoretical activity of deconstruction up with more directly political engagements and practices. By the time of *La Carte Postale* he is able to state that: 'I have often had to insist on the fact that deconstruction is not a discursive or theoretical matter, but practico-political, and it is always produced within what we call (rather summarily) institutional frameworks.'[85] And, in an interview from around the same date, he can explicitly state that deconstruction as a purely theoretical activity would fail in its aims: 'a deconstructive practice which did not bear on "institutional apparatuses and historical processes" . . . would reproduce, whatever its originality, the self-critical movement of philosophy in its internal tradition.'[86]

However, Derrida has not been noticeably successful in articulating the relationship between 'deconstruction' in its initial discursive sense, as concerned with the analysis of 'logocentrism' and the 'metaphysics of presence', and his more concrete political concerns. Throughout his work, Derrida hints at a complicity between the fundamental assumptions of Western thought and the violences and repressions which have characterized Western history, but the nature of this complicity is never truly clarified. One major reason for this, it might be suggested, is the disanalogy between texts and institutions, and Derrida's consequent inability to give an appropriate account of the latter. For Derrida cannot help but acknowledge that institutions are not simply textual or discursive structures, but rather consist of 'a powerful system of forces and multiple antagonisms'.[87] Yet this politically necessary recognition of a non-textual reality enters into conflict with Derrida's own contention that there is no 'outside of the text', since 'the generalized graphics has always already begun, is always grafted on to a "prior" writing'.[88] Furthermore, given that institutions are traversed by relations of force, it is difficult to see how deconstruction could be applied to them. For deconstruction is centrally concerned with exposing the mechanisms whereby texts generate effects of meaning and truth while, at the same time, undermining them – in other words, with logical contradictions. Political antagonisms, however, cannot be reduced to logical contradictions. In this context, it is worth observing that when Derrida, during the 1980s, begins to make more explicit statements of social and cultural criticism, he tends to revert to a conventionally Heideggerian account of technology and bureaucracy, and their dangers, although he had formerly undermined the possibility of an appeal to the experience of Being, upon which Heidegger himself relies.[89]

Ultimately, Derrida's difficulties in this respect can be seen to derive from his fundamental conception of what logocentrism – the prioritization of speech over writing – represses. For what is at stake in Derrida's work is the perpetual inadequation between a finite consciousness, whose experience is necessarily structured in terms of the oppositional categories of reflection, and the unconditioned source of these categories themselves; and it is difficult to see how meditation on this relation could lead to any kind of political aim. Derrida, of course, is aware of the difficulties of this position, and attempts to avert them, suggesting that dissemination is 'with all the risks, but without the metaphysical or romantic pathos of negativity'.[90] Yet his work as a whole does consist in what he himself admits is an 'interminable' attempt to subvert and evade a structure of thought which must perpetually renew itself: Levinas is surely right to suggest that 'the whole contemporary discourse of overcoming and deconstructing metaphysics is far more speculative in many respects than metaphysics itself'.[91] But, if this is the case, it seems legitimate to enquire whether there might not be other ways of conceiving the 'end of metaphysics', and what it might mean to move to a post-metaphysical mode of thought.

In this respect, one of the most striking features of Derrida's thought is his reluctance to take the path which has been taken by the majority of philosophers after Hegel. If Hegel represents the most ambitious and comprehensive attempt of philosophical thought to grasp the totality as human history, then, after Hegel, historical content can be said to burst through its philosophical integument: philosophy is obliged to abandon this claim to comprehensiveness, to admit its entwinement with a social and historical reality which it cannot claim to master alone. A move of this kind can, of course, be detected in Marx and in the Marxist tradition. But it is also present in Nietzsche, in hermeneutic thought, in post-Husserlian phenomenology, with its shift from foundationalism to an exploration of the life-world, and also – in a rather different way – in the work of the later Wittgenstein. In many cases, this move also entails a recognition of the reciprocal relation between philosophy and the empirical sciences, of the kind we have already seen sketched in Adorno. Philosophy still retains a crucial interpretive and interrogative, and also a critical role, but it can no longer pretend to stand above, and to legislate for, all other forms of knowledge. Philosophical concepts must be challenged and transformed in a confrontation with the results of concrete investigations, whether these take the form of empirical science or some other form.

For Derrida, however, as his critique of Merleau-Ponty makes clear, such a move would mean a collapse into pre-transcendental naivety: empirical knowledge can claim no autonomous authority, but is rather ceaselessly dissolved into the endless reflexive movement of *différance*. Any orientation towards truth, that of empirical science no less than that of philosophy, betrays a submission to the metaphysics of presence, so that Derrida's strategy becomes one of uncovering the process whereby both science and philosophy are constituted. Paradoxically, however, in order to achieve this, Derrida must lay claim to a form of *Wesensschau*, essential insight. He must argue that certain concepts have a *necessary* content which cannot be modulated by the uses to which they are put. Thus, in *Speech and Phenomena* he states: 'We have discovered the systematic solidarity of the concepts of meaning, ideality, objectivity, truth, intuition, perception, expression. Their common matrix is being as *presence* . . . '[92] Similarly, in *Margins*, he affirms that 'every time a question of *meaning* is posed, it can only be so within the closure of metaphysics', while in *Of Grammatology* he suggests that all Western methods of analysis are 'within logocentric metaphysics'.[93] Throughout Derrida's work it is possible to find pronouncements on the 'essentially' metaphysical content of certain concepts.

One way of understanding Derrida's move would be as an attempt to carry out an '*epoche*' on the Western philosophical tradition as a whole. Just as, in Husserl's phenomenological reduction, acts of consciousness are not negated, but rather suspended – placed in abeyance so that their meaning can be revealed – so Derrida's deconstruction does not seek to *challenge* or *transform* the relationship between subjectivity, truth and presence (for example), but rather seeks to lay bare its structure. Although this manoeuvre then generates for Derrida the difficulty of explaining the point from which he himself is speaking, perhaps even more importantly it represents – in a paradoxical sense – an attempt to *preserve* the security and priority of philosophical discourse. Derrida's conception of deconstruction as an eternal vigilance, as an incessant attempt to escape the illusion of presence, seems to support this interpretation. Deconstruction cannot learn from its objects, but occupies a position of superior insight, just as in Husserl the transcendental theory of constitution reveals the naivety of the natural attitude: in this way the successor to philosophy continues to evade the exposure of thought to the contingency of interpretation, and the revisability of empirical knowledge. But this then raises the question of whether it might not be possible to think the end of metaphysics in a different way – precisely in terms of this exposure. We might enquire whether it would be possible – rather than abandoning truth while retaining the a priori – to abandon the a priori while retaining truth.

Derrida, Adorno and Heidegger

The work of Adorno seems a good point of departure for such an enquiry since – as we have already seen – Adorno too is concerned to challenge the standpoint of transcendental consciousness, yet does so in a significantly different manner, by stressing an irreducible break between philosophical conceptuality and facticity. Adorno is aware, of course, that the obvious response to his insistence is to argue that such a break only exists *for* reflection – itself consists in a *conceptual* distinction. He argues, however, that such a response merely betrays again the constitutive illusion of philosophy – that the moment of non-identity in thought and experience, the necessity of thinking or experiencing *something*, can itself be reduced to a set of conceptual determinations. 'Philosophy', Adorno writes, 'has made a virtue out of the difficulty that, as soon as it wishes to give validity to experiences, in general it always only ever has a concept of experience, and not experience itself, and has deduced from this that experience, since it can only ever be expressed in a concept of experience, is itself only a concept, an essence.'[94] For Adorno, this illusion is grounded in the function of conceptual thought as a means of self-preservation. The drive of metaphysics as a whole to reduce what is non-identical in the object to mind, the fundamentally idealist bent of philosophy therefore, is a sublimated expression of the drive to conquer nature, which Adorno views as the motor of the 'dialectic of Enlightenment' which characterizes human history. Thus, in *Negative Dialectics* Adorno argues that, 'The system in which the sovereign mind imagined itself transfigured has its primal history in the pre-mental, the animal life of the species . . . The animal to be devoured must be evil. The sublimation of this anthropological schema extends all the way to epistemology. Idealism – most explicitly Fichte – gives unconscious sway to the ideology that the not-I, *l'autrui*, and finally all that reminds us of nature is inferior, so the unity of the self-preserving thought may devour it without misgivings . . . The system is the belly turned mind, and rage is the mark of each and every idealism.'[95]

At first sight, Adorno's position would seem to be reducible to a crude naturalism and pragmatism, which relies upon a dogmatic assumption concerning the function of conceptual thought. But, in fact, Adorno's argument is far more subtle than this. For he argues that the attempts of 'identity-thinking' to absorb the diffuseness and contingency of nature leave scars, in the form of inconsistencies and incoherences, within the philosophical text itself. The general form of these attempts consists in prioritizing subject over object, mind over nature, the interior over the exterior. In his analyses, Adorno shows that these very attempts are self-subverting. The subject, for example, severed from all determinate content of experience in the form of the transcendental subject, would lose the features which *distinguish* subjectivity, all spontaneity and individuality, and become merely a closed system of laws of possible experience: 'The constitutive subject of philosophy is more like a thing than the particular contents of the mind, which it excludes from itself as thinglike and naturalistic.'[96] In general, Adorno argues that 'there is no so-called principle which, in order to be thought at all, does not require precisely that which, according to its own determination, it excludes.'[97] The attempts of philosophy to deny this continually result in self-undermining dialectical reversals.

The parallels between this Adornian procedure of 'immanent critique' and Derridean deconstruction are clear. Yet it is also important to note the major contrasts. Both are concerned with demonstrating how apparent philosophical contraries surreptitiously depend on each other, and both are concerned with reversing the traditional hierarchical relations in which these contraries have been placed. In Adorno, however, the need for this reversal results from the genuine primacy of one of the terms, a primacy which is specified by the materialist critique of metaphysics which begins with Marx, and which places thought within the overall development of social-historical life. For Adorno, Marxist materialism is not an 'ontology', it is 'no longer a counter-position one may resolve to take; it is the critique of idealism in its entirety, and of the reality for which idealism opts by distorting it.'[98] The type of argument which Adorno develops in this context can perhaps best be illustrated by his discussion of the subject-object relation in *Negative Dialectics*. Fundamentally, for Adorno, the subject is always a 'piece of the world', it is *something*, despite its transcendental moment, whereas the object is not by the same token a subject. Thus, 'Due to the inequality inherent in the concept of mediation, the subject enters into the object altogether differently from the way the object enters into the subject . . . An object can be conceived only by a subject but always remains something other than the subject, whereas a subject by its very nature is always an object as well.'[99] It is important to note, however, that Adorno speaks of a dyssymmetry of mediation: he does not wish to abolish mediation altogether, to collapse the subject into the object, but rather to establish an emphasis which is the opposite of that maintained by the philosophical tradition: 'Mediation of the object means that it must not be statically, dogmatically hypostatized but can only be known as it entwines with subjectivity; mediation of the subject means that without the object it would be literally nothing.'[100] As a consequence of this argument, Adorno states that 'it is not the purpose of critical thought to place the object on the orphaned royal throne once occupied by the subject. On that throne the object would be nothing but an idol. The purpose of critical thought is to abolish the hierarchy.'[101]

What Adorno understands by abolition of the hierarchy, however, is *not* abolition of the subject-object distinction, or of any other philosophical opposition. And this is where he differs from Derrida. For, in Derrida's work, reversal of emphasis *within* the hierarchy is portrayed is being merely a stage on the way to its overcoming. Derrida argues that a moment of reversal is necessary – such as the moment in which he prioritizes writing over speech – since without this move it would be impossible to intervene on the existing philosophical terrain. But reversal is *only* a stage: simply to assert the 'priority' of writing over speech would be to remain within the metaphysical closure. Hence a second move must be made, in which the very opposition is disrupted and overcome: 'One must also, by this double writing, carefully stratified, displaced and displacing, mark the distance between the inversion which, by deconstructing the sublimating or idealizing genealogy, brings it lower, and . . . the irruptive emergence of a new "concept", one which no longer allows itself (not that it ever did) to be understood on the earlier ground.'[102] However, as our earlier analyses will have made clear, this second move in Derrida, which involves the introduction of 'unthinkable' concepts, is in fact a shift to the standpoint of speculation, with the consequent restoration of what would be – from an Adornian perspective – a 'philosophy of origins'. In his evocations of '*différance*', 'arche-writing', the 'trace', Derrida has still not escaped the 'idea of the first', even though this first cannot take the form of 'presence'. In this respect, Adorno's characterization of the vapidity of *Ursprungsphilosophie* well captures the weakness of the thought of *différance*: 'The first of the philosophy of origins must become more and more abstract; the abstracter it becomes, the less it explains, the less it is able to do its job of grounding.'[103] For Adorno, any reduction of opposition to a *single* principle must have this idealist consequence: it could be argued against Derrida, in fact with more justice than Adorno argues against Heidegger, that, 'The thought fascinated by the chimera of the absolutely first will be inclined to claim eventually even the irreducibility [of the subject-object relation] as such an ultimate.'[104] However, Adorno does not conclude from this that an 'abstract insistence upon polarity' is a sufficient antidote either. Rather, he argues that, 'The theoretical limit against idealism does not lie in the content of the determination of ontological substrates or primal words, but first of all in consciousness of the irreducibility of what is to a pole of uncancellable difference, whatever its nature might be. This consciousness must be unfolded in concrete experience.'[105]

This reference to concrete experience is crucial for an understanding of the distinction between Derrida and Adorno. For Derrida, an appeal to experience necessarily implies a lapse into the metaphysics of presence, a repression of *différance*, whereas for Adorno it is precisely *within* experience that the tension of nonidentity between subject and object is preserved, a tension which cannot be entirely eliminated even by the most extreme reification. It is for this reason that he can define negative dialectics as 'the logically consistent consciousness of non-identity (*das konsequente Bewusstsein des Nichtidentischen*)'.[106] For Derrida, of course, the term 'consciousness of non-identity' would be incoherent. As we have seen, he uses the term 'consciousness of difference' in the 'Introduction' to 'The Origin of Geometry', but thereafter drops it in his move towards a *différance* which 'is unthinkable on the basis of consciousness'. However, from an Adornian standpoint, Derrida's belief that 'perception is precisely a concept, a concept of an intuition or a given originating from the thing itself',[107] which encourages this move, is itself a reflection of the prejudices of identity-thinking. Derrida fails to question the transcendental and speculative interpretations of experience which he inherits from Husserl and Hegel, and is therefore obliged to jettison the concept altogether as tainted with presence. For Adorno, by contrast, it is necessary to maintain both that there is something *given* in experience, and that there is nothing given *immediately*. Experience must be seen as an interplay of the immediate and the mediated, of presence and absence, of the identical and the non-identical, since if all immediacy is shunned, then – paradoxically – mediation itself becomes immediate, swallowing up the particular. Something of this kind takes place in Derrida, where, as Manfred Frank remarks, *différance* tends to become 'totalitarian and destructive of meaning (*totalitär und sinnzersetzend*)'.[108] However, in some of Derrida's own work the non-necessity of this consequence is revealed. In the chapter of *Speech and Phenomena* devoted to Husserl's theory of time, Derrida's account of the play of protention and retention in time-consciousness leads him to speak initially of a 'compounding' and 'participating' of presence and absence, identity and difference. It is only towards the end of the chapter that Derrida makes the fatal slide towards an account of difference as logically prior to and constitutive of identity, a slide which generates insoluble problems for his philosophy.[109]

It is through considering the consequences of this basic Derridean move that the complex, and contested, question of the relation between Derrida's thought and that of Heidegger can perhaps best be clarified. Throughout our discussion so far it is Derrida's relation to Husserl which has been emphasized, despite the fact that Derrida's thought is most frequently seen as an extension and transformation of that of Heidegger. However, there is good reason for this emphasis, for – as we have seen – Derrida often interprets his own work as a search for the grounds of transcendental consciousness, and consequently employs a vocabulary of 'conditions', 'effects', and logical priorities which is alien to Heidegger. The fact that this vocabulary is employed to articulate what can be more appropriately viewed as a speculative position merely serves to underline the fundamental equivocation over the status of *différance* which informs Derrida's work, an equivocation over whether the difference between identity and difference is itself an 'effect' of *différance*. However, Heidegger's response to Husserl is very unlike this. From *Being and Time* onwards, Heidegger's tendency is to deepen the concept of experience, so as to reveal the poverty of transcendental and speculative models. In consequence, Derrida's determination to show that even the ontological difference can be seen as a feature or an effect of *différance* reveals a speculative drive towards identity which is absent from Heidegger's work. For Heidegger, Being is never the generative ground of beings, as *différance* can be said to be the generative ground of identity, but is rather revealed and concealed in its difference from beings and through such beings. Accordingly, Heidegger's vision of a belonging together of Being and human beings, with he significantly describes as '*die Konstellation von Sein und Mensch*', and in which each is 'assigned' (*übereignet*) to its other, without being merely posited by it, bears a far closer relation to Adorno's conception of philosophical experience than to anything to be found in Derrida.[110]

On the other hand, there is also an affinity between Adorno and Derrida, which aligns them in opposition to Heidegger, insofar as both are profoundly suspicious of the vein of nostalgia, of longing for a pre-modern and pre-urban unity, which runs through Heidegger's thought. Derrida, on a number of occasions, queries whether the history of the West might not be too differentiated to be thought of in terms of the 'destiny of Being', and indeed suggests that even to talk of Being implies an unacceptable orientation towards unity. There is an element of Nietzschean scepticism here, which Derrida shares with Adorno, and which entails a more antagonistic attitude towards the philosophical tradition than is to be found in Heidegger, where the tradition functions as a source of truth which can still be revealed if it is approached obliquely. Ironically, however, it is the very strategy which Derrida employs to outflank Heidegger, the strategy of suggesting that the ontological difference and the history of Being are themselves subordinate to *différance*, which prevents him from fully developing these criticisms. For, despite all appearances, *différance* is itself a powerful principle of unity. When Derrida speaks of the 'historico-transcendental scene of writing',[111] he continues – like Husserl and Heidegger before him – to erase the contingency of the historical process, a contingency which can only be approached through empirical investigation, and which alone can secure the genuine resistance of history to unifying philosophical schemas.

Once this contingency is admitted, however, a further aspect of the relation between Derrida, Heidegger and Adorno emerges, which reveals Adorno in opposition to both Derrida and Heidegger. For it is only if the distinction between contingency and necessity is preserved, if these categories are not blended in the unfolding of Spirit, the destiny of Being, or the play of *différance*, that political action directed towards the overcoming of those contingencies which take the form of senseless necessities even becomes a possibility. To present contingency and necessity as already reconciled is to rationalize the irrational, and to deny the anticipatory relation of thought to practice. Thus, it is the concept of political action which provides the link between Adorno's concept of experience, which in some respects brings him near to Heidegger, and his critique of the repressive and coercive features of metaphysical thought, which aligns him with Derrida. But precisely because for Adorno philosophical thought – even in the form of a critique of philosophy, or rather by virtue of its status as critique – is not autonomous, independent of the social context from which it emerges and the practices which it implies, a final decisive gap opens up between his thought and that of Derrida. For Derrida, there can be no other truth than truth as defined by metaphysics – an assumption which drives him into a posture of incessant harrying of an unbeatable enemy. Whatever the inconsistencies and self-contradictions of philosophical discourse may reveal, they cannot be read as signs of 'untruth', even though they are, in some sense, signs of illusion. But Derrida's resistance to the equation of contradiction and untruth derives from his assumption that the consequence of this must be the equation of truth and coercive identity. Adorno's position, however, reveals the falsity of this assumption. The fundamental illusion of philosophy is the illusion of the autonomy and primacy of the concept, but this illusion is not constitutive of thought as such. Rather, it is part of the structure of delusion generated by an antagonistic society. Thus, the very concept of truth points beyond philosophy, towards political practice, however despairing Adorno himself may be about the possibility of such practice. Furthermore, if social antagonism conceals itself behind the illusion of identity, then the overcoming of antagonism, contrary to Derrida's expectations, will also be the overcoming of identity. As Adorno writes: 'Reconciliation would release the nonidentical, would rid it of coercion, including spiritualized coercion; it would open the road to the multiplicity of different things and strip dialectics of its power over them.'[112]

2

Jacques Lacan:
A Philosophical Rethinking of Freud

It has long been commonplace in philosophical discussions of psychoanalysis to point out that the thought of its founder is characterized by a deep theoretical ambiguity.[1] Freud, who spent the formative years of his career as a physiologist in the laboratory of Ernst Brücke, could not fail to be influenced in his scientific outlook by the mechanism and determinism of the then dominant Helmholtz School of Medicine, in which Brücke himself was a leading figure. Indeed, Freud's early training moulded his views to such an extent that, throughout his life, he never entirely abandoned the expectation that the discoveries of psychoanalysis would ultimately be translatable into the scientifically 'respectable' vocabulary of neurology and physiology. Even when, during the 1890s, the centre of Freud's interests shifted from the physiological to the psychic, as he began to piece together his model of the mind from clinical evidence, he continued to assume that the processes with which he was concerned could be accounted for in purely causal and mechanical terms. In the opening sentence of an unpublished manuscript of 1894, the now celebrated *Project for a Scientific Psychology*, Freud announces his intention to 'furnish a psychology that shall be a natural science: that is, to represent psychical processes as quantitatively determinate states of specifiable material particles, thus making these processes perspicuous and free from contradiction'.[2] The *Project* attempts a theorization of the fundamental operations of the mind in terms of the increase, diminution, displacement and discharge of an energy or 'quantity' conceived of as flowing through and accumulating within a differentiated network of neurones. Freud's

45

subsequent abandonment of the already metaphorical neurology of the *Project* in favour of the postulation of an overtly psychic apparatus and topography, despite its far-reaching implications in opening the domain of psychoanalysis proper, produced no major alteration in his commitment to energetic and causal modes of explanation. Natural science was always to remain for Freud the only conceivable prototype for knowledge.

In practice, however, neither Freud's general theory of the mind, nor the methods employed in particular analyses, ever began to approximate to this epistemological ideal. Although Freud and his early followers perceived themselves as the founders of the first truly scientific psychology, it has become clear in retrospect that, far from suppressing our intentional vocabulary – the vocabulary of meanings, motives and purposes in terms of which the activities of human beings are ordinarily discussed – in favour of purely causal forms of explanation, the achievement of psychoanalysis was rather to extend the application of these concepts to a new domain of psychic activity, whose recognition had formerly been hindered by its unavailability to consciousness: Little Hans develops his phobia of horses in order to mask his own antagonism towards – and fear of the castrating power of – his father; Freud himself dreams the dream of Irma's injection in fulfilment of a wish to exonerate himself for the unsuccessful treatment of a patient. Freud's work presents us with fear, rivalry, love, anxiety, the whole range of human thought and emotion, operating at an unconscious level, while seeking disguised expression in conscious life in the form of dreams, symptoms, parapraxes. Freud's aim, however, is not simply to achieve the recognition of such a domain of unconscious psychic activity. The natural-scientific tenor of his work is maintained in his attempt to anchor the complexity of human behaviour in the biological needs and drives of the organism, which he sees as impinging forcefully upon, indeed – after much transmutation and ramification – as constituting the life of the psyche. Thus in Freud's work there always exists an interplay and tension between the hermeneutic foreground of his work, in which his concern is with the interpretation of human behaviour, and a metapsychological background, in which the fundamental processes of the psyche are described in terms of an economics and dynamics of libido.

Such a characterization of Freudian psychoanalysis may create the impression that Freud himself was fundamentally confused about the methodological bases and cognitive status of his work. Certainly, there has been no lack of philosophically sophisticated commentators on psychoanalysis ready to suggest that, because of his intellectual background, Freud was obliged to clothe what was in effect a new hermeneutics of human speech and action in the antiquated vocabulary of 19th-century scientism. It is remarkable that Freud's work betrays no awareness of the *Methodenstreit* between the proponents of causal explanation (*Erklären*) and of interpretive understanding (*Verstehen*) in the human sciences which occurred in the German-speaking world during his lifetime. And if one examines the detail of Freud's texts this inno-cence manifests itself on every level, from the overall structure of his metapsychology to the individual sentence, where Freud can be found fusing together both intellectual operations. In the dis-cussion of the dream of the burning child, for example, which opens the final chapter of *The Interpretation of Dreams*, Freud claims to have shown that 'the dream was a process with a mean-ing, and that it can be inserted into the chain of the dreamer's psy-chical experiences',[3] while in his 'Short Account of Psycho-analysis' he emphasizes simultaneously the 'thoroughgoing meaningfulness (*Sinnhaftigkeit*) and determination (*Determinie-rung*) of even the seemingly darkest and most arbitrary psychic phenomena'.[4] Yet, paradoxically, it is Freud's refusal to recognize the distinction between explanation and understanding which has endowed the discipline which he founded with its depth and power. For this refusal enabled psychoanalysis to do justice simultaneously to two profoundly rooted, yet apparently irrecon-cilable, views of human behaviour, to combine a realization that human action is moulded and impelled by biological and social forces, even – and especially – when these forces remain excluded from awareness, with an appreciation that no amount of scientific investigation could invalidate the treatment of human beings as responsible agents, capable of forming purposes and enacting intentions.

The history of post-Freudian developments in psychoanalysis, however, makes clear how fragile was the ambiguity – and equi-librium – which constituted the strength of Freud's work. The ori-ginal Freudian synthesis – a commitment to determinism in the domain of the psyche, a penchant for biological modes of explanation, an analytical practice founded in a hermeneutics of human speech, and (with *Beyond the Pleasure Principle*) even a certain return to the *Naturphilosophie* against which Helmholtz and his followers had rebelled – proved too complex and unstable to be sustained in its entirety by any of Freud's inheritors. During Freud's lifetime, with the major secessions of Jung and Adler, and to an even greater degree after his death, psychoanalysis began to fragment into a variety of different schools and tendencies, each laying claim to only a part of the Freudian legacy. At one extreme stands the work of Wilhelm Reich, who championed the Freudian theory of libido – of the fundamentally sexual nature of psychic energy – as the natural-scientific foundation of psychoanalysis, against what he saw as the increasing squeamishness of his fellow analysts. The adoption of this stance led Reich eventually to abandon the principle of the 'talking-cure' altogether in favour of a direct manipulation of the body, and culminated in the theoretical delirium of his final years, in which the apparatus of a naive scientism is applied to the pursuit of a cosmic libidinal energy.[5] Far more frequent and varied, however, have been those developments of psychoanalysis in which Freud's biologism, and his insistence on the sexual aetiology of mental disorder, are underplayed in favour of what is considered to be a less reductionist perspective. In the New York School of 'ego psychology' such anti-reductionism is reconciled with a broadly natural-scientific orientation by means of the postulation of a 'conflict- free' sphere of the ego, which has at its disposal sources of energy independent of the id.[6] In general, however, from Binswanger's marriage of psychoanalysis with the categories of Heideggerian *Daseinsanalyse* to the emphasis on social and cultural determinants of neurosis in the work of 'Neo-Freudian revisionists' such as Fromm and Horney, the critique of Freud's biologism has gone hand in hand with an aversion to the natural-scientific ethos, and a corresponding highlighting of the social and hermeneutic dimensions of analysis.

Some consideration of the history and of the divergent currents of psychoanalytical theory is an essential preliminary to an appraisal of the work of Jacques Lacan, since at the heart of Lacan's teaching – which began in earnest in 1953 with his departure from the International Psychoanalytical Association and the inauguration of the *Seminar* – is the call for a 'return to Freud', for a renewed close reading of Freud's original texts, a reaffirmation of the dislocating radicality of the concept of the unconscious, and a rejection of the dilutions and deviations which have characterized psychoanalysis since the death of Freud.[7] Moreover, Lacan himself has characterized the history of psychoanalysis, in a manner not dissimilar to the outline above, in a series of complementary departures from an original Freudian norm. In an article on 'Variants of the Standard Treatment', published in 1955, Lacan suggests that 'an external coherence persists in these deviations from analytical experience, which frame its axis as rigorously as the fragments of a projectile, in their dispersal, preserve its ideal trajectory at the centre of gravity of the cone which they trace'.[8] In Lacan's view this ability of psychoanalysis to preserve its fundamental coherence and efficacity is due to the fact that it is 'nothing other than an artifice of which Freud has given the constituents, while laying down that the notion of these constituents is englobed by their ensemble':[9] the theory of psychoanalysis, in other words, is internal to its practice, so that the 'purely formal maintenance of these constituents is sufficient to ensure the effectiveness of their overall structure'.[10] Yet if the effectiveness of analytical practice may thus be seen to possess a certain independence from the adequacy of psychoanalytical theory, this is not to imply that theory is of no importance. Lacan argues that 'the incompleteness of the analyst's notion of these constituents [of psychoanalysis] tends to become one with the limit which the process of analysis will not be able to pass in the analysand',[11] so that his call for a 'return to Freud' is ultimately of clinical significance. The major question which hangs over Lacan's work, therefore, is whether its self-presentation as a return to the complexity and radicality of Freud's original doctrine is sustainable, or whether Lacan too – for whatever reasons – was obliged to become a revisionist.

The Early Lacan

Lacan did not begin his professional life as a psychoanalyst, but trained first as a doctor of medicine, and subsequently entered psychiatry as a disciple of the distinguished French psychiatrist Clérambault. By the early 1930s he was a young *chef de clinique*, with a promising future before him. Yet, as his doctoral thesis on paranoid psychosis – first published in 1932 – makes clear, Lacan at this point was already in rebellion against the theoretical tradition in which he had been reared, at odds with the pervasive and deepset belief of his profession in the organic origins of mental illness. Centred upon the full-length case-history of a patient named 'Aimeé', *De la psychose paranoïaque dans ses rapports avec la personnalité* argues persistently that psychosis cannot be viewed as a physiologically grounded intrusion into – and disruption of – an otherwise 'normal' personality. This is not simply because psychosis can be shown to occur in the absence of any – even merely conjectural – organic lesion,[12] or because of the difficulties into which such theories run when confronted with the phenomenon of 'double delirium' (*délire à deux*).[13] Far more fundamental for Lacan is the argument that the phenomena of mental life cannot consist in chains of causally linked events, comparable to processes in nature, since these phenomena reveal an intentional character. 'Every phenomenon of consciousness', Lacan affirms, 'has in effect a *sense* (*sens*), in one of the two connotations which language gives to this term: that of meaning or that of orientation. The simplest phenomenon of consciousness, which is the image, is either symbol or desire'.[14] The task of the psychiatrist, therefore, cannot be to establish a putative aetiological chain which would ultimately lead back to organic factors, since such an orientation towards causal explanation neglects the 'human meaning' of the behaviour of the mentally disordered, which can only be made available through a methodology of understanding (*compréhension*). Lacan demonstrates in the course of his case history that the attempt to understand, rather than reductively explain, disturbed behaviour will show that psychosis – far from representing an alien intrusion into the inner life of the patient – stands in an intrinsic relation to the 'personality' of the patient, understood as 'the totality constituted by the individual and by their particular environment'.[15] This holistic and interpretive approach is confirmed in an article written shortly after the apperaance of *De la psychose paranoïaque*, in which Lacan explicitly includes his own research with that of Binswanger in the category of 'works of phenomenological inspiration on mental states' which 'do not detach the local reaction, which in the majority of cases is remarkable only because of some pragmatic discordance, and which can thereby be isolated as mental disorder, from the whole lived experience of the sick person, which they attempt to define in its originality'.[16] Since there can be no intrinsic or objective mark of mental disorder, any psychiatry which looks towards natural science must ignore the role of interpretation in the very definition of its object.

Although, at the time his thesis was published, Lacan was still working as – and considered himself to be – a psychiatrist (he joined the Paris Psychoanalytic Society in 1934, after an analysis with Rudolf Loewenstein), *De la psychose paranoïaque* deals sympathetically, and at considerable length, with Freudian theory. Lacan argues that his analysis of the case of Aimée, which involves a detailed examination of her life history and of her 'inspired' writings, has confirmed certain fundamental discoveries of psychoanalysis concerning the role, in psychopathology, of infantile

sexuality and childhood history. Furthermore, in the final theoretical section of the book, he claims that he has taken two very
general postulates of psychoanalysis as guidelines for the development of his own proposed 'science of personality': that there
exist 'certain typical stages of the development of the personality,
that is to say a certain equivalence or common measure between
the different phenomena of personality, an equivalence which is
expressed by the common use of the term – imprecise, but
imposed by the necessities of thought – "psychic energy"'.[17] As
the reticence of this final phrase indicates, however, for Lacan the
specifically sexual or biological content of libido-theory is far
from being the core of Freud's doctrine. It is crucial to note that
Lacan's initial gravitation towards psychoanalysis is not towards
an explanatory and reductive science of the mind, but rather
towards what he terms 'a semantics of behaviour and of representative phantasies'.[18] For Lacan psychoanalysis is primarily a
'method of interpretation', since far from engaging in a futile
attempt to trace mental disorder back to physical causes, it
reverses the relation of mind and body to reveal the 'psychogenic
meaning' not only of dreams and parapraxes, but even of organic
reactions.[19] From the very first psychoanalysis is considered by
Lacan as a means of countering the orientation of theories of the
mind towards the paradigm of natural science.

This early evaluation of psychoanalysis was not altered by
Lacan's official conversion to Freudianism. If a shift in attitude
can be detected in those writings of the 1930s and 1940s which
Lacan refers to as the 'works of our entry into psychoanalysis',[20]
it is simply that the conflict between organicism and reductionism, and a psychology of comprehension, which in *De la psychose paranoïaque* had been embodied respectively by psychiatry
and psychoanalysis, is now considered as an incoherence within
Freudian doctrine itself. Lacan perceives a fissuring of Freud's
work between a view of the human being as a solipsistic organism,
for whom other individuals figure only as sources of gratification
and frustration, and an understanding of the dimension of social
meaning inherent in neurosis and psychosis, between a tendency
towards biological reductionism and an implicit recognition that
the proper object of psychology is the 'specific reality of interhuman relations'.[21] Accordingly, Lacan now defends what he
terms 'the phenomenological advance of Freudianism', the grasp
of human behaviour as moulded by a series of identifications, as
'bearing the mark of a certain number of typical psychic relations
which express a certain social structure',[22] while deploring the

attempt ultimately to derive such typical relations, or 'complexes', from an underlying system of instincts.[23] For the young Lacan, the Freudian notion of a death instinct – in particular – testifies to 'the aporia that confronted this great mind in the most profound attempt so far made to formulate an experience of man in the register of biology',[24] while in his definitive critique of organicist aetiologies of madness ('Propos sur la causalité psychique'), dating from 1946, Lacan suggests that Freud remained – in opposition to the dominant movement of his thought – a victim of the prejudices of psycho-physical parallelism.[25] Yet this reading of Freud as providing primarily an account of the structuring of the domain of inter-human relations is not without its own difficulties. For while insisting on the irreducibility of images, social meanings, and identifications to any purely biological substratum, Lacan cannot afford to lose touch with the kernel of truth concealed in Freud's propensity for biologism: that human existence cannot be seen as centred on an essentially cognitive consciousness, but, even in its most non-physical reaches, is traversed by physical needs and appetites. The difficulty, therefore, becomes one of developing a non-reductionist critique of consciousness, or – to reverse the terms of the problem – of producing an account of the emergence of a *specifically human* form of desire.

Like so many other influential thinkers and writers of his generation, Lacan found, not the solution to this problem, but the fundamental mould within which his successive attempts at a solution would be cast, in Hegelian thought, and more specifically in the interpretation of the *Phenomenology of Mind* proposed by the emigré Russian thinker Alexandre Kojève. It was to prove of crucial importance for the subsequent development of Lacan's work that the period during which he produced his first psycho-analytical essays was also the period during which Hegel made his first major impact on French thought,[26] and that Lacan – along with Raymond Aron, Georges Bataille, Maurice Merleau-Ponty, and other future celebrities – attended the lectures on the *Phenomenology* given by Kojève at the *Ecole Normale Supérieure* between 1933 and 1939. For in his lessons on Hegel there is one particular section of the *Phenomenology* to which Kojève repeatedly returns, and which clearly forms one of the keys to his interpretation; it is the passage at the beginning of the chapter on 'Self-Consciousness' in which Hegel describes the transition from organic life to properly human existence, from 'sentiment of self' (*Selbstgefühl*) to 'self-consciousness' (*Selbstbewusstsein*). As rewrought by Kojève, the core of Hegel's argument is that self-consciousness – as opposed to a consciousness which is purely passive absorption in its object – can only emerge on the basis of animal life, out of the cycle of desire and of the satisfaction of desire. The first rudimentary experience of selfhood is made possible by the non-self-sufficiency of the organic, since to crave a particular external object for the satisfaction of physical need is at the same time to experience oneself as lacking that object. At the same time, however, the awareness of dependency upon external reality which necessarily accompanies such craving is experienced as an injury to this incipient sense of selfhood, so that the consumption of the object can be interpreted as its 'negation', a denial of dependency aimed at reinforcing the 'certainty of self' (*Selbstgewissheit*). Yet at the purely animal level such negations are doomed to failure: physical desire can provide no durable support for self-consciousness, since its temporary satiation leads to an extinction of the awareness of lack upon which the sense of self depends, while its re-awakening leads only to another futile repetition of the cycle. Hegel therefore concludes that self-consciousness can only truly emerge when desire is no longer oriented towards a perishable object, but rather towards another desiring subject, since only a second subject, in acknowledging the first, can negate itself without forfeiting its alterity; furthermore, only another self can support a self-consciousness which is individualized, rather than simply reflecting the generic natural object. True self-consciousness is therefore for Hegel dependent upon the mutual recognition of consciousnesses.[27]

However, although Hegel sketches such a form of reciprocity at the close of the introduction to Part Two ('The Truth of Self-Certainty'), fully mutual recognition does not, in the *Phenomenology*, follow directly upon the transition from consciousness to self-consciousness. Indeed, the remainder – and by far the larger part – of the *Phenomenology* is taken up with an account of the oscillations and diremptions through which consciousness must pass in order to attain its goal. For Hegel the primordial encounter of consciousness is inherently unstable: consciousness can grasp itself only through its reflection in and recognition by the other, yet – as was the case at the level of organic life – an inherent aspiration towards autonomy repugns against the dependency which this relation implies. The initial result of this dilemma is a comic stasis of mutual imitation, in which neither consciousness dares differ from its other for fear of losing the ground of recognition, and in which, therefore, neither can gain a significant advantage over its fellow and rival: 'Each sees the *other* do the same as it does; each does itself what it demands of the other, and therefore also does what it does only in so far as the other does the same.'[28] This deadlock can only be broken when one self-consciousness is prepared to grasp for universality by detaching itself entirely from the compulsions of physical existence, to risk death itself in what Kojève terms a 'struggle for pure prestige' in order to extract recognition from the other without being required to acknowledge the other in its turn. The result of this battle is therefore a constitution of the characteristic relation of master and slave, a relation which Hegel describes as 'the divergence of the centre into extremes, which as extremes are opposed to each other, and of which one is only recognized, while the other only recognizes'.[29] The master-slave relation, in other words, represents the maximal disequilibrium of self-consciousness, and it is from this point that the long peregrination of consciousness towards an adequate concept of itself will begin. Clearly, such a concept can only emerge when full reciprocity becomes possible, when consciousnesses can 'recognize themselves as *mutually recognizing* one another',[30] without coercion, and without abandoning their individuality in futile imitation. For Hegel such recognition involves the abandonment of total autonomy as a possible goal. Full reciprocity is only attained when human individuals cease to cling to the punctuality of self-certainty, and recognize themselves and each other as common participants in the practical unity of a social world, in that 'I which is We, and We which is I', which Hegel refers to as *Geist*.[31]

It would scarcely be an overstatement to affirm that the entire first phase of Lacan's work as a psychoanalyst, from his first address to the *International Psychoanalytic Association* in 1936 to the ceremonial announcement of his apostasy from official Freudianism in the *Discours de Rome* of 1953, is dominated by the elaboration of this Hegelian account of the dilemmas of self-consciousness and their resolution, a reworking in which the fundamental contributions of Freud and Hegel are enriched from sources as diverse as animal ethology and the phenomenology of Heidegger. The basic direction which Lacan's thought will take is already clear in his inaugural address, the celebrated paper on 'The Mirror Stage', unorthodox in its introduction of a phase of childhood development entirely absent from classical Freudianism. The child, according to Lacan, when somewhere between the age of six and eighteen months, and hence before the beginnings of articulate speech, is profoundly affected by the encounter with its own image as reflected in a mirror, despite its ability to verify the illusory nature of the image, the point at which a primate placed in this situation would lose interest. Through a 'flutter of jubilant activity', in which it tests the correspondence between its perceived movements in their reflected environment and its own body in relation to the persons and objects which surround it, the child demonstrates a first apprehension of bodily unity, as the support of the division between a coherent self and that which is other, before it is capable of concretely assuming such an identity in the actual control of its bodily movements. It is through this experience, Lacan argues, in 'a drama whose internal thrust is precipitated from insufficiency to anticipation',[32] that the 'I' or ego is consolidated in its primordial form. In contrast to the majority of Freudians, however, Lacan does not portray the emergence of the ego as the beginning of a reckoning with the demands of reality, and therefore as a step on the path to maturity. Lacan's parable of genesis rather marks the ego from the very start as a form which is both ominous and ineluctable. For the very exteriority of the image, its inverted symmetry, and the contrast between its height and apparent fixity and the turbulent sensations which the child experiences, presage what will become in Lacan's account the fundamental characteristics of the ego as a form of estrangement, a mirage of coherence and solidity through which the subject is seduced into misrecognition of its own truth. The mirror stage inaugurates the constitution of what Lacan describes as 'the armour of an alienating identity, which will mark with its rigid structure the subject's entire mental development'.[33]

The novelty, within the psychoanalytical tradition, of Lacan's account of the formation of the ego can only be fully appreciated if contrasted directly with that of Freud himself. Freud's initial conception of the ego, and – arguably – the conception which remained most fundamental throughout his career, is already to be found in the *Project*, when the ego is portrayed as a system which progressively differentiates itself from the rest of the neural network as a result of its perceptual contact with external reality, and which consequently becomes the representative of the demands of that reality, charged with controlling the spontaneous impulse of the organism towards a reckless or hallucinatory gratification. In Freud's later psychoanalytical thought the concept of the ego will always remain associated with the system of perception and consciousness, and with the function of reconciling the conflicting exigencies of the inner and outer worlds. From 1914 onwards, however, with the publication of 'On Narcissism: an Introduction', a new group of themes begins to overlay this primary, biologically grounded conception. Freud now suggests that the ego itself can become an object of libidinal cathexis, indeed, that a state of 'primary narcissism' should be assumed, in which the whole store of libido is focussed upon the ego, so that the development of the ego may be said to consist in a displacement of libido on to external objects. At the same time, this transformation of ego-libido into object-libido brings with it a dilemma, since the more libido is invested in the object, the more libidinally impoverished becomes the ego itself, a process which reaches its culmination in the state of 'being in love'. It is in order to counter this danger that there emerges what Freud terms 'narcissistic object-choice', the tendency of the ego to model its object on itself, or to select an object which possesses precisely those virtues which it feels itself to lack. 'To be loved,' affirms Freud, 'represents the goal and satisfaction of narcissistic object-choice . . . Dependency upon the loved object has a degrading effect (*wirkt herabsetzend*); whoever is in love is humble. Whoever loves has, so to speak, surrendered a part of their narcissism and can only obtain its replacement through being loved in return.'[34]

A little under a decade after 'On Narcissism: an Introduction', in his pivotal essay on *The Ego and the Id*, Freud advances even further in this direction. Although he now abandons the concept of a primary narcissism, arguing that the newly defined id must be seen as the initial reservoir of libido, Freud suggests that the ego not only chooses objects which resemble itself, but also models itself to a large extent upon its earliest objects. Specifically, the ego is formed by processes of identification which – as in Freud's account of the work of mourning – compensate for the loss of the loved object, the most important of these being the identifications with the parental figures, and especially the father, which form the nucleus of the super-ego. 'The character of the ego', Freud now suggests, 'is a precipitate of the abandoned object-cathexes, it contains the history of these object choices.'[35] However, these new theoretical developments do not entirely displace Freud's former views. He continues to describe the ego as having privileged access to external reality, and as the much-harassed mediator between the claims of reality, super-ego and id. The ego may be merely a 'constitutional monarch', severely limited in its autonomy and possibilities for action, yet through its control of motility and its development from 'obedience to drives' to the 'curbing of drives'[36] it retains a position of dominance which is by no means unwarranted. Indeed, for Freud 'Psychoanalysis is a tool which should make possible the ego's progressive conquest of the id.'[37]

This Freudian conception of the ego and its functions – confirmed by his final papers on analytical technique – is clearly at variance with Lacan's account of the ego as an alienating form, as the support of a register which he will soon come to characterize as that of the 'Imaginary'. This is one of the points at which Lacan's psychiatric formation, his original concern with psychosis rather than neurosis, has left an indelible stamp upon his work. Undoubtedly, Lacan's accession to the theory of the mind via the study with paranoia profoundly impressed upon him the characteristics of the ego which are salient in that disorder: projection and identification as forms of self-misrecognition, the aggressivity of attempts to dissolve the narcissistic tension of identification, alternating with a fundamental passivity.[38] Accordingly Lacan's tactic, from the very first, will be to detach the biologico-genetic account of the ego which persists throughout Freud's work from the theory of narcissism and identification to be found in 'On Narcissism: an Introduction' and *The Ego and the Id*: it is these texts which will form Lacan's touchstones in his discussions of the ego. Already in *De la psychose paranoïaque* Lacan had rejected the Freudian assumption of a progressive differentiation of the ego from the id, arguing that the 'reality principle can only be distinguished from the pleasure principle on a gnoseological plane, and it is therefore illegitimate to introduce it to the genesis of the *ego*, since it implies the *ego* itself in its role as subject of knowledge (*connaissance*).'[39] The cognition of which the ego is the support, however, is inseparable from a process of 'miscognition' (*méconnaissance*) which is rooted in the imaginary identification of the mirror stage. Lacan will persistently denounce 'the deceptive obviousness of the notion that the self-identity which is supposed in the common awareness of the ego has anything to do with a presumed instance of the real'.[40] 'The ego of which we speak,' says Lacan, clearly echoing the arguments of *The Ego and the Id*, 'is absolutely impossible to distinguish from the imaginary captivations which constitute it from head to toe, in its genesis as in its status, in its function as in its actuality, by another and for another.'[41]

It will be clear by now that Lacan's procedure in this first phase of his work is to reformulate what he takes to be the central insights of the Freudian theory of the ego in terms of the Hegelian dialectic of self-consciousness. In Freud's own work these multiple insights – into identity-construction as an identification with the love-object, into the contradictions between self-love and object-love, into the frequency of oscillations between affection and hostility – are couched in the terminology of the libido theory, of alternating ego- and object-cathexes, and of a fundamental duality of Eros and the death-drive. In his discussion of the phenomenon of ambivalence, for example, of the interplay of love and hatred within a single relationship, Freud takes special care to refute the suggestion that what is involved is a direct transformation of one emotion into another. He argues, rather, that what takes place is an alternation in predominance between two qualitatively distinct sources of impulse, one libidinal and the other destructive. Naturally, Lacan's opposition to organicism and reductionism – whether inside or outside psychoanalysis – leads him to oppose this view: the oscillation between love and aggression, fascination and rivalry, which is characteristic of many human relationships, cannot be traced back to a biological foundation, but is rather a consequence of the ontological precariousness of the ego, of its fundamental alienation or being-other. When Lacan wishes to illustrate the phenomena of alternation and ambivalence he turns most spontaneously not towards the Freudian theory of drives, but towards the analyses of the dialectic of self and other, of seeing and being seen, of humiliation and domination to be found in Sartre's *Being and Nothingness*.[42] Despite his strictures on the absolute autonomy of the self assumed by existentialism,[43] Lacan recognizes in Sartre a fellow Hegelian.

If Lacan's reworking of the concept of the ego as the form of the subject's entanglement in the *impasses* of identification is deeply indebted to Hegel, his account of the resolution of the dilemmas of the imaginary is no less so. In the *Phenomenology of Mind*, as we have seen, the successive alienations of consciousness – the Stoic's retreat from the world into the empty freedom of thought, the longing of the Unhappy Consciousness of religion for an unattainable beyond, the inability of the revolutionary's 'general will' to generate concrete social institutions – can only be definitively overcome when self-consciousness abandons its insistence upon its own absolute autonomy, and accepts its belonging to and dependence upon the human community which constitutes its substance. Conversely, however, such a community can only be adequate to the aspiration towards autonomy inherent in self-consciousness when it embodies a recognition of the subjective freedom of each social member. Thus for Hegel and – following Hegel – for Kojève the discrepancy between the self-certainty of consciousness and the truth of *Geist* can only be resolved politically, through the emergence of a society in which the individual is recognized as such, rather than as a member of a caste or class, through the appearance – as a result of the immanent dialectic of history – of the modern state. Lacan follows this conception insofar as he argues that the dilemmas of the ego cannot be resolved by retrenchment, by its insistence on its own autonomy and self-identity, but only by the acceptance of its implication in the domain of 'intersubjectivity', maximally defined as the 'total acceptance by the subject of the other subject'.[44]

It is important to note, however, that Lacan differs from Hegel and Kojève in his suggestion that conflict, far from requiring a historical and political solution, has always been potentially resolved through the prior possibility of mediation inherent in language. Although both predeccessors stress the importance of language in the self-formative process of Spirit (for Hegel 'language is self-consciousness existing *for others* . . . which *as such* is immediately *present*', while Kojève argues that language is one of the preconditions of self-consciousness[45]), neither gives language an absolute primacy over labour and social conflict. Lacan's difference in this respect is evident in his adaptation of the Hegelian theory of desire. In his development of this theory Kojève had emphasized the symbolic focus of human conflict: the mere fact of its possession by the other can transform an otherwise worthless thing into an object of contention; human desire is always mediated by the desire of the other, so that all struggle is fundamentally a fight for recognition, and human history becomes – aphoristically – 'the history of desired Desires'.[46] Lacan's account of the crystallization of an initially 'shifting field stretched in accordance with the lines of animal desire'[47] into a world of knowable objects makes fundamental use of this Hegelian-Kojèvian argument. The human object, distinguished by its 'neutrality and indefinite proliferation', its 'instrumental polyvalence and symbolic polyphony',[48] is dependent for its identity upon an identification of the ego. 'It is around the wandering shadow of his own ego', Lacan suggests, 'that will be structured all the objects of [man's] world.'[49] Yet this relation of subject and object is itself caught up in an anterior intersubjective relation. 'What makes the human world a world covered with objects,' Lacan affirms, 'is grounded in the fact that the object of human interest is the object of desire of the other'; and, as in Kojève's thought, this entails that, 'A primitive otherness is included in the object, in so far as it is primitively an object of rivalry and competition.'[50] Yet for Lacan human speech has the power to still the quarrel of rival consciousnesses, since the contractual nature of language requires that, in order for two subjects to name the same object, they must recognize each other as recognizing the same object, thereby transcending the struggle for possession. 'Speech', Lacan argues, 'is always a pact, an accord, one comes to an agreement, one is of the same mind – this is yours, this is mine, this is this, this is that.'[51] Conversely, it is 'at the limits where speech resigns that the domain of violence begins'.[52]

Language, Subjectivity and Historicity

By the early 1950s, therefore, Lacan has developed a philosophical position – arrived at by this largely Hegelian route – which rejects the view of language as a representation of a world of pre-given objects, and which places great emphasis on the relation established by language between speaking subjects. If, as Lacan argues, 'No linguist or philosopher can maintain any longer a theory of language as a system of signs which doubles a system of realities, the latter being defined by the common accord of sound minds in sound bodies',[53] if the mutual recognition of subjects precedes the cognition of objects, this is because no fixation of linguistic meaning, no act of naming, can be accomplished in isolation from the system of language as a whole, and therefore from the continuous intersubjective coordination of language use which sustains this system. Even at the most elementary level, that of ostensive definition, the attempt to establish a privileged point at which language would hook directly on to the world is condemned to failure. 'There is only one gesture,' Lacan argues, 'known since Augustine, which corresponds to nomination: that of the index-finger which shows, but . . . by itself this gesture is not even adequate to designate what is named in the object indicated.'[54] No definition of a linguistic term can be self-explanatory, so that the explication of meaning involves the potentially indefinite series of interpretive substitutions made possible by the language as a whole: 'the unity of signification . . . proves never to be resolved into a pure indication of the real, but always refers back to another signification. That is to say, the signification is realized only on the basis of a grasp of things in their totality.'[55]

One major consequence of this conception of language, evident both in Lacan's work and in the hermeneutic thought to which it is closely allied, is the erosion of the distinction between reference and meaning, between the object of discourse and what is communicated about that object. For if there can be no purely ostensive definition of objects – although this does not preclude a pre-linguistic experience of objects – the identification of objects, and therefore the meaning of the terms by which they are designated, will depend upon what theories are currently held by members of a speech community. It is for this reason that Lacan refers to the 'signified' neither as the reality which is referred to, nor as the meaning communicated in language, but as 'the diachronic set of concretely pronounced discourses'.[56] 'The object', argues Lacan, 'is not unrelated to speech. It is from the very first partially given in the objectal, or objective, system in which must be included the sum of prejudices which constitute a cultural community':[57] the meanings sedimented in language are inseparable from shared patterns of knowledge and belief. But, conversely, any introduction of new information will have its effect upon the distribution of meanings by contributing to the 'diachronic set of concretely pronounced discourses'. Intersubjective communication, therefore, cannot be simply the transferral of concepts from one mind to another, an exchange of tokens which already have their meaning clearly stamped upon them.

If Lacan's grounding of meaning in intersubjective agreement, rather than in a relation of representation between language and reality, blurs the dividing-line between speech and its objects, it has a no less crucial effect on our understanding of the subject implied by speech. For if 'speech is essentially the means of being recognised',[58] if 'language, before signifying something, signifies for someone',[59] it must be concluded that any utterance not only presupposes an addressee, another subject who is capable both of grasping its meaning, and of grasping this meaning as intended by a subject, but that a position in relation to the speaking subject is implicitly attributed to the addressee by the utterance. 'If I call the person to whom I am speaking by whatever name I choose to give him,' Lacan writes, 'I intimate to him the subjective function that he will take on in order to reply to me, even if it is to repudiate this function.'[60] 'In its symbolising function,' therefore, 'speech is moving towards nothing less than a transformation of the subject to whom it is addressed by means of the link that it establishes with the one who emits it . . . '.[61] But since, in accordance with the dialectic of recognition, the very being of the subject is dependent upon its recognition by other subjects, the subject's stance towards the addressee will eventually rebound to determine the position of the subject him- or herself. Lacan's oft-repeated paradigms of this transaction are the statements 'You are my wife', or 'You are my master', in which 'speech commits its author by investing the person to whom it is addressed with a new reality': the attribution of a new status to the other is in fact an indirect transformation of one's own status.[62] Thus every instance of speech is not simply a confirmation, but at the same time the transformation of an intersubjective pact, and thereby of the subjects engaged in this pact. It is in this 'intersubjective logic' of speech that Lacan will discern one of the 'essential dimensions' of psychoanalytical theory and technique, to be set alongside the 'historical theory of the symbol' and the 'temporality of the subject'.[63]

In the second of these two other 'essential dimensions' of analytic experience which Lacan mentions in the *Discours de Rome*, the influence of Hegel is again unmistakable. In the narrative of the *Phenomenology of Mind* Hegel embodies a conception of the relation between consciousness and history which has remained influential ever since, and whose relevance to psychoanalysis Lacan has not been alone in perceiving.[64] Firstly, although Hegel does not deny that forms of consciousness are entwined with determinate historical and social conditions, he argues that the understanding of the past is fundamentally a matter of grasping conceptual rather than causal relations; the ultimate motor of historical development is a recurrent disjunction between the self-comprehension of human subjects and their actual social and historical positions, between the ostensible intentions embodied in the practical compact of social life, and the processes which this practice sets in motion. Secondly, and even more importantly, in interpreting the past in this way we do not grasp a process which is purely external to ourselves: for the categories in terms of which we interpret the past are themselves a product of that past, so that historical knowledge is at the same time a process of self-discovery and self-comprehension. Lastly, in Hegel's view, the beliefs which human beings hold about themselves and their world at any specific moment in history cannot be the embodiment of truth in the fullest sense of the word. Such beliefs do reveal an aspect of the truth, yet this aspect can only be understood when their determination becomes apparent from a more comprehensive position, which emerges from the conflict between such limitation and the absoluteness of the claim to truth. Thus Hegel argues that in the *Phenomenology of Mind* – which reconstructs the experience of consciousness as it passes through these conflicts and transformations – 'each moment is the difference between knowledge and truth, and the movement in which this difference is superseded (*sich aufhebt*)'.[65] Since it is the unconditionality of truth which necessitates the – often painful – abandonment of what was formerly knowledge, truth itself may be said to be the motor of a historical process which takes the form of its own progressive emergence.

This Hegelian conception of the relations between historicity, subjectivity and truth is clearly at the heart of the account of the psychoanalytic process at which Lacan has arrived by the early 1950s. In the opening chapter of the first *Seminar* Lacan stresses that the aim of analysis cannot be to provoke a direct reliving of the past, since such a catharsis could not essentially alter the relation of the patient to his or her history. If, in analysis, 'the restitution of the wholeness of the subject . . . takes the form of a restoration of the past',[66] this restoration must be understood not as an affective reanimation of the past, but as a 'reconstruction'. 'It is less a question of remembering,' Lacan affirms, 'than of rewriting history.'[67] Furthermore, if such conceptual ordering can have the practical effects which are experienced in analysis, this is because history cannot be reduced to a sequence of external vicissitudes which function as the causal antecedents of neurosis, but rather constitutes the subject in its very being. History, says Lacan, is 'that present synthesis of the past' which forms 'the centre of gravity of the subject'.[68] Finally, psychoanalysis for Lacan, as philosophy for Hegel, is concerned with the disjunction between knowledge and truth, the one being constituted by the relation between the ego and its objects, while the other resides in the relation to other and former selves in which the subject is caught up, but which, in the inertia of its imaginary identifications, it misconstrues. For Lacan, analysis is not a question of establishing certain objective 'truths' about the life-history of the patient – all the more so, as the dividing-line between phantasy and reality can never be conclusively established – but of interpreting this recalled life-history as an expression of the 'truth' of the subject whose drama it represents. This interpretation will then in turn alter the patient's stance towards the past, so that for Lacan, as for Hegel, 'Truth is not a given that can be seized in its inertia, but a dialectic in movement.'[69]

Clearly, one of the primary aims of this Lacanian account of historicity is – once again – to criticize the biologistic and reductionist aspects of psychoanalysis, to debunk what Lacan terms the 'mythology of instinctual maturation',[70] and to effect what he calls 'a disentanglement of the deciphering of the unconscious from the theory of instincts'.[71] This is not to imply that Lacan denies the reality of biological or physiological processes. His argument is rather that no event of this order can have an unmediated effect upon the formation of the subject, since its effectivity will depend upon the way in which it is interpreted *by* the subject, and this in turn will depend upon the web of interhuman relations in which the subject is caught up. The infant's attitude towards its own faeces, for example, will be inescapably influenced by its mother's attitude towards them, and this intersubjective dimension will be operative no matter how far one returns in the patient's history: Lacan points out that even a new-born child responds differently to an accidental knock than to a deliberate slap. From this point of view, Freud's quasi-biological account of successive stages (oral, anal, phallic) in the development of libido, and of fixation as an attachment of a part of the libido to a particular stage, to which the libido as a whole will tend to return if blocked at a later date, can only be rejected as mythical. Lacan argues that 'every fixation at a so-called instinctual stage is above all a historical stigmatum: a page of shame that is forgotten or annulled, or a page of glory that constrains'.[72] And he continues: 'the instinctual stages, when they are being lived, are already organized in subjectivity . . . the subjectivity of the child who registers as victories and defeats the heroic chronicle of the training of his sphincters, enjoying the imaginary sexualization of his cloacal orifices, turning his excremental expulsions into aggressions, his retentions into seductions, and his movements of release into symbols – this subjectivity is *not fundamentally different* from the subjectivity of the psychoanalyst . . . '.[73] For Lacan, the importance of bodily functions in psychoanalysis is not biologically grounded, but derives from their early centrality as sites of intersubjective negotiation. It is consistent with this view that Lacan should argue that 'there is no relation of engendering between one of the partial drives and its successor'.[74] Whatever the reality of human biological development, 'in psychoanalysis history is a different dimension to that of development – and it is an aberration to attempt to reduce the former to the latter. History only pursues its course in a syncopated, untoward relation to development (*en contretemps du développement*).'[75]

One of the important consequences of this argument in Lacan's work is that any notion of analysis as following a predetermined path, or relying upon a preconstructed schema of explanation, is decisively rejected. For Lacan psychoanalysis, like history, is a 'science of the particular',[76] condemned to wrestle with all the paradoxes which flow from such a definition; it proceeds by means of a 'series of revelations which are special to each subject'.[77] Lacan is fond of pointing out that Freud went so far as to suggest that the entirety of analytic theory should be put in question by each new analysis, and insists that this openness to the unforeseen in analytic experience is not simply a matter of cognitive punctiliousness, but is essential to the success of psychoanalysis. 'Any intervention will fail,' Lacan argues, 'which is inspired by a prefabricated reconstitution, forged on the basis of our idea of the normal development of the individual.'[78] The goal of analysis should not be to coerce the subject into conformity with some preconceived model of psychological well-being, an error which is pushed to its extreme in the view that analysis should encourage the patient to identify with the ego of the analyst,[79] but to enable the patient to avow the idiosyncrasy of his or her desire.

Yet despite the magnitude of its debt to Hegel, there is one crucial facet of Lacan's theory of historicity which differs from its model. For Hegel, the dimension of remembrance and reappropriation of the past is essentially retrospective. Since, as we have seen, the movement of history consists in successive dialectical displacements of the gap between truth and knowledge, truth and knowledge can only become one, the implicit can only be made fully explicit, when history itself has in some sense come to a close. Consciousness, in the form of *Geist*, now attains complete freedom since, comprehending the historical process as a whole as its own process of self-formation, it no longer suffers the restriction of dependence upon a reality external to itself. In a psychoanalytical perspective, however, this account is clearly unacceptable. For an analysis can be no more than an episode in the life-history of a patient; any more adequate comprehension of the past which it makes possible must be oriented towards enabling the patient to lead a less impeded or tormented life when it has ended. The aim of analysis can only be 'the advent of true speech and the realization by the subject of his or her history in relation to his or her future'.[80]

It is no accident that, in emphasizing this dimension of analysis against Hegel, Lacan makes considerable reference to the work of Heidegger, and specifically to the 'existentialist' Heidegger of *Being and Time*. For although the conception of historicity which Heidegger develops in that work is clearly indebted, both directly and via the thought of Dilthey, to the Hegelian view of human existence as permeated by the human past, Heidegger sharply contests the exclusively retrospective orientation of historical understanding in Hegel. In Heidegger's view, human thought can never elevate itself from its immersion in the past into a position of panoramic survey. Our relation to the past is not one of *Erinnerung*, of 'recollection in tranquility', but rather of 'repetition' or 'recapitulation' (*Wiederholung*: etymologically, 'bringing-back'), in which our attempt to grasp our own rootedness in the past is driven by the urgency of a need to establish an authentic relation to our still to-be-realized possibilities of being.[81] This Heideggerian view of the primacy of the temporal dimension of the future is one with which Lacan's thought has a natural affinity. For already in the paper on the 'Mirror-Stage', Lacan had suggested a 'specific pre-maturation' of the human infant, which makes possible a precocious apprehension of unity and identity in 'a drama whose internal thrust is from insufficiency to anticipation'.[82] From the very first, therefore, one of the functions of the Lacanian imaginary will be to paper over a gap inherent in the subject's relation to the future, and by the early 1950s the concept of this gap or lack is being formulated in the vocabulary of *Being and Time*. 'The subject,' Lacan argues, in his uncollected paper on 'The Neurotic's Individual Myth', 'always has an anticipatory relationship to his own realization which in turn throws him back onto the level of a profound insufficiency and betokens a rift in him, a primal sundering, a thrownness, to use the Heideggerian term.'[83]

In terms of the theory of the 'temporality of the subject', most fully developed in the *Discours de Rome*, this Heideggerian element in Lacan's presentation once again underlines the fact that the actions of the subject cannot be seen as causally determined by his or her past. For the effectivity of the past, like that of any present event in the subject's life, is determined by the manner of its interpretation: it is the way in which we understand our past, for Lacan, which determines how it determines us.[84] But since this understanding is itself intimately related to our orientation towards the future, it can be argued that, 'What is realised in my history is not the past definite of what was, since it is no more [this would be the objectivist view], or even the present perfect of what has been in what I am [as argued by Hegel], but the future anterior of what I shall have been for what I am in the process of becoming.'[85] However, if Lacan agrees with Heidegger that the primary dimension of self-understanding is the future, he draws back – under the influence of Hegel – from the Heideggerian portrayal of the search for an 'authentic' relation to past and future as an essentially solitary quest pursued against the levelling anonymity of collective life. As both the text of *Being and Time* and Heidegger's brief political engagement make clear, such a conception courts the twin dangers of fatalism and decisionism. For Lacan, by contrast, for whom the Hegelian dialectic of the 'law of the heart' remains a paradigm of madness,[86] the truth of the subject's interpretation of its own past cannot be guaranteed by any Heideggerian notion of 'authenticity' or 'resolute decision' (*Entschlossenheit*), but must be put to the test in the intersubjective medium of dialogue. An insistence upon the primacy of inwardness belongs to the illusions of the ego.

By the early 1950s, therefore, Lacan has developed a complex and philosophically sophisticated reformulation of the theory and practice of psychoanalysis, implying a critique of the biologistic elements of Freudian thought, and including a corresponding emphasis upon the primacy of intersubjectivity and the efficacy of speech. The central inspiration of this reformulation, as we have seen, is Hegelian thought. Indeed, in the *Discours de Rome* Lacan goes so far as to claim that the principles which govern Freud's speech 'are nothing other than the dialectic of self- consciousness, in the form in which it is realized from Socrates to Hegel, which starts from the ironic supposition that everything which is rational is real in order to jump to the scientific conclusion that everything which is real is rational'.[87] The analyst, by taking the patient 'at his word', yet refusing to provide a collusive support for the rationalizations which are thus produced, forces the patient into an articulation of ever deeper levels of presupposition, until the rationality of the apparently 'irrational' symptoms is revealed. This is a process which Lacan describes as a transition from 'empty' to 'full speech', in which the subject progressively abandons the imaginary autonomy of the ego, in order to accept its true location in the domain of intersubjectivity. To attain full speech means to cease to speak of oneself as an object, it implies what could be termed a 'recognition of recognition'. 'The subject,' says Lacan, 'begins analysis by speaking about himself without speaking to you, or by speaking to you without speaking about himself. When he can speak to you about himself, the analysis will be over.'[88]

It will also be clear by this point that, despite his portrayal of his work as a 'return to Freud', as a heretical reassertion of psychoanalytical orthodoxy, and a challenge to the complacencies of philosophy, Lacan's reformulation of the theoretical foundations of psychoanalysis is in fact part of a broader movement of criticism of the reductionist and deterministic elements of Freud's thought, both inside and outside analytical circles. Among Lacan's philosophical neighbours and contemporaries, both Sartre and Merleau-Ponty were concerned to refute the biologism and scientism of Freud's work, and both turned to the same sources as

Lacan in order to support their critiques: the thought of Hegel and Heidegger. In *Being and Nothingness* Sartre interprets the Freudian theory of the unconscious as referring to a domain of purely causal processes, as being a 'mechanistic theory of condensation and transference', concerned with 'complexes plunged deep in semi-physiological darkness'.[89] It is then an easy matter for him to argue that the concept of repression implies both, on the side of consciousness, an awareness of what is being repressed, and, on the side of the unconscious, an awareness of having been repressed, so that the supposed division of the psyche introduced by the barrier of censorship can be seen to belong to a 'reified mythology'. Sartre's alternative explanations in terms of bad faith have the merit – he claims – of acknowledging the unity of consciousness which psychoanalysis vainly seeks to challenge. Merleau-Ponty, more sympathetic to psychoanalysis, nevertheless seeks to blunt the edge of Freud's reductionism, arguing, in *The Phenomenology of Perception*, that 'the significance of psychoanalysis is less to make psychology biological than to find a dialectical process in functions thought of as "purely bodily", and to reintegrate sexuality into the human being'.[90] Conversely, Lacan's attempt to distinguish the historicity of the subject in psychoanalysis from any quasi-biological theory of development clearly echoes in its philosophical intent the efforts of Merleau-Ponty and Sartre in the domain of collective history to temper the determinism of orthodox historical materialism.

Within the international arena of psychoanalysis itself, Lacan's revision of Freudianism can also be provided with numerous parallels. The work of such neo-Freudians as Fromm and Horney involves a systematic critique of Freud's theory of instincts, of his anchoring of neurotic conflict in supposedly archaic and infantile layers of the mind, and a rejection of the tendency towards solipsism in Freud's view of the individual. For Fromm, 'Freud's *homo sexualis* is a variant of the classic *homo economicus*. It is the isolated, self-sufficient man who has to enter into relations with others in order that they may mutually fulfil their needs . . . In both variants the persons essentially remain strangers to each other, being related only by the common aim of drive satisfaction.'[91] In a very different way, the British analyst R.D. Laing produced during the 1960s a series of works which sought to attack the reifying effects of Freudian metapsychology, indeed of any theory which 'begins with man or a part of man abstracted from his relation with the other in the world'.[92] Like Lacan, Laing is concerned to debunk organicist aetiologies of madness, although his specific concern is with schizophrenia, rather than paranoia, and to demonstrate the intrinsic meaningfulness of the speech and action of those labelled insane. Furthermore, in the course of this enterprise Laing develops a theory of intersubjectivity and its dilemmas which is in many ways similar to that of Lacan. Despite the fact that Laing places the emphasis on 'experience', whereas for Lacan intersubjectivity is primarily linguistic, both theories are ultimately derived from Hegel, Lacan's more directly, and Laing's via the philosophy of Sartre.

The existence of these parallels to the fundamental thrust of Lacan's thought points to the fact that for Lacan, at this stage of his intellectual development, psychoanalysis is pre-eminently a humanistic discipline, a body of theory whose great initial merit was to have achieved 'the recreation of human meaning in an arid period of scientism'.[93] It is in this spirit that Lacan compares psychoanalysis not to a science in the modern sense, but to the 'liberal arts' of the Middle Ages: 'What characterizes these arts and distinguishes them,' he argues, 'from the sciences that are supposed to have emerged from them, is the fact that they maintain in the foreground what might be termed a fundamental relation to human proportion. At the present time, psychoanalysis is perhaps the only discipline comparable to those liberal arts, inasmuch as it preserves this proportional relation of man to himself – an internal relation, closed on itself, inexhaustible, cyclical, and implied pre-eminently in the use of speech.'[94] Thus, at this point, the very primacy which Lacan accords to language within his doctrine is founded in a – Hegelian – view of language as the domain of 'properly human reality, of that which is communicable'.[95] 'If one had to define the moment when man becomes human,' says Lacan, 'let us say that it is the moment when, however little, he enters into the symbolic relation.'[96] Not surprisingly, therefore, Lacan evokes the aims of analysis, during this period, in the vocabulary of post-war philosophical humanism. Analysis should be oriented towards 'the reconquest by the subject of the authentic reality of the unconscious'.[97] On occasion Lacan will go so far as to suggest that 'full speech is defined by its identity with that of which it speaks',[98] thus fully adopting a Hegelian conception of a coincidence of subject and object as the proper goal of the dialectic of analysis.

The Influence of Structuralism

The centrality of the *Discours de Rome* to Lacan's *oeuvre* can in large part be attributed to the fact that it both represents the culmination and announces the decline of this 'humanist' phase in his work.[99] Shortly after the *Discours de Rome*, a rapid and remarkable shift of emphasis begins to take place in Lacan's teaching, clearly visible in the disjunction between the first (1953-54) and the second (1954-55) *Seminars*, in which the theory of the ego and the imaginary, which had been the central concern of the first phase of Lacan's work, is displaced from its primary position by the theory of a new register which Lacan refers to as the 'Symbolic'. Lacan ceases to portray psychoanalysis as the crown of contemporary humanistic learning, and to present the goal of analysis as a restoration of the lost integrity and authenticity of the subject. He now argues that the notion of humanism is 'sufficiently weighed down with history for us to be able to consider it as a particular position realized in a distinctly limited domain of what we continue imprudently to call humanity'.[100] Not only this, Lacan begins to suggest that Freud himself has dealt a fatal blow to a humanism which is inseparably intertwined with the notion of the primacy of consciousness. Hegel had advanced a long way along this path, since throughout the course of history as Hegel understands it there exists a gap between the concept consciousness has of itself, and its actual content. Yet, in the *Phenomenology*, this disjunction is ultimately resolved in absolute knowledge, whereas for Freud, Lacan argues, the disjunction is perpetual.[101] The new emphasis of Lacan's thought will be on the extent to which the human subject is irredeemably fractured, decentred, condemned to a permanent dispossession of self.

This shift in Lacan's intellectual orientation, marked by a break with the phenomenological-existentialist terminology which had echoed through his earlier work, was undoubtedly in large part the result of a growing awareness of the methodological principles of structuralism, initially as presented by Lévi-Strauss in *The Elementary Structures of Kinship* (1949) and in his *Introduction à l'oeuvre de Marcel Mauss* (1950), a little later – with the publication of the *Course in General Linguistics* in 1955 – as formulated by Saussure himself. It is remarkable that, over a decade before structuralism attained the height of its popularity in France, Lacan had already absorbed what he understood to be the principal advances of structuralist theory. Furthermore, unlike many later converts of the 1960s, Lacan – despite his considerable debt to structuralism – never paid uncritical homage either to Lévi-Strauss, or to structuralist principles in general. Indeed, by the mid 1950s he had already stated the fundamental lines of argument of the critiques of structuralism which only began to be widely accepted in the late 1960s. This cautious, discriminating reception of structuralism on Lacan's part was entirely to be expected. For Lacan's fundamental insistence on the *intersubjectivity* of language excluded from the very start his acceptance of any account of language as a code, or formalizable system of signs. This is not to say that Lacan denies the possibility of specific formalized languages, such as those of mathematics, or even of the formalization of parts of natural language. It is simply that he always makes the elementary 'hermeneutic' point that any such formalization must itself be grounded in intersubjective agreement, and that the terms of this agreement cannot themselves be formalized. This insight underlies Lacan's oft-repeated dictum that 'there is no meta-language',[102] since 'it is necessary that all so called meta-languages be presented to you with language. You cannot teach a course in mathematics using only letters on the board. It is always necessary to speak an ordinary language that is understood.'[103] Hence Lacan's encounter with structuralism produces not an unqualified conversion, but rather a complex pattern of interference with his original Freudian and Hegelian assumptions. The result is a novel synthesis in which each contributory current of thought tends to subvert and modify each of the others. It is precisely this confluence of – and competition between – the philosophical themes of the immediate post-war era and the more recent innovations of structuralism which makes for the richness and ambiguity of Lacan's work from the early 1950s onwards. It is from this point – which coincides with his emergence as the *maître* of the *Seminar* – that one may date the inception of Lacan's mature thought.

It is unlikely, however, that a thinker as persistent as Lacan in his central concerns could have 'changed direction' in this way, had there not been present in his earlier work certain assumptions and tendencies favourable towards the theoretical opening offered by structuralism. This conjecture is confirmed if we turn once again to the doctoral thesis on paranoid psychosis. If Lacan appears to be deeply attracted to Freud's thought in this work, as we have already noted, this is precisely because of Freud's respect for the *meaningfulness* of psychic phenomena, even – and especially – for the processes and creations of the disordered mind. There is, however, a subordinate, yet persistent strain of argument in *De la psychose paranoïaque*, in which Lacan appears anxious to deny that a semantic and psychogenic account of mental illness must entail the ruin of scientific objectivity. Thus he writes: '*To understand (comprendre)*, by this we mean to give to the behaviour that we observe in our patients in its human meaning . . . But it should be noted that if the method makes use of relations of meaning (*rapports significatifs*) which are grounded in the consent of the human community, their application to the determination of a given fact can be governed by purely objective criteria.'[104] At one or two points Lacan goes so far as to suggest that the meaning grasped by the procedure of *Verstehen* may be as ill-founded as 'the homogeneous (*participationist*) interpretation which the primitive gives to the totality of natural phenomena';[105] as a method of analysis comprehension is 'in itself too tempting not to present grave dangers of illusion'.[106] In order to counter these dangers, he argues, a science of personality must begin from the hypothesis that 'there exists a determinism which is specific to the order of phenomena defined by relations of human comprehensibility'.[107] In itself this hypothesis is simply a postulate, but like the hypotheses which found the object, the method and the autonomy of any science, its *prima facie* acceptance is unavoidable. For 'if there were no psychogenic determinism, it would be useless to speak of human behaviour other than in poetic figures'.[108] Throughout *De la psychose paranoïaque*, therefore, Lacan's persistent rejection of the mock-scientificity of organicism and psycho-physical parallelism is counterbalanced by an assertion of the potential objectivity of a purely psychological and semantic account of mental disorder.

In Lacan's doctoral thesis, however, the defence of the autonomy of the domain of social relations of meaning jostles uneasily with his claims to scientific rigour. Indeed, Lacan is caught in a severe dilemma. For it is impossible for him to elucidate how the comprehension of psychic phenomena, even if the results of such a procedure do not coincide with the significance attributed to his or her own acts by the subject, can result in anything other than the grasping of an implicit meaning, of the underlying logic and purpose of the patient's behaviour, so that the problem of interpretation, and all the attendant dangers of imaginary identification, simply recur at a new level. The notion of a form of explanation, in other words, which is not itself simply the understanding of unconscious meaning, is not supported by any specific theoretical resource in Lacan's early work. Accordingly, it is the critique of biologism and reductionism – rather than of the potential illusions, the endless mirror-play of meaning – which dominates the first phase of Lacan's work. As late as the opening pages of the first *Seminar*, Lacan can suggest that it is the reintroduction of 'something with a different essence, with a concrete psychological density . . . namely meaning', which distinguishes Freud from the scientistic century in which he was born,[109] while in the *Discours de Rome* the 'deliverance of imprisoned meaning' is presented as central to the enterprise of analysis.[110]

Once the latent anti-hermeneutic current in Lacan's early work has been perceived, it is no longer difficult to understand how structuralism could so rapidly reverse the relation of forces between this undertow and a formerly predominant anti-scientism. The single most important idea which Lacan adopts from structuralism is that of the – in Saussure's terminology – 'arbitrary' relation between signifier and signified. For what this arbitrariness entails is that there can be no natural, automatic, or self-evident transition from signifier to signified, from language to meaning, or from human behaviour to its 'psychological' significance. The bar between signifer and signified in Lacan's transcription of what he terms the Saussurian 'algorithm' – S/s – may therefore be described as 'a barrier resisting signification',[111] since it blocks the intuitive grasp of meaning which Lacan now associates with a misleading, imaginary identification with the other, and the attendant dangers for analytical practice. The Saussurian conception will also provide the basis for a newly emphasized distinction between the 'signifier' and the 'sign'. For Lacan the sign belongs to a codified system in which meanings have been rigorously specified, or implies a natural or unalterable relation between indicator and indicated, such as exists – for example – between smoke and fire, or such as is exemplified by the 'language' of the bees.[112] As a vehicle of a stable meaning, the sign may be defined as 'representing something for someone'.[113] The signifier, such as a term of everyday language, by contrast, 'has no need to justify its existence in terms of any signification whatsoever';[114] such signification is not its 'content' – as in the case of the code – but is determined by its relations to other signifiers. More paradoxically, it can be said that – as the title of a chapter of Lacan's third *Seminar* puts it – 'The signifier, as such, signifies nothing'[115] – the signifier in itself is simply a mark or a sound: it is only its location within the differential system of a language, rather than an intrinsic relation with an object or signified, which endows it with the capacity for signification, and only its actual use by a speaker which realizes this capacity in a unique way.

Seen in terms of Lacan's earlier theoretical dilemma, the most important aspect of this dissociation – or arbitrary relation – between signifier and signified, is that it offers the possibility of an escape from the immersion in meaning implied by comprehension. If the link between language and meaning can be broken for the purposes of analysis – as appears to be the case in structural linguistics, with its masking out of semantics – then it becomes possible to study the structure of the signifier, and consequently the determination of meaning – Lacan's original ambition – without becoming embroiled in the problems and dangers of interpretation. 'It is impossible to study how the phenomenon called language, and which is the most fundamental of interhuman relations, functions, if one does not distinguish from the start between signifier and signified. The signifier has its own laws, independently of the signified.'[116] In the chapter of the third *Seminar* from which this remark comes Lacan explicitly connects this new conception of the signifier with the reversal of his previous subordination of explanation to understanding: 'You are acquainted with the so-called opposition between *Erklären* and *Verstehen*. In relation to it, we must maintain that there is no scientific structure except where there is *Erklären*. *Verstehen* is an invitation to all kinds of confusions. *Erklären* does not at all imply mechanical signification, or anything of that kind. The nature of *Erklären* is the recourse to the signifier as the sole foundation of any conceivable scientific structuration.'[117]

Although these developments in Lacan's thought would have been impossible without Saussure's division of the linguistic sign into signifier and signified, the general shift of theoretical outlook which they mark is more directly indebted to Lévi-Strauss. For it is Lévi-Strauss who claims most insistently that structuralist methodology has opened the possibility of a new, rigorously objective treatment of data in the human sciences. Not only does Lévi-Strauss argue that a society may be seen as 'an *ensemble* of symbolic systems, in the first rank of which would be language, marriage-rules, economic relations, art, science, religion',[118] he also suggests that in the analysis of such systems, significance – the lived experience of meaning – may be seen as a secondary and derivative phenomenon, that 'since meaning is always the result of a combination of elements which are not themselves significant . . . behind all meaning there is a non-meaning'.[119] It is this belief in the reducibility of meaning to non-meaning which opens up the objectivist perspective of conventional structuralism, since it appears to permit the anthropologist to escape from a concern with the understanding of native experience, and therefore to eliminate the 'hermeneutic' danger of an interpretation predetermined by the expectations of the investigator. 'For too long,' Lévi-Strauss complains, echoing the Lacanian critique of the imaginary relation of ego to ego, 'philosophy has succeeded in keeping the human sciences imprisoned in a circle, permitting them to perceive no object of study for consciousness other than consciousness itself.'[120]

In Lévi-Strauss's anthropological work, the doctrine that 'symbols are more real than what they symbolize, the signifier precedes and determines the signified',[121] broadens out into the view that social life is constituted and determined by a 'universe of rules'. According to such a view, explanations of social phenomena cannot have reference to individual or collective experience or affectivity, since the content of experience is itself determined by an unconscious system of shared categories. Thus, in his study of *Totemism*, Lévi-Strauss points out that the kind of explanation employed by Malinowski, in which magical ritual is seen as an attempt to ward off an anxiety produced by consciousness of risk, could just as easily be reversed: it could be argued that it is rather because an object is associated with magical ritual that it generates such feelings.[122] Lévi-Strauss's development of this separation between psychological and biological considerations and symbolic structure, in his analysis of totemism, is of particular relevance to the thought of Lacan, since the central phenomenon at issue is the 'identification' between social groups and an animal or other totemic object. Lévi-Strauss contends that any theory of totemism which takes this identification as primary, seeing it as the outcome of a particular physical dependence upon the natural environment, or as the expression of some putative primitive mentality, must remain within the circle of the 'totemic illusion'. This circularity can only be broken when it is appreciated that totemic systems do not consist of a sequence of one-to-one relations between terms (human groups and natural species), but rather of two parallel series of *differences* between terms.[123] Totemism, for Lévi-Strauss, is simply a symbolic articulation of social structure: any phenomena of affective identification with the totemic object are determined by this symbolic articulation, rather than being its foundation.

This Lévi-Straussian argument for the primacy of symbolic systems is central to the shift in Lacan's theoretical position which takes place during the early 1950s, and in which the problem of relation between the ego and intersubjectivity is reformulated as that of the relation between the imaginary and the new order which Lacan – following Lévi-Strauss – refers to as the 'symbolic'. In explicating the concept of this order Lacan adopts almost without qualification the Lévi-Straussian account of the rules of matrimonial exchange – circumventions of the incest taboo – as the foundation of human sociality, of the nature of all social systems as signifying systems, and of the paramount position of language as the paradigm and mediator of these systems. 'The primordial Law', Lacan argues, 'is therefore that which in regulating marriage ties superimposes the kingdom of culture on that of a nature abandoned to the law of mating. . . . This law, then, is clearly revealed as identical with an order of language. For without kinship nominations, no power is capable of instituting the order of preferences and taboos that bind and weave the yarn of lineage through succeeding generations.'[124] At the same time, a new sense of fatality enters Lacan's work, closely linked with the 'heteronomy' of a symbolic order which is 'irreducible to human experience' and which therefore 'cannot be conceived of as constituted by man, but as constituting him'.[125] The 'little freedom', the narrow but decisive leeway which the subject formerly possessed in adopting a stance to his or her own past, thus making it possible to 're-order past contingencies by bestowing upon them the sense of necessities to come'[126] is abolished. And in his or her relation to the signifier the subject is compared with 'the messenger-slave of ancient usage, who [although he] carries under his hair the codicil that condemns him to death knows neither the meaning of the text, nor in what language it is written, nor even that it had been tattooed on his shaven scalp as he slept'.[127]

At the same time as Lacan introduces this conception of the determination of the subject by the symbolic, he reveals a new enthusiasm for the apparently scientistic and reductionist aspects of Freud's work. He now argues that the ethos of 19th-century determinism and materialism which pervades Freud's work cannot be dismissed as simply the anachronistic clothing of the humanistic core of his thought. 'It is this very scientism,' Lacan suggests, 'if one wishes thus to designate his adherence to the ideals of a Brücke . . . which lead Freud, as his writings show us, to open up the path which will forever bear his name.'[128] It is a token of this new sympathy that Lacan now offers a positive exegesis of the biologistic aspects of Freud's thought, and in particular of the concept of a 'death-drive', dismissed by the majority of post-Freudian analysts – with the notable exception of Melanie Klein – as hopelessly speculative. He argues that Freud's obstinate maintenance of a duality of instincts (in the form of Eros and the death-drive) at the point at which it was ceasing to be plausible to argue for a qualitative distinction between ego and sexual drives may be attributed to his intuitive grasp of the relation of the human subject to a symbolic order which is 'irreducible to human experience'.[129] In Lacan's view, one should 'recognize in the metaphor of the return of the inanimate (which Freud attaches to every living body) that margin beyond life that language gives to the human being by virtue of the fact that he speaks'.[130] More generally, if Freud continued throughout his work to emphasize the 'energetic function', this is because the 'energetic myth' was his means of evoking 'what is beyond the interhuman reference, what is properly speaking a symbolic beyond'.[131]

This association of the symbolic with what is 'beyond' the interhuman relation indicates what is perhaps the most important transformation which the new concept effects in Lacan's thought. Up to this point Lacan has logically traced language back to a 'pact of nomination' in which subjects agree to recognize – and to recognize each other as recognizing – an object which had formerly been the focus of intersubjective rivalry. The notion of a pact of nomination therefore depends upon a coordinate of intentions between a minimum of two subjects. What the encounter with the theory of the symbolic forces Lacan to recognize, however, is that any such coordination depends upon a prior understanding of language, since the major clue to what subjects intend is the meaning of what they say, as determined by the structure of language. Hence linguistic meaning cannot be founded in the prelinguistic intentions of speaking subjects.[132] For Lacan this does not entail, however, the abandoning of the concept of the subject altogether. From the very beginning, Lacan perceives clearly that the Lévi-Straussian and – in general – structuralist attempt to abolish the problem of the subject leads merely to the instatement of the symbolic system itself, self-enacting and self-perpetuating, as a kind of meta-subject. 'The symbolic function,' Lacan affirms, 'has absolutely nothing to do with a para-animal formation, a totality which would turn the whole of humanity into a kind of collective animal – because in the final analysis that is what the collective unconscious is.'[133] Lacan's difficulty, therefore, is to avoid the absorption of the individual human subject into a collective subject, without relying upon the assumption that social order is dependent upon a compact between individual subjects. He must find a means of theorizing the subject as dependent upon – but not reducible to an effect of – the social-symbolic order. It is in order to achieve this aim that Lacan introduces the distinction between the 'Other' (*le grand Autre*) and the 'other' of imaginary identification.

Lacan's distinction between the 'other' and the 'Other' is based on the assumption that, in the relation between subjects, each will attempt to discover a confirming image, a reinforcement of his or her own ego in the response of the other. 'The subject always imposes on the other,' Lacan suggests, 'in the radical diversity of modes of relation, which range from the invocation of speech to the most immediate sympathy, an imaginary form which bears the seal, or the superimposed seals, of the experiences of powerlessness through which this form was modelled in the subject: and this form is nothing other than the ego.'[134] What this means is that the arbitrariness of the relation between signifier and signified – and here the signifier need not be linguistic, but can be any form of human action or self-expression – makes inevitable a process of interpretation which is not simply a matter of 'reading off' meanings, and that – since this interpretation of *what* is communicated is inseparable from the addressee's conception of *who* is communicating – the 'message' of the subject with whom the addressee is in relation will have the form of the latter's ego imposed upon it: the 'other', in this sense, is an echo of the self. In the course of communication, we may come to realize that our construal of what is meant does not correspond with what the other subject intends, indeed the intersubjectivity of communication consists precisely in a continuous adjustment of assumptions about the partner in communication. But what Lacan wishes to signal by his distinction between the 'other' and the 'Other' is that our preconceptions can never be replaced by a definitive grasp of who the other subject truly is. For any evidence of the other subject's authentic intentions is no less open to interpretation than what has preceded. 'What the subject says to me,' Lacan remarks, 'is always in a fundamental relation to a possible dissimulation, in which he sends me or I receive the message in an inverted form.'[135] Hence, 'The subject is separated from the Others, the true Others, by the wall of language.'[136]

By introducing the concept of the Other in this way, Lacan finally eliminates the belief of his earlier work in a possible coincidence of self-conception and intersubjective position, which would be realized by the mutual recognition of subjects in language. For in order for the dialectic of recognition to come to rest in such an equilibrium of acknowledgement, it would be necessary for me to recognize the other as recognizing me. But this, Lacan now suggests, is impossible. Certainly, *I* must recognize the other, since every act of speech implies a plea to be heard. Yet I can never be certain that this request has been acceded to, I can never be fully confident of my interpretation of the Other's reply or lack of reply. To illustrate this, Lacan returns to his favoured examples of the intersubjectivity of speech: '*You are my wife* – but after all, what do you know about it? *You are my master* – but in fact, are you so sure?* Precisely what determines the founding value of these words is the fact that what is aimed at in the message, like what is manifest in dissimulation, is the fact that the other is there as absolute Other. Absolute, that is to say recognized (*reconnu*) but not known (*connu*).'[137] This irreparable dissociation of cognition and recognition, of knowledge and acknowledgement, now provides the basis for critique of Hegel's position, in which the inherent ambiguities of dialogue are ultimately resolved in the monologue of a reason which recognizes itself to be universal. In Lacan's view, this ultimate reinstatement of consciousness, after its long historical 'decentring', simply repeats the error of the self-consciousness which mistakes its own immediacy for the universal, which Hegel himself denounces. The Hegelian dialectic, he now argues, 'cannot shake the delusion of the presumption to which Hegel applied it, remaining caught in the trap offered by the mirage of consciousness to the *I* infatuated with its feelings, which it erects into a law of the heart'.[138] The concept of Other indicates the point at which 'the recognition of desire is linked with the desire for recognition', but this point has now been removed to an unattainable 'beyond'.[139]

Yet if the concept of the Other finally stills the echoes of Hegelian reconciliation to be found in Lacan's early work, it proves to be a double-edged weapon, which can be turned just as effectively against the objectivist claims of structuralism. As we saw in our initial discussion of the dialectic of recognition, the meaning of speech cannot be seen as bestowed by the intentionality of the subject, but is dependent upon the response of the addressee, since it is this response which situates the subject in relation to its own speech. But since this response, despite the ego's attempt to frame it as the confirming reply of a fellow ego, in fact comes from the unattainable Other, the concept of the Other introduces a radical semantic uncertainty into language, and produces an endless reflexive movement of speech endeavouring to grasp its own meaning. 'Language', Lacan remarks, 'is constituted in such a way as to found us in the Other, while radically preventing us from understanding him.'[140] Furthermore, since this Other, whom the subject takes to be absolute though unattainable, is in fact another subject 'founded in the Other', and is therefore only unattainable because believed to be absolute, it is language itself, interposed between subjects as the medium of intersubjectivity, as the 'locus of the treasure of the signifier',[141] which may be described as the absolute Other with which all subjects are confronted. Thus, although it may at first appear that the other subject is perpetually hidden 'behind' the wall of language, it becomes apparent that all subjects are on the same side of this wall, although they are able to communicate only indirectly by means of the echo of their speech upon it.[142]

This argument naturally leads to an unsparing critique of the claims of structuralism to produce an objective decoding of linguistic messages through the application of a formal system, a critique which is perhaps most ingeniously expressed in Lacan's 'Seminar on the ''Purloined Letter'''. For in searching systematically and repeatedly through the Minister's apartment for the stolen missive, the police in Poe's story carry out what Lacan terms an 'undoubtedly theoretical exhaustion of space',[143] comparable to a structuralist dissection of a text into a system of differentially related elements. But, as the story makes clear, this neutral 'scanning' – as Lacan terms it elsewhere – bears no relation to what will be found or not be found. The object of the quest is in fact defined by the subjective expectations which are brought to the quest, and which the objectivity of structural analysis was believed to have excluded. In this case these expectations are determined by an imaginary identification with the 'criminal mind', which is assumed to have concealed the letter in the most unlikely and inaccessible hiding-place. The letter remains undiscovered therefore simply because, even as the police held it in their hands, it 'did not correspond to the description which they had (*ne répondait pas au signalement qu'ils en avaient*)'.[144] But as the embodiment of a reply which thwarts the expectations of the ego, in its 'oddness' which eludes the systematicity of the search, the letter clearly represents the non-objectifiable alterity of the Other, in other words – of the unconscious. Like the signifier, which has no intrinsic meaning, the message contained in the letter is not known by the participants in Poe's story and it is precisely this mystery which constitutes its power: each invests it with an imaginary meaning which reflects his or her own fears and ambitions, whereas in fact, 'In coming into possession of the letter – admirable ambiguity of language – it is its meaning which possesses them'.[145] For Lacan, therefore, meaning cannot be objectified: rather, it is characterized by a fundamental elusiveness and unpredictability. 'The meaning of meaning in *my* practice', he states, 'can be grasped in the fact that it runs away: in the sense of something leaking from a barrel, not in the sense of "making tracks". It is because it runs away (in the barrel sense) that a discourse assumes a meaning, in other words: by virtue of the fact that its effects are impossible to calculate.'[146]

Lacan's Reformulation of Basic Concepts

So far we have examined the development of Lacan's views on language and interpretation, and the manner in which these intersect with his conception of the dialectic of intersubjectivity, but we have yet to consider how – within this framework – he retheorizes the basic concepts of Freudian psychoanalysis: the concepts of the unconscious, of castration, and of the Oedipus complex. Perhaps the best way to approach these issues is to return to the Hegelian starting point of his thought, where self-consciousness is portrayed as emerging from the awareness of physical need. Having arrived, by the early 1950s, at his conception of the human subject as divided between ego and 'true subject', Lacan will begin to employ a version of this Hegelian account in order to theorize the formation of the unconscious, a version in which a stress on the Saussurian bar between signifier and signified ultimately 'subverts' the conclusions arrived at by Hegel. Like his philosophical mentor, Lacan begins from the experience of physical need (*besoin*), not in relation to the living organism in general, however, but specifically in relation to the child, who, because of the 'prematurity' of human birth, is for a long time dependent upon others for the satisfaction of its basic wants (this is a point which Lacan follows Freud in emphasizing). Lacan argues that a crucial transformation takes place when the child's plea for satisfaction begins to be expressed in language, since the request for satisfaction is now accompanied by a plea for recognition as the *subject* of the need to be satisfied, which Lacan terms *demande*. It is at this point, however, that the subject encounters a paradox. For, however sedulously its physical requirements are attended to, he or she can never be sure that this attention is the expression of the recognition which is craved, rather than simply a pacification, the quietening of speech treated merely as an intrusive signal of animal discomfort. 'In this way,' Lacan argues, 'demand annuls (*aufhebt*) the particularity of everything which can be granted by transmuting it into a proof of love, and the very satisfaction that it obtains for need is reduced (*sich erniedrigt*) to the level of being no more than the crushing of the demand for love.'[147] It is out of this process that there emerges what Lacan terms 'desire' (*désir*), which he understands as resulting from the gap between the unconditionality of demand, and the inadequate particularity of whatever is proferred in reply. Through the experience of the incapacity of the object of need to function as an unequivocal signifier of love, the subject is thrown back into the quest for an impossible particular object which would satisfy the universality of the demand made manifest in language. 'Thus desire', Lacan argues, 'is neither the appetite for satisfaction, nor the demand for love, but the difference that results from the subtraction of the first from the second, the phenomenon of their splitting (*Spaltung*).'[148] For Lacan it is through this splitting that the unconscious is formed. 'We must posit', he writes, 'that it is the concrete incidence of the signifier in the submission of need to demand which, by repressing desire into the position of the misrecognized, gives the unconscious its order.'[149]

One of the most important consequences of this account of the formation of the unconscious is that, for Lacan, 'The unconscious *is not* a type defining within psychic reality the circle of that which does not possess the attribute (or virtue) of consciousness.'[150] Initially, Lacan may here appear to be simply reiterating Freud's argument that it is not the absence of the quality of being conscious which defines a content as unconscious, but rather its belonging – under repression – to a specific psychical system. Lacan's position, however, is less orthodox than this, since he goes on to suggest that 'the presence of the unconscious, being situated in the place of the Other, is to be sought in every discourse, in its enunciation.'[151] The import of this definition can best be understood by returning to Lacan's account of the relation between the subject and the Other. As we have seen, Lacan stresses that speech is not simply a conveyor of information, but establishes a relation between speaker and hearer; it is this duality, present from the beginnings of his work, which the later Lacan describes in terms of a distinction between 'statement' (*énoncé*) and 'utterance' (*énonciation*), between what is said and *the fact that* the speaker says it. It is the latter, the utterance of a particular statement in a particular situation, which reveals the position which the speaker wishes to take up in relation to the hearer, or – in other words – what the subject wishes the Other to recognize him or her as being, but the content of the desire for recognition conveyed by the utterance is not – for reasons we have already examined – determined by an intention of the speaker: it is only the response of the Other which determines what the situation is. But since this response is submitted to the same conditions as the original utterance, the desire for recognition which motivates speech is condemned to remain implicit, and therefore 'unconscious'. Or, to reverse the terms of this description, the specificity of desire *is* articulated through the intersubjectivity of language, but this intersubjectivity itself cannot be articulated. Hence the many passages in Lacan's work where he equates the unconscious with the transindividual dimension of language, suggesting that the unconscious is contained in the meaning which exceeds subjective intention.[152] For Lacan, the 'exteriority of the symbolic in relation to man is the very notion of the unconscious';[153] or, more famously and more aphoristically: 'The unconscious is the discourse of the Other.'

This conception of the unconscious as 'language which escapes the subject in its operation and in its effects'[154] makes clear why so many of Lacan's theoretical emphases, in relation to the unconscious, differ so sharply from those of Freud. For Lacan, the unconscious is 'a self (*un soi-même*) and not a series of disorganised drives, as a part of Freud's theoretical work might lead one to think, when you read that within the psyche only the ego has an organization'.[155] Lacan repudiates any conception of the unconscious as linked with the instinctual, the archaic, or the regressive, as the 'place of the divinities of night'. For, although Lacan does not deny the reality of biologically-based needs, his contention is that such needs can only enter into communication as symbolized, and therefore as *symbolizing*, obliquely representing the subject who represents. The instinctual foundations of the soul do not 'resonate in depth', he suggests 'except by reflecting back the echo of the signifier'.[156] Furthermore, and even more dramatically, Lacan denies that the unconscious possesses any determinate content, or that the unconscious is the 'real place of another discourse'.[157] For any expression of wishes, emotions, thoughts or drives must be treated by the analyst as a signifier, must be interpreted in its status as an utterance, an appeal to another subject, rather than as a revelation of the 'psychological' condition of the speaker. Such an interpretation, in which the meaning of an utterance becomes the object of a statement, can of course be produced. But this interpreting statement will have its own dimension of utterance, and will therefore transform the intersubjective relation which it attempts to determine. This does not entail, it should be noted, that such attempts at determination are futile and should be abandoned, but it does require an appreciation of the paradox that to grasp the unconscious is, at the same time, to fail to grasp it. In *The Four Fundamental Concepts of Psychoanalysis* Lacan remarks that 'twice-lost Eurydice is the most striking image we can give, in terms of myth, of the relation between Orpheus the analyst and the unconscious'.[158]

Given the radicality of this reformulation of the Freudian unconscious, it is perhaps surprising that Lacan is able so loudly to proclaim his orthodoxy. For many 20th-century thinkers, most notably philosophers of the hermeneutic tradition stemming from Heidegger, to whom Lacan frequently refers, could agree that 'there is always on the level of language something which is beyond consciousness',[159] or that 'the range of meaning infinitely exceeds the signs manipulated by the individual',[160] without being thereby committed to the other major concepts of Freudian theory, such as the Oedipus complex, and the castration complex. Paradoxically Lacan himself is only able to retain the full panoply of Freudian concepts, abandoned by other analysts, by reinterpreting them as a theorization of the *ontological* predicament of the subject – as a want-to-be – in its dependence on the signifier. The key to this reinterpretation is Lacan's theory of the phallus, and in this context it is helpful to refer to a passage of 'Inhibitions, Symptoms, Anxiety', where Freud remarks that, 'The high degree of narcissistic value which the penis possesses can appeal to the fact that the organ is a guarantee to its owner that he can be united with his mother – i.e. to a substitute for her – in the act of copulation.'[161] Lacan carries this interpretation one stage further by arguing that copulation with the mother is not the real aim of the subject, but is itself merely an image of fully mutual recognition. The phallus, which Lacan distinguishes from the physical organ, the penis, functions as the assurance of this recognition, and may therefore be described as 'the signifier intended to designate as a whole the signifieds as effects, in that the signifier conditions them by its presence as signifier'.[162] Since the relation to the Other founded in language is radically uncertain, only a signifier outside the 'locus of the treasure of the signifier' could enable the subject to grasp the meaning of his or her own speech, by specifying how all the other signifiers produce their meaning. Such a signifier is, of course, impossible, so that the phallus is destined to appear to the subject as eternally lost. It is this loss which Lacan theorizes as castration.

Lacan suggests that it is through the realization of the mother's lack of the phallus that the child first confronts the reality of castration. It is only because of a prior symbolization, however, that a perception of the absence of the real organ can trigger the child's realization that the mother is not able to substantiate its being through full recognition, since she herself has no such plenitude to bestow, is submitted to the 'scission' of the symbolic order. The child's initial response to this discovery is to attempt to become the adequate object of the mother's own unfulfilled desire, and it is the series of these attempts which characterizes the Oedipus complex: 'The child . . . experiences the phallus as the centre of the desire of the mother, and situates himself in different positions, through which he is led to deceive this desire: he can identify with the mother, identify with the phallus, identify with the mother as bearer of the phallus or present himself as the bearer of a phallus. He testifies to the mother that he can complete her, not only as a child but as regards what she lacks: he will be, as a totality, the metonymy of the phallus.'[163] Eventually, however, the child will be obliged to accept the paradoxical nature of these efforts, and to come to terms with its own symbolic castration, with the loss of the imaginary phallus. This castration, equivalent to full entry into the symbolic order, takes place by means of what Lacan terms the 'paternal metaphor' or the 'Name-of-the-Father'. The function of this metaphor is not to be confused with the role of real father, since the paternal metaphor signifies the ultimate authority which upholds the symbolic order as a whole. 'In all strictness,' Lacan affirms, 'the Symbolic father is to be conceived of as "transcendent" – an irreducible given of the signifier. The symbolic father – he who is ultimately capable of pronouncing these words: "I am who I am" – can only be imperfectly incarnate in the real father.'[164] Lacan believes that the father is suited to play this role of 'author of the Law' (the symbolic order in its ineluctable, imperative aspect) by the fact that the relation of paternity does not possess the same biological obviousness as that of maternity. 'It requires a reversal,' Lacan remarks, 'in order for the human fact of copulating to receive the meaning which it really has, but to which no imaginary access is possible, that the child is really the father's as much as the mother's.'[165] Hence, to accept the Name-of-the-Father is to accept subordination to an order which cannot be grounded in experience, and to abandon a relation of imaginary complementarity with the mother, since it is the father who is the bearer of the phallus of which both mother and child are deprived.

From all that has been said so far, it will be clear that Lacan's theorization of psychoanalysis implies a very different conception of the aim of analysis from that proposed by Freud. In line with his dual conception of the ego, as both a system of identifications and the psychic agency which mediates between the drives and the demands of the external world, Freud, even in his late work, suggests that neurotic conflict is resolved when 'the drive is brought completely into the harmony of the ego, becomes accessible to all the influences of the other trends in the ego and no longer seeks to go its independent way to satisfaction.'[166] Behind this argument there clearly lies a conception of self-determination which stands within the tradition of liberal individualism, even if Freud provides an immeasurably more complex account of what the barriers to such autonomy might be than earlier thinkers. For Lacan, however, the dependence of the subject on the signifier debars autonomy in this sense from being a conceivable goal. Rather than being enabled to master wayward drives, the patient – at the end of the analysis – comes to recognize that his or her desire cannot be satisfied. This is why Lacan argues that 'in psychoanalysis it is a question raising powerlessness (that which accounts for phantasy) to the level of logical impossibility (that which incarnates the real). In other words, of completing the share of signs in which human fate is played out.'[167] Accordingly, and with great ingenuity, Lacan interprets Freud's dictum, 'Wo es war, soll ich werden', in a manner which sharply contrasts with its 'Enlightenment' interpretation, as a condensed expression for the conquest of the irrational by the rational, of compulsion by freedom. In a series of virtuoso exegeses, he associates the 'es' not with the id, but with the opacity and inertia of the reflexively constructed ego, while the 'ich' becomes the subject of the unconscious.[168] For Lacan, in other words, there is a spontaneity of the self which can be released, at least asymptotically, from the constraints of the imaginary. But this spontaneity cannot be equated with the freedom of conscious reflection. The dissolution of alienating images is not achieved through any *prise de conscience*, and psychoanalysis does not culminate in a more adequate *knowledge* of the self. 'The pretentions of the spirit', Lacan writes, 'would remain unassailable, if the letter had not demonstrated that it produces all its effects of truth in man without the spirit needing to become involved at all.'[169]

3

Lacan and Derrida:
Individuality and Symbolic Order

One way of regarding Lacan's comprehensive re-theorization of psychoanalysis would be as an attempt to recentre psychoanalysis on the problem of the 'self' – this translation of Lacan's term 'le sujet' recommends itself, since it helps to make clear the connection between Lacan's work and developments in the object-relations tradition, such as the work of Donald Winnicott. Furthermore, as the centrality of the 'mirror-stage' to Lacan's account of the formation of the subject might suggest, from such a standpoint Lacan's work appears as crucially concerned with the problems of the reflection theory of selfhood, which we have already encountered in connection with Derrida. Like Schelling, Lacan clearly perceives that the supposedly immediate certainty of self-identity is imaginary, that the capture of the 'I' by the image in the mirror is inseparable from a misrecognition of the gap between the viewer and what is viewed. Self-coincidence, far from being an unshakeable point of departure, is the outcome of an activity: ' . . . if, turning the weapons of metonymy against the nostalgia which it serves, I refuse to seek any meaning beyond tautology, if in the name of 'war is war' and 'a penny's a penny' I decide to be only what I am, how even here can I elude the obvious fact that I am in that very act?'[1] Accordingly, Lacan emphasizes that the reflection theory leads to an infinite regress, and cannot give us any insight into the nature of the subject. To demonstrate this, he employs the model of an observer standing *between* two mirrors, arguing that the 'false recurrence to infinity of reflexion' which is thereby generated cannot be taken as representing any 'progress in interiority'. This is because, however many times it is reduplicated, the image of the observer seeing him- or herself, which appears in the mirror, must always remain the object of an uncaptured *pre-existing gaze*. 'In seeing his image repeated . . . ', Lacan suggests, '[the observer] too is seen by the eyes of another when he looks at himself, since without this other, which is his own image, he would not see himself seeing himself.'[2]

Significantly, from 1801 until his death in 1814, Fichte was haunted, even in his dreams, by the idea of a look which sees itself. For, as we have already discovered, he believed that it was only through a mode of awareness which contained the immediate unity of subject and object that the regression of self-reflection could be brought to a close. Recently, the hermeneutic philosopher Manfred Frank, who is highly conscious of the connections between post-structuralism and German Idealism, has employed arguments derived from Fichte and Schelling in order to suggest that Lacan can have no coherent theory of consciousness and subjectivity. Frank acknowledges the importance of Lacan's distinction between the ego and the subject of the unconscious, the latter being understood as engaged in a quest for adequate representation which is the motor of the movement from signifier to signifier, but he suggests that Lacan is unable to provide a coherent account of the relations between them. The reason for this, Frank argues, is that, having exposed the failings of the reflection model of self-consciousness, Lacan fails in his obligation to explain the criterion which enables identification to take place at all. In some of his accounts of the mirror stage, Lacan describes the child as looking anxiously towards the mother, the Other, for recognition of its own self-recognition. However, since for Lacan the response of the Other is inherently ambiguous, since recognition cannot itself be recognized, no criterion of identity can ever be discovered. Lacan could only overcome this difficulty if he possessed the concept of a pre-reflexive self-acquaintance which could furnish a criterion of identity, which could explain why the subject is captured by a *specific* sequence of images. However, his account of the subject as the spontaneous principle of movement of the signifying chain, contains no suggestion of self-relation. Indeed, Frank suggests, Lacan is caught in a dilemma. For, if all self-relation takes the form of a specular consciousness, then an *unconscious* subject cannot be self-related, and therefore forfeits any right to be considered a *subject* at all.[3]

In fact, although Manfred Frank's criticism pinpoints a crucial difficulty in the theory of the subject, it is one of which Lacan is fully aware. It is precisely in order to resolve this difficulty, it can be argued, that Lacan, from the early 1950s onwards, begins to develop the theory of what he terms the '*objet petit a*', the object of desire which appears in unconscious phantasy. Perhaps the best way of introducing the function of this object is to consider once more the role which the phallus plays in Lacan's thought. The concept of a phallus which is not purely and simply 'non- existent', but which can rather only perform its function as 'veiled', or always lacking, can be seen as Lacan's means of theorizing an assumption which is a necessary precondition of any hermeneutic activity, of any understanding of meaning, and which can be said to define the basic structure of the hermeneutic circle: in order for the interpretation of any part of a text or discourse to be specified there must already be an anticipation of the meaning of the whole. However, this anticipation can itself never be specified, since the contribution of each partial interpretation at the same time alters the preconditions of any new interpretation. It is this circular structure within which interpretation is caught which Merleau-Ponty evokes when he suggests that 'all signs together allude to a signification which is always in abeyance when they are considered singly, and which I go beyond them towards without their ever containing it.'[4] For Lacan, the signifier of this impossible 'signification in abeyance' is precisely the imaginary phallus: the 'signifier intended to designate as a whole the signifieds as effects, in so far as the signifier conditions them by its presence as a signifier.'[5] However, this account of the phallus still leaves one important question unanswered. For, if all subjects, within the intersubjective economy, are defined simply in terms of their search for the phallus, we have no account of the *individuality* of interpretation, of why a text should mirror back a particular meaning for a particular subject, or – in more specifically Lacanian terms – why the subject should be captured by a specific series of identifications, produce a chain of signifiers which is irreducibly idiosyncratic, like no other. It is in order to account for this *style* of the subject that Lacan introduced the *objet petit a*.[6]

According to Lacan, 'The object *a* is something from which the subject has separated itself, in the form of an organ. It functions as the symbol of a lack, that is to say of the phallus, not as such, but insofar as it is lacking.'[7] The need for this stand-in for the missing phallus arises from the fact that, if the subject *simply* accepted castration, this would imply acceptance of the impossibility of finding itself within the symbolic order, and thus its own disappearance as subject. To counter this danger, therefore, the subject sacrifices a part of itself, the impossible point of overlap between subject and Other which cannot appear in reflection, and which it is therefore able to define itself as lacking even when threatened by total absorption into the universality of language. 'Analytical experience', Lacan suggests, 'does not define the object in its generality as correlative of the subject, but in its singularity, as that which supports the subject at the moment when it has to confront its existence (in the radical sense of ex-isting in the signifier), at the moment when, as subject, it must efface itself behind a signifier. At this panic point it clings to the object of desire.'[8] The structure which results from this process, notated $\$ \diamondsuit a$, is for Lacan the structure of phantasy.

The importance of this account of phantasy for the solution of the problems raised by Frank can be indicated by a comparison between the relation of the ego to its other, and the relation of the barred subject to the object a. For Lacan, both these relations are imaginary, in the sense that they imply a delusory immediacy, an overlooking of the gap between subject and object, but in all other respects they are radically opposed. The imaginary other, as the support of the ego, is characterized by an arbitrariness and reduplicability, whereas the object a is a 'paradoxical, unique, specified object'. As we have seen, the object a is 'non-specularizable' – it cannot appear in the mirror. But, although it cannot be reflected, made an object of consciousness, it is that which the subject is in search of in every self-representation. The object a therefore provides the criterion of identification which Frank argues is required in order to explain why the subject *recognizes* itself in a particular image or sequence of images: it defines the particularity of this sequence for any subject.

In this way, Lacan's theory of phantasy obviates the difficulty which Frank raises, that a 'totally non-reflexive subject – a subject without a double, without a counterpart – would fundamentally have no essence, if "essence" means "to be something", "to have characteristics".'[9] For, as we have seen, it is not correct to state that for Lacan the true subject has no 'inner double'. The theory of phantasy is rather an ingenious attempt to define a *non-reflexive* form of interiority. The losange, the screen of the imaginary, which Lacan places between the barred subject and the object a can be understood, he suggests, as a composite of the mathematical signs for 'greater than' and 'less than', and therefore as registering a paradoxical relation of 'internal exclusion' between the subject and its object. As in the original Fichtean act of positing, subject and object are both united and split simultaneously, since it is its very lack of the object a which constitutes the existence of the subject. Unlike Fichte, however, who believes that the structure of the originally unconscious act can be articulated through philosophical reflection, Lacan argues that the unity of subject and object cannot be reflected, in other words is *constitutively* unconscious, since in any self-reflection it is already presupposed. Although the subject is presented in phantasy with its object, it can never be, simultaneously, present to itself with the lost part of itself which would make it whole, a point which Lacan underlines with his suggestion that 'the notation $ expresses the necessity that* S *be eclipsed at the precise point where the object* a *attains its greatest value'.*[10] Thus, the subject of the unconscious is not without internal duality, as Frank suggests. It is characterized by a self-acquaintance (the object *a* is the missing part of the body, the result of the splitting of an original unity) which brings the regress of reflection to a close, but which can never be articulated at the conscious level. The object *a*, Lacan argues, can function as the ' "stuff", or rather the lining or stand-in (*doublure*), although not on this account the reverse, of the very subject who one takes to be the subject of consciousness.'[11]

Lacan and Derrida on Language and Meaning

As the discussion up to this point will have made clear, there are numerous similarities and convergences between Lacanian psychoanalysis and the thought of Derrida. At first sight, this may appear surprising, since the two thinkers belong to entirely different intellectual generations. Lacan's philosophical roots are to be found in the new French enthusiasm for Hegel of the 1930s: his contemporaries are Sartre, Merleau-Ponty, Hyppolite, Bataille. Derrida's first published article, by contrast, dates from 1959, and is therefore contemporaneous with the initial breakthrough of structuralism to wider public attention in France. The parallels become less puzzling, however, if one considers that both bodies of work are the product of a similar overlap between the phenomenological currents of the immediate post-war period, and the theoretical innovations of structuralism. Despite the fact that Lacan's major influences are Freud, Hegel, Lévi-Strauss, while Derrida looks first to Husserl, and then to Heidegger, Nietzsche, Saussure, it was the confluence of phenomenological and structuralist modes of thought which enabled them both to develop a critique of structuralism without returning to a philosophy of consciousness. It is no accident that both Lacan and Derrida gained their first wide popular acclaim just over half-way through the 1960s; Lacan with the publication of the *Écrits* in 1966, and Derrida with his first trilogy – *Of Grammatology, Speech and Phenomena, Writing and Difference* – in 1967: the time was ripe for a philosophically sophisticated response to the objectivist and positivist assaults of the first half of the decade, which would not involve a return to 'humanism', to the philosophies of consciousness and freedom which appeared to have been so thoroughly discredited.

Viewed from this perspective, numerous common themes can be seen to run through the two *oeuvres*. At the most general level, both are centrally concerned with the revision of traditional understandings of the relation between language, meaning and consciousness. Since subjectivity is inconceivable prior to language, the subject can no longer function as the intentional bestower of meaning upon the otherwise empty shell of the signifier, and – in particular – the notion of a transcendental subject must be rejected. For Derrida, the 'movement of *différance* is not something that happens to a transcendental subject. It is what produces it',[12] while Lacan argues that, since the self-consciousness in which the ego assures itself of an incontestable existence is not immanent, but supported by a gap-bridging process of identification, 'the transcendental ego is relativised, implicated as it is in the *méconnaissance* in which the ego's identifications take root'.[13] Once subjectivity has been made dependent on language, then consciousness can no longer function as the self-identical support of the unity of signifier and signified: meaning itself becomes a transient 'effect' of the signifier rather than its ideal content.[14] Moreover, within this broad similarity of approach there are numerous parallels between Lacan and Derrida in the very metaphors in which the argument is played out. In both thinkers there is a constant emphasis on the relation between the anonymity of language and death: it is writing which threatens the living self-presence of speech, it is the signifier, always on loan from the Other, which reminds the subject of its own dependency and finitude. Similarly, in both bodies of work, the image of the dead father plays an important role. Derrida, in his analysis of Plato, shows how writing is experienced as parricidal, as the destroyer of the paternal Logos, while Lacan – via the theory of the 'paternal metaphor' and the Freudian mythology of *Totem and Taboo* – links the concept of the dead father – the unattainable author of the Law – with the debt paid by a castration which binds the subject to the Symbolic order. [15] At an even finer level of detail, both Lacan and Derrida attack the notion of a purely ideographic writing as symptomatic of nostalgia for a lost immediacy. Lacan's argument that, 'A form of writing, like the dream itself, can be figurative, it is always, like language, symbolically articulated',[16] is paralleled at the many points in Derrida's work where the spatiality of writing is emphasized, its resistance to absorption by an instantaneous, totalizing perception.

Yet despite the fact that the breakdown of positivist structuralism was marked by the simultaneous rise to pre-eminence of both Lacan and Derrida in the late 1960s, and despite the fact that for the succeeding half-decade a good deal of theoretical work was produced which employed elements from both thinkers,[17] by the mid 1970s it was becoming clear that Lacan's popularity – notwithstanding the increasing hermeticism of his seminars – was continuing from strength to strength, while Derrida's influence was already beginning to wane. This was not simply an external phenomenon of fashion. Lacan, now increasingly concerned with the elaboration of mathematical models of the unconscious, undoubtedly continued to innovate, even if he left successive waves of mystified and disenchanted followers behind him as he did so. But Derrida's thought, after the hectic wordplay of *Glas* (1974), appeared in certain respects to flag, to settle back into the well-worn grooves of the French tradition of *explication de texte* from which it had clearly emerged. Even the new political initiative represented by the founding of GREPH (*Groupe de recherches sur l'enseignement philosophique*),[18] in which Derrida played a central role, failed to halt the comparative decline of public attention to his work: it can be no accident that it was about this time that Derrida published his major onslaught on his leading rival in *Le facteur de la vérité* (1974).[19] There is no doubt that significant work continued to be done by writers grouped around Derrida's perspectives, including a critical exposition of one of the *Écrits*, by Jean-Luc Nancy and Philippe Lacoue-Labarthe, *Le titre de la lettre* (1973). And in 1980 a full-scale colloquium was held on his work, although even here the breakthrough of themes incompatible with Derrida's basic premises is apparent.[20] In general, however, the enterprise embarked on under the Derridean aegis could not be compared in range and depth to the research – including the output of an entire university department at Vincennes – carried out within a fundamentally Lacanian framework, both inside and outside the *Ecole Freudienne de Paris*. It seemed for a while as though Lacan had realized the Freudian dream of gathering together researchers in a wide range of disciplines – philosophers, mathematicians, historians, linguists, theorists of film and literature – under the banner of psychoanalysis.

This greater amplitude and durability of Lacan's success, which persisted undiminished until his death in 1981, can perhaps partly be explained by the institutional – and, given the nature of the institution, affective – resources which were available to the head of a major psychoanalytic school: the charisma of Lacan's personality and the mesmeric power of his lecturing style are legendary. Yet it is difficult to escape the impression that such considerations cannot furnish the entire explanation. On closer comparison of the two bodies of work it becomes apparent that Lacan's theory is more nuanced and discerning in what must be considered the central area of their common concern: the relation of language and meaning to subjectivity and consciousness. For whereas Derrida is obliged to consign the concept of the subject to a kind of theoretical limbo, neither able to make use of it, nor to 'abolish' it in the structuralist fashion, Lacan had been developing – ever since the 1950s – precisely what a public no longer satisfied with the philosophically inadequate formulas structuralism would be looking for: a theory of the subject which no longer took the form of a philosophy of consciousness.

As we have seen, Derrida's critique of the Husserlian transcendental ego – and, by implication, of the philosophical concept of the subject in general – hinges on the incoherence of the notion of a consciousness which could grasp its own self-identity prior to and independently of language. There can be no domain of 'phenomenological silence' in which consciousness would be directly acquainted with itself, since the determination of any object of knowledge – including consciousness as an object for itself – must always be mediated by the differentiating system of language. But since, in Derrida's view, the concepts of self-identity and unmediated self-presence are central to any philosophical account of subjectivity, Derrida – no less than his structuralist contemporaries – has no alternative but to abandon the concept of the subject. It is true that Derrida continues to refer to the 'subject' on occasion; at the close of the discussion which followed the delivery of his lecture on 'Structure, Sign and Play in the Human Sciences', he insists that his aim is to 'situate' rather than 'destroy' the subject.[21] Yet since Derrida is also adamant that the subject is entirely subjugated to the play of language, that 'Subjectivity – like objectivity – is an effect of *différance*, an effect inscribed in a system of *différance*',[22] the retention of the *term* 'subject' alters nothing in the fact that the *concept* of the subject plays no autonomous role in his thought. For Derrida, as

for Foucault during the 1960s and 1970s, despite their philosophical remoteness in other respects, the subject is purely an effect of
the text, a function of discourse.

However, this erasure of the subject as an operative concept in
Derrida's thought is not without its difficulties, as becomes
apparent when Derrida begins to formulate his own critique of
structuralism. For if the impossibility of applying a formal system
to the decoding of texts results from the fact that linguistic
terms – being diacritical and intertextual in their functioning –
lack supralinguistic criteria of identity, and therefore cannot be
endowed with a determinate, immutable meaning, Derrida must
still provide some explanation of the *movement* of the signifier, of
the incessant process of semantic displacement which he describes, and he must do so without recourse to notions of the
initiative or creativity of speaking subjects. In the first step
towards such an explanation, Derrida accepts the structuralist
argument that language is not a function of the speaking subject.
'This implies', Derrida argues, 'that the subject (self-identity or
in some cases consciousness of self-identity, self-consciousness)
is inscribed in language, is a "function" of language, only
becomes a *speaking* subject by conforming its speech, even in so-
called "creation", even in so-called "transgression", to the system of prescriptions of language as a system of differences.'[23] But
at the same time, Derrida cannot accept this 'system of prescriptions' itself as determinate and immutably given, for this would be
to revive the notion of semantic self-identity: the system of
prescriptions must itself be historically transformed and reconsti-
tuted. In Saussure's work, this takes place through the dialectic of
langue and *parole*; indeed, Saussure goes so far – in a passage
which Derrida quotes – as to argue that 'historically, the fact of
speech always comes first'.[24] But since Derrida has already
described the role of the speaking subject as fully prescribed by
langue, his only recourse is to make *différance* the name of an
activity which is logically prior to, and which generates, the
dialectic of speech and language as a whole. 'Retaining at least the
schema,' says Derrida, 'if not the content of the exigence formulated by Saussure, we will designate by *différance* the movement
in accordance with which language, or any code, any system of
relays in general constitutes itself "historically" as a tissue of differences, "constitutes itself", "produces itself", "creates itself",
"movement", "historically", being understood beyond the
metaphysical language in which they are caught up, along with all
their implications.'[25] In other words, Derrida can only resolve the

problem of the relation between language and the speaking subject by recourse to what we have already discovered to be a speculative principle.

Given Derrida's initial assumptions, however, the course of the argument is ineluctable: if subjectivity is equated with the self-presence and self-identity of consciousness, and if this identity is then shown to be dependent upon the perpetual lack of self-identity in language, the only recourse is to surpass the originating role of transcendental subjectivity towards the new and 'higher' principle of this lack. The characterization of this principle as non-self-identical makes no substantial alteration to its status, since absolute difference – which is what Derrida's term '*différance*' indicates – is ultimately indistinguishable from absolute identity; *différance* is no less inwardly unified, though historically deployed, than Heidegger's *Sein* or Hegel's *Geist*. Furthermore, Derrida's abrupt ascent to the stratospheric levels of historico-transcendental and speculative thought has deleterious effects upon his more modest aim of providing a critique of traditional philosophical conceptions of language. This can be seen in the fact that many of the concepts which Lacan thoroughly investigates – the concepts of 'desire', of the 'law', or 'castration' – emerge in Derrida's thought – but in a desultory, inadequately theorized, way – in order to account for what Derrida sees as the fundamental movement of occidental history: he suggests, for example, that the rupture marked by the questioning of the 'structurality of structure' reveals the need to 'think the law which governed, as it were, the *desire* for the centre in the constitution of structure and the process of signification prescribing its displacements and its substitutions for this law of the central presence'.[26] In addition, as we have already seen, Derrida's strict subordination of identity to non-identity leaves him deprived of any serious theoretical resources in order to cope with the multiplicity of questions which arise at the level of the individual utterance. What, for example, can be the status of the 'illusion' of expression, of the 'effect' of meaning in speech? Indeed, if the syntax of *différance* has always already outmanoeuvred semantic self-identity, how does meaning emerge at all? Even if not considered as determinant, the role of pre-linguistic intention in relation to linguistic meaning can scarcely be avoided. With regard to many of these questions Derrida simply reserves judgement. He suggests, for example, that 'what we need is to determine *differently* (*autrement*), according to a differential system, the *effects* of ideality, of signification, of meaning, and of reference',[27] but in fact is unable to move beyond such programmatic statements in order to produce an account of these 'effects' which would be beyond what he considers to be the 'closure of metaphysics'.

In the light of Lacan's work, it becomes even clearer that many of Derrida's difficulties stem from his initial orientation towards Husserlian phenomenology, and his consequent automatic and incautious equation of subjectivity with the self-presence and self-identity of consciousness. In assuming this equivalence Derrida tends to overlook that other tradition of thought in which the subject is theorized not in terms of self-presence or self-identity, but in terms of non-identity and pre-thetic identity: the tradition which includes Schelling, Schleiermacher, Sartre – and Lacan. Perhaps the most crucial divergence from Derrida which this approach to the problem of the subject makes possible in Lacan's thought is that human beings remain the empirical bearers of a quasi-transcendental, but not constitutive, subjectivity. For Lacan, it is only the appearance of language-using beings which sets limits to any purely causal account of reality, and demands the supposition of a subject. 'A physics is conceivable,' he suggests, 'which would explain everything in the world, including its animated part. A subject only becomes unavoidable by virtue of the fact that there are in this world signifiers which have no meaning, and are therefore to be deciphered.' Hence, 'No subject has any reason to appear in the real, except if there exist speaking beings.'[28] Furthermore, although Lacan stresses the priority of the symbolic order over the individual human being who enters into it, the distinction between *langue* and *parole*, between the 'treasure of the signifier' and the speaking subject, cannot be *aufgehoben* in the Derridean manner, into the night of *différance*. Rather, Lacan insists that the concepts of psychoanalysis must be reformulated in terms of the subject's *encounter* with the signifier – an encounter which would be unthinkable if subjectivity were a mere 'effect' of the text – to the extent that he can present the fact that 'language is not the speaking subject' as the very 'foundation' of his discourse.[29] As a result of this, Lacan is able to provide a theory of the relation between conscious intention, language and meaning as these are interlinked in the process of enunciation, while obviating the difficulties which Derrida rightly perceives in traditional philosophical theories of language.

Lacan's most complete exposition of this theory is to be found in 'Subversion of the Subject and Dialectic of Desire', where it takes the form of a commentary on a graph that he introduced and elaborated in his *Seminar* for the year 1958-59 (see below). In

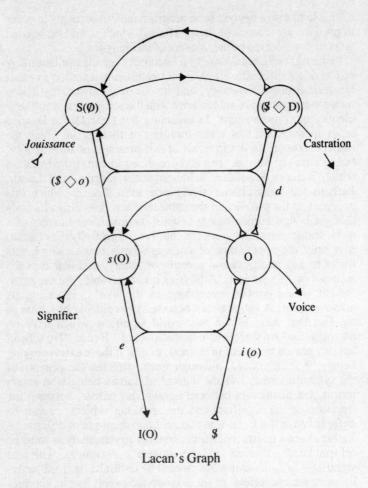

Lacan's Graph

Derrida's thought the terms *espacement* and *temporalisation* are employed to describe the fact that writing must be unfolded in space and time, and that the meaning conveyed by language cannot therefore be grasped in a single, unitary moment of perception. But because, for Derrida, these processes are aspects of *différance*, of a perpetual deferral of meaning, he is unable to explain how the experience of meaning is able to occur at all. Derrida – as we discovered through a comparison with German Idealism – offers no alternative between the illusory immediacy of speech and the endless delay of writing. Lacan's graph, however, takes account of the relation between intention and meaning, without assuming that, as in Husserl's classic phenomenological account, the meaning-bestowing intentionality of the subject takes the form of 'a certain sequence of mental experiences which are associatively linked to the [verbal] expression'[30] – precisely the illusion which Derrida denounces in the philosophical valorization of speech. The line which passes from Signifier to Voice on Lacan's graph represents the utterance in its diachronic dimension, inescapably required by the fact that language consists in a system of differentially articulated elements. This 'vector of enunciation' is then portrayed as being bisected in a *reverse* direction by the line of intentionality which passes from the barred subject (\$) to the ego-ideal (I(O)). At the level of the signifier this line must pass through the Other (O), or the 'place of the code', since the subject is initially confronted with the battery of signifiers out of which it must attempt to forge a meaning. The resultant 'clinching of a signification by the retroactive effect of the signifiers on their antecedents in the chain'[31] occurs in the 'place of the message', where a signified is depicted as appearing in the domain of semantic uncertainty instituted by the Other (s(O)). No such 'punctuation in which the signification is constituted as a finished product'[32] could occur, however, were it not supported in the imaginary register, represented by the shorter circuit which runs from \$ to I(O) via the imaginary other and the ego. Every act of speech, Lacan suggests, must be supported by a self-conception of the subject, but this conception is merely an expectation, which will only be confirmed by what the subject discovers itself as 'having meant'. Lacan speaks of 'a retroversion effect by which the subject becomes at each stage what he was before and announces himself – he will have been – only in the future perfect tense.'[33] Thus the founding drama of the ego, whose 'internal thrust is precipitated from insufficiency to anticipation' is repeated in miniature as the imaginary dimension of every act of enunciation. 'In this "rear view",' Lacan remarks, 'all the subject can be certain of is the anticipated image coming to meet him that he catches of himself in the mirror.'[34] Even in order to reflect upon itself as 'having meant', however, the subject must bracket the intersubjective relation which in fact determines the meaning of its discourse. This *epoche* is indicated by the symbol for the ego-ideal – I(O): an imaginary unbarred Other – which stands at the end of the vector of intentionality, as the imaginary point from which the subject could see itself whole, without distortion.

At the moment in which the subject grasps its intended meaning, however, there takes place a process which Lacan describes as the 'fading' of the subject, a realization that whatever it represents itself as being will fail to capture its 'non-being'. The Lacanian subject is therefore confronted with a cruel dilemma, described in terms of a fundamental 'splitting' of the subject between the subject of the statement (*sujet de l'énoncé*) and the subject of the utterance (*sujet de l'énonciation*). For, before it begins to speak, the subject is simply a lack, a nothingness, which finds itself confronted with 'the given of the signifiers which cover it in an Other which is their transcendental place'.[35] In order to 'spring forth', in order to be recognized and therefore to *be* at all, the subject must make use of these signifiers, yet none of them can adequately represent the subject as the subject who makes use of these signifiers in order to represent itself. 'The subject', Lacan can therefore state, 'is the emergence (*surgissement*) which, just before, as subject, was nothing, but which, scarcely having appeared, congeals into a signifier.'[36] This makes clear how remote the Lacanian subject is from the notions of self-presence and self-identity denounced by Derrida, since the desiring subject, the subject of the utterance, is eclipsed by the subject of each successive statement, each 'fading' becoming the occasion for a renewed attempt at self-representation. Lacan reserves some of his most evocative prose for this process: 'There where it was just now, there where it nearly was, between this extinction which still glows, and this blossoming forth which comes to grief, I can come to be by disappearing from what is said by me.'[37] As this description suggests, however although the subject cannot be represented by any single signifier, it can make itself known obliquely in the succession of signifiers; since no signifier follows automatically from that which precedes it, in the very *gap* between signifiers something of the subject is revealed. It is this possiblity which is indicated in the upper half of Lacan's graph, which represents the unconscious level of speech, as the lower half depicts the level of consciousness. In the imaginary register enunciation is guided by the relation between desire (*d*) and the object of the phantasy ($\mathcal{S} \diamondsuit a$), the fixity of this relation being made manifest in the signifying chain in the form of a demand of which the subject is unaware ($\mathcal{S} \diamondsuit D$), and which is persistently repeated, since the response to this demand reveals the Other who could meet it as barred (S($\emptyset$)). In this way, Lacan is able to explain the unique consistency of the subject's discourse, while making clear that this is not the consistency of a self-conscious, self-identical subject.

It is worth noting that the problem of the singularity of the subject, which Lacan addresses through his concept of the object *a*, is central to the disagreement between Lacan and Derrida which is recorded in 'Le facteur de la vérité', the essay in which Derrida attempts a rival deconstructive reading of Poe's 'The Purloined Letter'. Throughout this text, Derrida questions Lacan's insistence on the 'indivisibility' of the letter, arguing that this is Lacan's means of preserving the security of meaning and truth, and countering with the assertion that the materiality of the letter, far from implying its indestructibility, rather implies its 'ever-possible partition', the danger of its being 'broken up irrevocably'.[38] For Derrida, the assertion of indivisibility can only be based upon an idealization: *'This "materiality", deduced from an indivisibility which is not found anywhere, corresponds in fact to an idealization.* Only the ideality of a letter resists destructive division. "Cut a letter into small pieces, and it remains the letter it is", as this may not be said of empirical materiality, an ideality (intangibility of self-identity travelling without alteration) must be implied therein.'[39] However, Derrida's argument is based on a failure to distinguish between unity as *sameness*, as reflexive identity, and and the unity of an *individuality*. For Lacan, the unity of the letter is not constituted reflexively, rather the signifier – which the letter symbolizes – 'is a unity by virtue of being unique (*le signifiant est unité d'être unique*)'.[40] In order to make his argument succeed, therefore, Derrida would be obliged to show that the individuality of the subject could be analysed into elements, despite the fact that individuality is defined precisely by its intrinsic resistance to conceptual dissection. A literary style, for example – or indeed the 'style' of any speaking subject – is 'one thing', yet it cannot be reduced to a set of components. Accordingly, Lacan is far from committed to the 'intangibility of a self-identity travelling without alteration'. As we have already seen, for Lacan self-identity is inherently unstable, caught up in a process of intersubjective exchange. What Lacan is committed to, however, is the view that there must be an underlying principle of the very transformation of self-identity, no matter how elusive this principle might be. Derrida's assertion that the letter is always divisible in fact amounts to the destruction of subjectivity.

Significantly, in some of his more recent work, Derrida has been obliged to acknowledge, albeit indirectly, the force of this argument, and has consequently begun to grapple with the problem of singularity. In an interview dating from 1983, for example, Derrida states: 'I feel as if I've been involved for twenty years, in a long detour, in order to get back to this something, this idiomatic writing whose purity I know to be inaccessible, but which I continue, nonetheless, to dream about.' And, when asked by the interviewer what he means by idiomatic, he replies: 'A property you cannot appropriate; it somehow marks you without belonging to you. It appears only to others, never to you – except in flashes of madness which draw together life and death, which render you at once alive and dead. It's fatal to dream of inventing a language or a song which would be yours – not the attributes of an "ego", but rather the accentuated flourish, that is the musical flourish of your own most unreadable history.'[41] It is difficult not to read this passage as a highly evocative and penetrating description of the Lacanian object *a* and its role in phantasy, for the object *a* – too – is precisely that which 'marks you without belonging to you', 'a property you cannot appropriate'. The very use of this latter phrase suggests the need for Derrida to revise his earlier attempts to deconstruct *any* concept of the proper, an attempt whose logical consequence was the dissolution of the subject. Yet Derrida has not carried out any explicit revision, but rather half-moved on to a new terrain, where new concepts and positions clash with the old. In his *Schibboleth pour Paul Celan*, for example, he is centrally concerned with the relation between the singularity of a date or an individual and language; the latter is not conceived as a medium of generality which erases the singular, but rather as the place of encounter *between* singularities. 'This you', Derrida states, 'which should be an I, like the *Er, als ein Ich* of a moment ago, always figures an irreplaceable singularity. Only another singularity, just as irreplaceable, can take its place without substituting itself for it. This you, one addresses oneself to it as to a date, to the here and now of a commemorable provenance.'[42] One is reminded of Lacan's dictum that the signifier does not represent a meaning, but rather 'represents the subject for another signifier': a deepened meditation on the concept of 'irreplaceable singularity' introduced here would surely oblige Derrida to revise his insistence on the destructibility of the letter, and indeed his whole account of dissemination.

The Symbolic, Power and Desire

It is important for an understanding of the development of French thought in the 1970s to note that the work of Derrida and Lacan, despite sharp divergences over the status of the subject, is united in its emphasis on the priority of the text, or what Lacan terms the 'primacy of the symbolic'. Recently, Derrida has repudiated interpretations of deconstruction which endorse a linguistic idealism: 'I never cease to be surprised by critics who see my work as a declaration that there is nothing beyond language, that we are imprisoned in language; it is, in fact, saying the exact opposite. The critique of logocentrism is above all else the search for the "other" and the "other of language".'[43] Yet, as we have seen, Derrida has also stated directly that, 'There is nothing before the text; there is no pretext which is not already a text.'[44] This second statement must surely be considered more consistent with his basic philosophical position, since – for Derrida – if what is before the text were not itself a text, it could only take the form of a presence, and would thereby be demoted to an *effect* of the text. Derrida's work can best be seen not as a search for the other *of* language, but rather for the other *as* language. He is concerned to show that language cannot be made *present*, as a self-enclosed totality, rather than that there is a reality outside of language, which language seeks to erase.

It might be argued that the Lacanian emphasis on the primacy of the symbolic does not have the same philosophical consequences. For in Lacan's thought, the symbolic is merely one of three orders, to be set alongside the imaginary, whose nature we have already explored, and the real – which we have yet to examine. What is perhaps Lacan's most lucid general statement about these three orders occurs in the third *Seminar*, where he outlines three distinct ways in which the colour red can be regarded. Firstly, it can be regarded at the level of sensation, as a physical process (the level at which we can enquire whether an individual is colour blind); secondly, at the level of perception, where the colour appears to bear within itself an intrinsic expressive quality (suggested by the expression 'seeing red'); and lastly, at the level of *conventional* significance (the level at which red is opposed to black in a pack of playing cards).[45] The distinctions which Lacan draws here are not entirely without parallels in the work of other thinkers. One might point, for example, to Habermas's distinction between three 'domains of reality': outer nature, inner nature, and society, to which correspond the objective, the subjective, and the intersubjective dimensions of rationality. For Habermas, as for Lacan, these three domains are irreducible to each other, although they are interwoven in complex ways, and it is significant that Lacan is the only post-structuralist thinker to respect this irreducibility, which Habermas considers to be the mark of modernity, whereas Derrida, Foucault and Lyotard, in their different ways, constantly strive to break down these distinctions.

One consequence of this irreducibility, for Lacan, is that the symbolic order cannot be seen as *representing* the real. Lacan always emphasizes that there is no point at which language abuts directly on to the real, since the reference of a term always requires interpretation: 'What characterizes, at the level of the signifier/signified distinction, the relation of the signified to what is there as an indispensable third, namely the referent, is precisely the fact that the signifier always misses it. The collimator doesn't work.'[46] Yet this does not lead Lacan to deny that the real may have an *effect upon* the symbolic. Rather, the real, as 'the domain of that which subsists outside of signification', is capable or disrupting the fragile equilibrium of the imaginary and the symbolic, which constitutes what the subject understands to be reality: 'The real does not wait, and in particular not for the subject, since it expects nothing from speech. But it is there, identical with its existence, a noise in which anything can be heard, and ready to burst in and submerge what the "reality principle" has constructed under the title of the "external world".'[47] In general, Lacan connects the concept of the real with an irreducible contingency, to which our interpretations are obliged to accommodate, and which can always unexpectedly overturn any given interpretation. Thus, in *The Four Fundamental Concepts of Psychoanalysis*, Lacan states that, 'The real is the collision, it's the fact that things don't work out straight away, as the hand which reaches towards external objects would like.'[48] This characterization also helps to make clear why, in his later work, Lacan increasingly connects the object *a* with the register of the real. For this object also belongs to 'the domain of that which subsists outside signification'; Lacan describes it as a 'remainder', (*un reste*) or a 'piece of waste' (*un déchet*): it is that which is always left behind in every attempt of the subject to represent itself. As such, it suggests the singularity, the non-rationalizability, of the metonymic sequence of signifiers which is desire.

Although Lacan's theory of the three registers makes clear that he cannot be regarded in any sense as a 'linguistic idealist', it might still be legitimate to query the manner in which he conceptualizes the relation between the discursive and the non-discursive. For any consideration of Lacan's views in this area cannot fail to observe the closeness with which he follows Lévi-Strauss's account of the social as constituted by relations of communication and symbolic exchange. The difficulty here, as has been noted on numerous occasions, is that Lévi-Strauss's analyses of primitive societies leave relations of power and domination almost entirely out of account: the question of the *function* of a symbolic system in maintaining a certain distribution of power is neglected in favour of the question of its *meaning*. As Dan Sperber has argued, ' . . . when [Lévi-Strauss] identifies in turn social life and communication, communication, language and exchange; exchange and reciprocity, there is hardly any place left for the political within the social domain.'[49] Lévi-Strauss characteristically overestimates the internal logic and coherence of symbolic systems, failing to consider the possibility that a symbolic system, rather than defining the categories of a collective unconscious, might be traversed by incoherences which betray its political function of speciously universalizing the interests of a specific social group.[50]

In Lacan's adaptation of Lévi-Strauss, which transforms the latter's multiple 'symbolic systems' into a single symbolic order, this neglect of the possibility of systems of meaning promoting or masking relations of force remains. As we have already seen, in his fusion of the Lévi-Straussian concept of exchange with the Hegelian dialectic of recognition, Lacan neglects the view of both Hegel and Kojève, that this dialectic is intertwined with those of labour and political struggle, and suggests that the 'pact of speech' alone can put an end to the oscillating antagonism of the relation between ego and other. Accordingly, for Lacan the essential features of the symbolic order are exemplified by the password, which lacks any meaning *apart* from that of embodying the pact of speech itself, and which defuses through this pact the threat of violence. In a text not collected in the *Écrits*, he refers to 'the point of convergence of the material which is most void of sense in the signifier with the most real effect of the symbolic, a place which is occupied by the password under the double aspect of the non-sense to which it is customarily reduced, and the truce which it brings to the enmity of man for his fellow. This is no doubt the zero point of the order of things, since nothing has yet appeared here, but which already contains everything which man is entitled to expect from its power, since he who has the word avoids death.'[51] In a similar vein, in one of his later discussions of the Hegelian struggle for pure prestige, Lacan argues that 'death, precisely because it has been drawn into the function of stake in the game, . . . shows at the same time how much of the prior rule, as well as of the concluding settlement, has been elided. For in the last analysis it is necessary for the loser not to perish, in order to become a slave. In other words, the pact everywhere precedes violence before perpetuating it, and what we call the symbolic dominates the imaginary.'[52] It will be noted that here Lacan does not affirm an incompatibility between the symbolic and violence. But he does suggest that if a certain relation of force can be institutionalized, if the pact can *perpetuate* violence, this can only take place on the basis of an agreement.

It is precisely this argument, however, and the corresponding attribution by Lacan of talismanic power to the word, which is open to question. In the case of the password, for example, its recitation cannot produce an automatic protection from violence, since hidden tensions may at any moment break out amongst those who were formerly allies. Similar concrete objections could be raised to other Lacanian examples of the primacy of the symbolic. Thus, in the second *Seminar*, during a discussion of Poe's 'The Purloined Letter', Lacan suggests that the police are mistaken in believing their power to be based upon sheer force: 'the police, like all other powers, also rests on the symbol. As you have seen for yourselves in periods of unrest, you would have let yourselves be arrested like little lambs if a guy had said to you *Police!* and showed a card, otherwise you would have punched him in the face as soon as he laid a finger on you.'[53] Here again, the conclusion is improbable: there is no unbreakable prior pact between police and demonstrators, and the showing of a police identity card could just as easily invite attack as induce submission in the person to whom it is shown. Although Lacan's position is more sophisticated than that of Lévi-Strauss, since he does not neglect the question of power, his view that all power must ultimately be founded in consensus, that 'All legitimate power, like any kind of power, is always based on the symbol'[54] cannot be made plausible, although this is not to deny that power has a symbolic dimension.

At first sight the problem of the relation of power and the symbolic might appear to be tangential to Lacan's central concerns, yet it is of immeasurable significance for our understanding of the politics of psychoanalysis. For, if the structure of discourse – the structure of what is possible to say and *not* possible to say – is not considered as overdetermined by relations of power, then the nature of the social order cannot be understood as a factor in the level of unconscious repression, if we take the concept of repression ultimately to imply a clash of forces, however symbolically mediated. This is already clear from Lacan's construal of the Oedipus complex, since Lacan does not portray desire as a *force* which the paternal prohibition contains. Indeed, for Lacan the Oedipus complex is a 'myth' which 'gives epic form to the operation of a structure'.[55] In Lacan's view, for the subject to accept the Name-of-the-Father means to accept his or her own inscription within the symbolic order: by symbolically possessing the phallus, the mythical father who is invoked by the Name-of-the-Father assures the subject that desire can be reconciled with the symbolic order, while making clear that the fulfillment of desire cannot be obtained by the short-circuit of identification with the phallus. Indeed, since the subject only exists as desiring subject, as both excluded from and represented in the signifying chain, far from thwarting the desire of the subject, the acceptance of the Name-of-the-Father as support of the Law (the symbolic order in its imperative aspect) rather assures the subject of the possibility of a place within the symbolic order. In Lacan, the Law *both* institutes and represses desire; indeed he goes so far as to state that the law and repressed desire are 'one and the same thing'.[56]

There is in Lacan's work, in other words, nothing of that conflict between nature and culture – a conflict which frequently takes on a tragic dimension – which is so central to Freud's original vision. The unconscious is not understood as the locus of a more primitive or rudimentary type of mental activity, or of a demand for sensuous fulfilment which is incompatible with civilization, and which disrupts the coherence of conscious discourse in order to make its message known. Indeed, Lacan goes further than this. In his first *Seminar*, for example, he urges his pupils to abandon the idea that 'resistance is coherent with this construction according to which the unconscious is, in a given subject, at a given moment, contained and, as they say, repressed.'[57] For Lacan, the unconscious is not the 'real place of another discourse', a discourse which is forcibly excluded from consciousness. He suggests that it is precisely the overcoming of such a conception of the unconscious, as a set of mental contents which could be detected and defined, which sets Freud apart from thinkers who are often taken to be his precedessors: 'If Freud has contributed to the knowledge of man nothing more than the truth that there is such a thing as the true (*cette vérité qu'il y a du véritable*) there would be no Freudian discovery. Freud would then take his place in the line of moralists in which is embodied a tradition of humanist analysis, a milky way in the sky of European culture, where Balthazar Gracian and La Rochefoucauld shine as stars of the first order, and Nietzsche figures as a nova whose brightness matches the speed with which it fades back into darkness.'[58]

By contrast, for Lacan the 'exteriority of the symbolic in relation to man is the very notion of the unconscious'.[59] Lacan abandons Freud's conception of a clash and interference between two principles of mental functioning, or the notion that there are two distinct languages, that of consciousness and that of the unconscious, in favour of the view that 'the presence of the unconscious, by virtue of the fact that it is situated in the place of the Other, is to be sought in every discourse, in its enunciation.'[60] The unconscious is not another discourse, but simply another way of reading the *same* discourse. The consequence of this argument, however, is that the incompatibility between desire and speech cannot be given any social content: it follows simply from the nature of language as such. Hence Lacan writes of 'the prohibition which the subject has brought to bear on himself by his own words', and suggests that desire is simply the impossibility of a further speech which could lift this prohibition, since any such speech, 'in replying to the first can merely reduplicate its mark of prohibition by completing the split (*Spaltung*) which the subject undergoes by virtue of being a subject only in so far as he speaks.'[61]

Despite the profundity and ingenuity of Lacan's theoretical reconstruction of psychoanalysis, such a conclusion clearly eliminates the – albeit ambivalent – potential for a critique of modern society and culture which was built into Freud's original model. Despite Lacan's suspicion of all forms of naturalism and essentialism, in a curious sense, his interpretation of psychoanalysis as concerned with the relation between the subject and language *as such*, returns psychoanalysis to a historical and political vacuum ultimately no less debilitating than the most crudely naturalistic interpretation of Freud. It is scarcely surprising, therefore, that during the early 1970s, in the wake of the political upheavals of the late 1960s, new conceptions of the unconscious will begin to emerge in France, which will lay stress on the heterogeneity of desire and language, and which will emphasize the capacity of desire to dislocate and disrupt symbolic and social order.

4

Jean-François Lyotard:
From Perception to Desire

We have already seen that the history of French philosophy in the 1960s can be divided into two distinct phases. In the first, structuralist-dominated phase many key themes were introduced (the suspicion of meaning, the 'decentring' – in effect, the erasure – of the subject, the reflexive concern with, and attempt to side-step, the traditional status of philosophical discourse), but this introduction took place within the framework of a naive scientism and objectivism inherited from the French positivist tradition. In the second phase, inaugurated by the success of Derrida and Lacan, and which can also be viewed as the first phase of post-structuralism, this positivism in turn becomes the target of a critique. But, at the same time, the initial themes are not abandoned: rather they are taken up and developed in a far more sophisticated way. This twinning of Lacan and Derrida should not, of course, be allowed to obscure the profound differences we have discovered between the two. There is a crucial distinction between Lacan's argument that meaning is never where we take it to be, and Derrida's *reduction* of meaning to an 'effect' of the ultra-transcendental movement of *différance*, just as there is between the Lacanian 'splitting' of the subject and its Derridean abolition as an effective reality. But, beyond these distinctions, both are united in an awareness of the inadequacy of the positivist response to the challenge of reflexive thought. And both conclude that this challenge can only be met by travelling much of the Hegelian road, yet – at the last moment – deflecting Hegel's argument so that the illusion of absolute knowledge is dissipated. In Derrida's case this effect is achieved by prioritizing the non-signifying gap between signifier and signifier to produce the shattered dialectic of *différance*, while in Lacan's work it is the supposition of a non-reflexive subject which jams the progress of consciousness towards absolute knowledge. In both cases, however, a form of theoretical discourse is produced which could only appear to die-hard adherents of structuralist method as a mystifying lapse into speculation and metaphysics. By the time he came to write the 'Finale' of *Mythologiques* in 1971, Lévi-Strauss was already denouncing the belief in the possibility of a philosophy 'beyond' structuralism, and lamenting the emergence of a new 'metaphysics of desire'.[1]

Even as Lévi-Strauss was fighting this rearguard action, however, a second phase of 'post-structuralism' was already beginning to emerge, and would eventually make necessary a revision of the conception adopted by 'early' post-structuralism of its own relation to the immediate past. For despite their critique of the objectivism of structuralist accounts of meaning, Derrida and Lacan remain tied to the structuralist assumption of the primacy of the textual, the discursive, the symbolic, understood in a minimal sense as the differentially articulated. Indeed it is precisely their belief in this primacy which motivates the critique of objectivism: a 'science of meaning' which lays unconditional claim to objectivity must, of necessity, overlook its own linguistically-mediated status. In both Derrida and Lacan, however, the argument presses on ineluctably beyond this point. If not only semantic theory, but all knowledge of a language-independent reality is linguistically mediated, then there can be no non-linguistic determinations of – although there may be non-linguistic conditions of – linguistic mediation (Lacan), or perhaps even the very notion of a language-independent reality is incoherent (Derrida). It is precisely against this 'imperialism of the signifier', however, that the second phase of post-structuralism turns. Attention begins to shift from language as all-embracing medium to the determinations which bear upon language; discourse starts to be seen as patterned and disrupted by non-discursive forces.

As might be expected, the nascent theorizations of this philosophical shift were inextricably bound up with the political impact of the events of May '68 and their aftermath. For what this rebellion had decisively brought to attention was that social structures could not be viewed, in the naive structuralist manner, as placid, self-perpetuating systems of 'communication' or 'symbolic exchange'. What sustains or rebels against a given social structure cannot be simply an effect of that structure itself. Social systems are both imposed by force from above – they embody relations of *power* – and are adhered to or rejected from below – they are invested or disinvested with *desire*. Throughout the 1970s these two terms will become, increasingly, the focus of philosophical debate.

Although, initially at least, Gilles Deleuze was far better known as a critic of pure semiology and philosopher of desire, it is the work of philosopher Jean-François Lyotard which most clearly embodies the intimate relation between this second phase of post-structuralism and political concerns. In Lyotard's case the interest – and active engagement – in politics preceded many years his emergence as one of the leading figures of post-structuralism. During the 1950s and early 1960s he had been a member of the small far-left group *Socialisme ou Barbarie*, whose most intellectually prominent members were Claude Lefort and Cornelius Castoriadis, and many of his earliest writings were political contributions to the organ of the group, rather than essays on philosophical topics. Although both Lefort and Castoriadis had Trotskyist backgrounds, *Socialisme ou Barbarie* distanced itself from orthodox Trotskyism, developing a state-capitalist theory of the USSR, a critique of Leninist forms of political organization, and a defining emphasis on the extension of the self-management principle to all domains of social life. In this way *Socialisme ou Barbarie* anticipated, and may even have directly influenced, many of the key themes of the May student uprising. Having left *S ou B* in 1963, Lyotard, at that time a philosophy teacher at Nanterre, and therefore at the epicentre of the revolt, became active in the *Mouvement du 22 Mars*, the spontaneist, anti-authoritarian wing of the May movement. 'The Movement of '68', Lyotard wrote, in the introduction to his first anthology of essays, 'seemed to us to do and say on the grand scale what we had sketched out in words and actions in miniature and by anticipation . . .'.[2] Nor was he slow to learn the anti-structuralist lessons of this political experience: ' . . . an approach solely guided by the model of structural linguistics makes it impossible to understand the functioning of symbolic systems like those described by Mauss, or the appearance of ("revolutionary") events in a semantically "well-regulated" system like contemporary capitalism. In the first case, as in the second, there is a dimension of *force* which escapes the logic of the signifier.'[3] It is this insight which will lie at the heart of Lyotard's first major contribution to the post-structuralist debate: *Discours, Figure*.

Discourse and its Other in Lyotard

Although it was only in 1971, with the publication of *Discours, Figure*, that Lyotard made his first significant impact, the roots of his philosophical opposition to the first wave of post-structuralism may be traced back as far as 1954, to his introductory monograph on phenomenology.[4] Here Lyotard argues that, because of its founding project of an intuitive capture of 'the things themselves' prior to all predication, phenomenology may be described as 'a combat of language with itself in its effort to attain the originary'.[5] The phenomenological project must be described as 'fundamentally *contradictory*', the effort of language to capture a prelinguistic world is foredoomed, since 'as the designation of a pre-logical signified which is there in being itself, it is forever incomplete, because referred back dialectically from being to meaning via intentional analysis'.[6] For Lyotard, however, the appreciation of this inherent contradiction leads to precisely the opposite conclusion from that which will be drawn to structuralism and early post-structuralism. Derrida's work probably offers both the most extreme and the most coherent version of this conclusion: since, in any attempt to capture a world prior to – or independent of – language, language is always already presupposed, there cannot be 'a truth or an origin escaping the play and the order of the sign',[7] indeed there can be 'nothing before the text . . . no pretext which is not already a text'.[8] For Lyotard, however, there is an illicit jump in this argument: rather than revealing the ultimate illusoriness of any language-independent reality, why should not the impossibility of a linguistic grasping of the originary rather reveal the inherent limitations of language itself, its ultimate powerlessness when confronted with the non-linguistic? If 'the defeat of philosophy is certain',[9] this is not because philosophy remains shackled to an illusion of presence, but because philosophy is unable to acknowledge the world of sense in which it is immersed and from which it emerges, because 'the originary is no longer the originary in so far as it *is* described'.[10] For Derrida, in other words, it is *différance* as the transreflexive origin of reflexivity which cannot itself be reflexively grasped, whereas, for Lyotard, 'There is always a pre-reflexive, an unreflected, an antepredicative upon which reflection, science must lean, and which it conjures away every time it wishes to justify itself.'[11]

Nearly two decades later, in the introduction to *Discours, Figure*, Lyotard will take up again on a broader front this defence of the world of perception against the imperialism of language.

'This book', he writes on the opening page, 'protests: that the given is not a text, that there is within it a density, or rather a constitutive difference, which is not to be read, but to be seen: and that this difference, and the immobile mobility which reveals it, is what is continually forgotten in the process of signification.'[12] By this time, however, Lyotard's argument, though still rooted in phenomenology, has begun to acquire the overtones of Nietzsche's denunciation of the philosophers' obliteration of the world of sense. Lyotard declares his target to be: 'the penumbra which, after Plato, speech has thrown like a grey veil over the sensible, which has been constantly thematized as less-than-being, and whose side has very rarely truly been taken, taken in truth, since it was understood that this was the side of falsity, of scepticism, of the rhetorician, the painter, the *condottiere*, the libertine, the materialist . . . '.[13] One succinct phrase summarizes the gulf between Lyotard's position and the orthodoxy of the 1960s: 'one does not at all break with metaphysics by putting language everywhere'.[14]

However, this continued defence of the distinction between language and the perceived world, between – as Lyotard will express it – 'the letter and the line', should not be taken to imply that Lyotard's understanding of language has remained at the phenomenological stage. Rather he admits that structuralism has made a decisive advance in its account of the system of language as a pattern of differential relations which precedes and makes possible the speech of the individual speaking subject. 'Within the anonymous system,' Lyotard suggests, 'there are intervals which maintain the terms at a constant distance from each other, so that this "absolute object" is – so to speak – full of holes, and encloses within itself a dialectic which is immobile, and yet generative, and which causes the definition and value of a term to pass via the other terms with which it is in correlation.'[15] For Lyotard the crucial point is that the existence of this anonymous system renders inadequate any phenomenological attempt to ground linguistic meaning in a logically prior intentionality or gesture. Any 'dialectical' account of language in the Sartrian sense – as 'the inert depository of a power of speech which would be logically anterior to it' – is impossible, since it must be recognized that 'language precedes speech in as much as no speaker can claim, even modestly, to have founded the former, nor dream of instituting another, and . . . any attempt to reform language comes up against the circle that it is our tool, the only tool we possess for the purposes of transforming it'.[16]

For Lyotard, however, the structuralist acquisition that *parole* cannot be considered anterior to *langue*, as phenomenology in its diverse forms had always been tempted to claim, does not entitle us to dispense with a consideration of *parole*, of the specific dimension of language in use. While the view of language as an autonomous system of purely internal relations may be accepted as the basis of a structuralism which confines itself to its strictly scientific tasks, it becomes misleading when presented as a characterization of language *tout court*. For what is omitted in the understanding of language as a closed system of signifiers doubled by a system of signifieds is any sense of the referential dimension of language. 'There is a fact', Lyotard suggests, 'which our experience of speech does not permit us to deny, the fact that every discourse is cast in the direction of something which it seeks to seize hold of, that it is incomplete and open, somewhat as the visual field is partial, limited and extended by an horizon. How can we explain this almost visual property of speaking on the basis of this object closed in principle, shut up on itself in a self-sufficient totality, which is the system of *langue*?'[17] In Lyotard's view such an explanation is impossible. He argues that, in order to account for the fact that 'it is not signs which are given, but something to be signified',[18] we must consider language in use as characterized by two distinct forms of negativity. Saussure was undoubtedly correct to insist that, since the value of a linguistic term is constituted by its differences with other terms, since what a term *is* is defined purely by what it is not, 'in language there are only differences'. But, at the same time, this negativity must be set in relation to what Lyotard calls the 'negativity of transcendence', the fact that 'the speaker is torn away from that of which he speaks, or this is torn away from him, and he continues to hold it at a distance in speaking, as the object of his discourse, in a "vision"'.[19] From this standpoint both subject and object may be seen as 'fragments deriving from a primary deflagration of which language itself was the starting spark'.[20]

At this point it might appear possible to reply that Lyotard has misconstrued the post-structuralist case. It might be argued, for example, that Derrida does not deny that we experience a referential dimension of language; he remarks, at one point in *Positions*, that we should avoid 'an indispensable critique of a certain naive relation to the signified or to the referent, to meaning or to thing, becoming fixed in a suspension, or a pure and simple suppression of sense and reference'.[21] And yet, the logic of Derrida's position pushes him inevitably towards the conclusion that the referential can possess only a secondary and derivative status, for he immediately goes on to suggest that: 'What we need is to determine in *another way*, in accordance with a differential system, the *effects* of ideality, of signification, of meaning, of reference.'[22] Since Derrida is operating with a simple opposition between identity and difference, and since he argues that, 'Nothing – no present and in-different entity – precedes spacing and *différance*',[23] he is obliged to consider the perceived world as being itself no more than a system of traces, or – alternatively – if perception is considered as a subject-centred and unmediated form of awareness, to admit that 'I don't believe that there is any perception.'[24]

Nothing obliges us, however, to accept Derrida's initial dichotomy between identity and difference. It is possible to argue that the perceived world does not possess the structure of a text, without accepting its being flattened out into the immediacy of sensation or the pure presence of entities. Thus Lyotard points out that the perceived does not possess the interchangeable relativity of the linguistic; that the relation between here and there, above and below, in front and behind, to the right and to the left, is not assimilable to the diacritical relation between terms within a linguistic system: 'the place indicated, the *here*, is grasped in a sensible field, without doubt as its focus, but not in such a way that its surroundings are eliminated, as is the case with the choices made by a speaker; they remain there, with the uncertain, undeniable, curvilinear presence of that which maintains itself on the borders of vision, a reference absolutely essential to the indication of place . . . but whose nature marks a complete break with that of a linguistic operation: the latter refers back to a discontinuous inventory, sight to a topological space, the first is subordinated to the rule of the spoken chain which requires the uniqueness of the actual and the elimination of the virtual, the second determines a sensible field ruled by the quasi-actuality of the virtual, and the quasi-virtuality of the actual.'[25] If this distinction is accepted then any attempt to absorb the exteriority of the perceived world into the interiority of language – Lyotard's target is Hegel, but the argument applies equally to Derrida – must be seen as falling prey to a 'logophiliac presupposition'. 'It is all very well to affirm that everything is sayable,' suggests Lyotard, 'this is true; but what is not true is that the signification of discourse can gather up all the sense of the sayable. One can say that the tree is green, but the colour will not have been put into the sentence.'[26] Language may be seen as the *phenomenological*, but not as the *ontological* ground of the perceived world.[27]

Throughout *Discours, Figure* this awareness of an 'unsuppressible gap' between the sensible and the intelligible is expressed in terms of a contrast between the 'letter' and the 'line', between a graphic and a figural space. 'The letter', Lyotard argues, 'is the support of a conventional, immaterial signification, in every respect identical with the presence of the phoneme. And this support effaces itself behind what is supported: the letter only gives rise to rapid recognition, in the interests of signification.'[28] In Jacques Derrida's work, the return from the spoken to the written signifier is seen as a means of blocking this process of effacement, but since the letter is composed of a group of highly stereotyped traits which therefore tend towards the suppression of their own materiality and plasticity, the letter no less than the phoneme is intrinsically oriented towards intelligibility. It is only the line, by contrast, which thwarts easy recognition and assimilation – which obstructs the eye and forces it to linger. 'The manner in which meaning is present in the line (in any constituent of a figure),' affirms Lyotard, 'is felt as an opacity by the mind habituated to language. An almost endless effort is required in order for the eye to let itself be captured by the form, to receive the energy which it contains.'[29] In an interview dating from 1970, Lyotard explicitly turns this contrast against the all-engulfing Derridean concept of 'arche-writing', by means of a simple reference to the visual arts: 'One cannot at all say that the line which Klee's pencil traces on a sheet of paper is charged with effects of meaning in the same way as the letters which he writes under this line, and which say simply: "Fatal Leap".'[30]

As Lyotard's phenomenological background would lead one to expect, the argument in these opening chapters of *Discours, Figure* is heavily indebted to the work of Merleau-Ponty. Lyotard can be seen as taking up in a post-structuralist context some of the advantages of a Merleau-Pontyan position, which attempts to move beyond the categories of subject and object, not by a process of speculative sublation, but by returning below the subject-object relation to uncover 'our mute contact with things, when they are not yet things things said'.[31] In Merleau-Ponty's late work the key notions of 'depth' and 'opacity' – applied to what is perceived and to the act of perceiving – are employed to suggest that perception can never entirely possess either its object or itself. The world upon which perception opens is not a domain of pure presences – and therefore, in structuralist terms, a domain of illusion – but 'an ambiguous field of horizons and distances',[32] an overlapping of the visible and the invisible. Throughout his career Merleau-Ponty remained stubbornly opposed to the view that whatever meaning the world possesses must be bestowed by language, but – because of the rootedness of his thought in phenomenology – he also resisted the possibility that there might be an unbridgeable hiatus between language and the world. In Merleau-Ponty's thought there are meanings implicit, concealed in the world's dimension of depth which language does not determine, but brings to light; there is a spontaneous cooperation or affinity between the world of perception and that of language. 'To understand', he suggests, 'is to translate into available significations a meaning initially captive in the thing and in the world itself.'[33] And again: ' . . . language realises, in breaking the silence, that which silence wished for, yet could not obtain'.[34]

This 'tenderness' towards the perceived world, a *parti pris* which lies at the heart of Merleau-Ponty's philosophy, is clearly irreconcilable with structuralist and early post-structuralist thought, where there can be no doubt that, even granted the existence of a language-independent reality, it is language which segments it and determines its meaning. But significantly, it is also the point at which *Discours, Figure*, which up to this point could almost have been read as a phenomenological critique of structuralism, begins to question the work of Merleau-Ponty, and therefore may be said to mark the shift into a form of post-structuralism in Lyotard's thought. Lyotard, as we have seen, cannot accept the structuralist view that saying is purely determined by linguistic structure: language cannot speak itself. But neither can he accept Merleau-Ponty's attempt to 'introduce the gesture, the mobility of the sensible directly into the invariance characteristic of the system of language, in order to say what is constitutive of saying, in order to restore the act which opens the possibility of speaking'.[35] If, as structuralism contends, the anonymous system of *langue* is irreducible to individual acts of speech, then neither the 'horizontal' nor the 'vertical' dimension of negativity can be reduced to its complement, and 'the gesture of speech which is assumed to create signification can never be seized in its constitutive function'.[36]

Yet to abandon Merleau-Ponty's thought, in this way, as the 'last effort of a transcendental reflection', is not – for Lyotard – to dissolve the autonomy of the dimension of reference across which speech emerges. Lyotard's objection is principally to the notion that there exists a 'co-naturality', or elective affinity between language and the world. Perception is phenomenologically grounded in language, but language itself is a 'deflagration', a tearing asunder of our original unity with the world: the perceived object – far from embodying a semantic potential – is inherently resistant and opaque, it can never be grasped as it is 'in itself'. Lyotard elaborates this argument through an exploration of Frege's distinction between sense and reference, pointing out that – for Frege, and in contrast to the structuralists – the opening of language on to the non-linguistic cannot be simply ignored or suspended: 'We expect a reference of the proposition itself, it is the striving for truth which drives us to advance toward the referent.'[37] Yet at this point a difficulty arises. For the result of advance toward the object, of moving from the ideality of meaning to the reality of things, is simply the production of another proposition, the presentation of the object from a new viewpoint, which will in turn require verification. Thus language, far from articulating the implicit meaning of the world, perpetually excludes what it seeks to possess. It is in the gap left by this exclusion, Lyotard suggests, that there emerges what we call 'desire'.

This argument marks the midstream transition in *Discours, Figure* from a phenomenological to a psychoanalytical vocabulary. But it should not be taken to imply a parallel between Lyotard's position and that of Lacan. For although *Discours, Figure* is a consciously fragmented work, broken between a 'before' and an 'after' of structuralism, there is nevertheless a deep continuity between its phenomenological and its Freudian argument. In his critique of the Hegelian (and not only Hegelian) absorption of seeing into saying, Lyotard had emphasized the contrast between the mobility of the referential 'eye which maintains itself on the edge of discourse', and the process of selection and combination in language, between the continuous and asymmetrical nature of the visual field, and the articulated and differential nature of *langue*. But he goes on to point out that, in a certain sense, this set of contrasts also lies at the heart of Freud's work: 'Freud's reflections are, from the beginning to the end of his career, from the *Traumdeutung* to *Moses*, centred on the relation of language and silence, of signification and meaning, of articulation and the image, of the commentary which interprets or constructs and the desire which figures.'[38] From this standpoint, the non-articulated, perpetually shifting nature of the perceptual field may be taken as a kind of analogue for what Freud describes as the 'primary process', the mobility of cathexis in the unconscious. There is, Lyotard suggests, 'a radical connivance between the figural and desire'.[39] But just as the phenomenological argument of the first part of *Discours, Figure* had brought Lyotard into conflict with both structuralism and the philosophy of writing, so Lyotard's emphasis on the figural nature of desire leads him into conflict with the Lacanian interpretation of psychoanalysis as a 'logic of the signifier'. In the chapter entitled 'Le travail du rêve ne pense pas', this battle takes the explicit form of an elucidation of Freud's account of the 'dream-work' in *The Interpretation of Dreams*.

Lyotard and Lacan on the Unconscious

In order to appreciate the full import of Lyotard's argument, in an intellectual milieu largely dominated by the Lacanian account of the unconscious as 'structured like a language', we must first examine the manner in which Lacan himself characterizes the four fundamental aspects of the dream-work – condensation, displacement, considerations of representability, and secondary elaboration – described by Freud in the sixth chapter of *The Interpretation of Dreams*. In the introduction to this chapter Freud compares the manifest content of the dream to a 'pictographic script', and – a few lines later – to a 'picture puzzle' or 'rebus'. He points out that if we attempt to make sense of an image of 'a house with a boat on its roof, a single letter of the alphabet, the figure of a running man whose head has been conjured away, and so on' as if it were a 'pictorial composition', then such a jumble of images is bound to appear 'nonsensical and worthless'. It is only if we 'try to replace each separate element by a syllable or word that can be presented by that element in some way or other' that we begin to discover meaning beneath the apparent chaos: 'The words put together in this way are no longer nonsensical, but may form a poetical phrase of the greatest beauty and significance.'[40] Lacan begins his most systematic commentary on the nature of the dream-work by arguing that these Freudian similes establish definitively 'the agency in the dream of that same literalising (in other words, phonematic) structure in accordance with which the signifier is analysed in discourse'.[41] Within the dream, in other words, the images or components of images have no figurative function whatsoever: the dream is composed – to employ Lyotard's distinction – of 'letters' rather than 'lines'. Lacan reinforces his point by an elaboration of the references to pictographic script made by Freud, remarking that – in deciphering hieroglyphs – 'it would be ludicrous to deduce from the frequency with which a vulture, which is an *aleph*, or a chicken, which is a *vau*, signify the form of the verb to be and the plural, that the text is in any way interested in these ornithological specimens.'[42]

Having established that, despite its visual, pictorial form, the dream is essentially a kind of writing, an organization of signifiers, Lacan can present his reformulation of the dream-work procedures discussed by Freud. The overall operation of 'disguise, necessitated by the censorship', which Freud refers to as *Entstellung* (distortion), is translated by Lacan as 'transposition', and is equated with the 'sliding of the signified under the signifier', the semantic instability, overlooked by the ego in its inertia, which – for Lacan – is characteristic of all discourse. Within this general process of transposition Lacan aligns the operations of *Verdichtung* (condensation) and *Verschiebung* (displacement) with the two fundamental axes of language discerned by Roman Jakobson, the axis of selection and the axis of combination, which give rise to 'metaphor' and 'metonymy'. Although there has been much puzzlement about the relation between Jakobson's theory and the use made of this theory by Lacan, the manner in which Lacan's formulations both extend and diverge from those of Jakobson can in fact be characterized fairly straightforwardly. Lacan continues the linguist's argument in so far as he views metaphor and metonymy as two fundamental processes of all discourse (rather than two specific rhetorical figures – although these figures provide the most vivid exemplifications of these processes); but he goes beyond Jakobson in viewing metaphor as the mark of the relation of discourse to the subject, and metonymy as the mark of its relation to the object. Thus Lacan employs poetic examples to illustrate his definition of metaphor as 'the substitution of one signifier for another, by which is produced an effect of signification which is of poetry or creation',[43] but the creativity to which he refers is actually inherent in all discourse, since no appearance of a signifier can be deduced from the preceding signifiers in the chain. What this definition of metaphor points to, therefore, is Lacan's insistence that *langue* as a virtual system, the 'treasure of the signifier', cannot actualize itself, that discourse requires a speaking subject. But although each successive signifier reveals the *existence* of a subject, the signifier which appears cannot be seen as an unambiguous representation of the subject: the bar between signifier and signified, on which Lacan lays so much stress, blocks any automatic determination of meaning, so that it is the emergence of a further interpreting signifier, a crossing of the bar in which the first signifier now becomes the signified, which may be 'provisionally merged with the place of the subject',[44] since this reveals how the subject is revealed to itself. But since this second signifier appears under the same conditions as the first, there can be no absolute determination of the place of the subject: each signifier is a 'metaphor or the subject', a representation of the subject mediated by another signifier.

Lacan's corresponding definition of metonymy is: 'the connection from signifier to signifier, which permits the elision through which the signifier installs a lack-of-being in the object-relation, by making use of the reference-value of signification to invest this relation with a desire aimed at the lack which it supports'.[45] For Lacan, to attach a predicate to, or offer a description of, an object is always to present that object from a specific point of view. But since no single predicate or description can claim to exhaust the being of the object, and since there is a potential infinity of points of view, the attempt to grasp the object in language becomes an endless process: each description points toward further possibilities of description, but none can capture the object as it is 'in itself'. The relation between this account and the traditional definition of metonymy as a figure in which a part is taken for the whole is clear, as is the connection between the metonymic process and the Lacanian notion of desire: in Lacan desire is attached to a lost object which language permanently excludes. In metonymy, therefore, in contrast to metaphor, the bar between signifier and signified is not crossed: the object always appears 'beyond' or 'on the other side of' discourse, as the underlying coherence of the sequence of signifieds which cannot itself be signified. The *objet petit a* in Lacan, to which the subject entrusts its being at the 'panic point' when the singularity of this being is threatened by absorption into the universal dimension of language, is the sole object which is presumed to elude these linguistic conditions for the representation of objects. But it is precisely the belief in the possibility of the absolute presence of the *objet petit a* which condemns it to a permanent absence, and marks the phantasy relation to the *objet a* as imaginary. Since, for Lacan, the dream is essentially a text like any other, no more than any other sequence of signifiers can it embody or portray this object.

For Lyotard, Lacan's linguistic version of condensation and displacement is fully in continuity with the denegation and subordination of the dimension of the visible in Western thought. If Merleau-Ponty was mistaken in assuming that language could be opened up to and capture what was already implicit in the domain of the sensible, Lacan is equally at fault for relegating the perceived object to the register of the imaginary, of an immediacy which can only be grasped as already lost from the standpoint of the symbolic, and which can therefore have no independent *effect upon* the symbolic. Certainly, there is a relation between the entry of the subject into language and phantasy, but the object of phantasy does not function merely as the impossible, imaginary end-term of the metonymic chain of any discourse. Rather, the entry into language is a genuinely traumatic event, a 'primal repression' which establishes an irrecoverable phantasy in the unconscious: this phantasy will then seek to reveal itself through a disruption and overturning of the order of language, rather than through operations which are themselves merely linguistic. 'The supposed doubling of the pre-world [by language]', Lyotard argues, 'does not simply open up the distance in which the eye is installed on the edge of discourse. This tearing-away produces *in* discourse effects of distortion. A figure is installed in the depths of our speech, which operates as the matrix of these effects; which attacks our words in order to make them into forms and images. . . . By the *Entzweiung* the object is lost; by means of the phantasy it is re-presented.'[46] For Lyotard the work of the dream is the clearest example of such an irruption of the primary process into the secondary process, of the manner in which a 'figure-matrix', by its twisting of the order of language, traces – through the very distortions which it imposes – a figuration of the unfigurable. 'The dream', he suggests, 'is not the speech of desire, but its work . . . it results from the application of a force to a text. Desire does not speak, it violates the order of speech.'[47]

Clearly, such a standpoint imposes a very different understanding of what Freud means by 'condensation' and 'displacement' from that of Lacan. 'Condensation', Lyotard argues, 'should be understood as a physical process by which one or more objects occupying a given space are reduced to inhabiting a smaller volume. . . . To crush the signifying or signified unities against each other, to confuse them, is to neglect the stable gaps which separate the letters, the words of a text, to disregard the invariant distinctive graphemes of which they are composed, ultimately to be indifferent to the space of discourse.'[48] In support of this argument, Lyotard points to some of the 'amusing and curious neologisms' which Freud reports in *The Interpretation of Dreams* (the adjective '*norekdal*', for example, is decomposed into a parody of German superlatives such as '*kolossal*' or '*pyramidal*', and the names of two Ibsen characters – 'Nora' and 'Ekdal'), or to the tangle of associations attached to the 'botanical monograph' in Freud's dream of the same name[49]. Lyotard's account is unquestionably closer to Freud than the Lacanian reformulation of condensation as the metaphorical relation between a latent and a patent signifier. Lacan explicitly excludes the view of metaphor as 'the presentation of two images, that is, of two signifiers, equally actualized', whereas in Freud's writings condensation frequently takes the form of an overlapping of disparate traits to form a single composite figure, as if – as Lyotard puts it – 'the place where one dreams [were] narrower than the place where one thinks'.[50]

The gulf between Lyotard and Lacan is equally wide in their respective understandings of displacement. In *The Interpretation of Dreams* this concept refers to the manner in which, in the course of the formation of a dream, 'essential elements, charged, as they are, with intense interest, may be treated as though they were of small value, and their place taken in the dream by other elements, of whose small value in the dream thoughts there can be no question'.[51] In order to illustrate this aspect of the dream-work, Lyotard takes the example of a poster advertizing a film of the Russian Revolution, on which the letters of the phrase '*Révolution D'Octobre*' are written in an undulating manner, suggesting a banner blowing in the wind. The process of displacement can then be represented as a reinforcement of certain areas of the text, so that, if the speed of the wind were to increase, only these strengthened sections would remain visible on the flapping standard. There could remain visible, for example, merely the letters: *Révon D'Or*, which can be read as '*Rêvons d'or*' ('let us dream of gold'). In this sense, displacement – as Freud suggests in his discussion of the topic – is a preliminary process which provides the conditions for condensation or overdetermination. Again, we are remote from Lacan's account of displacement as the metonymic circling of discourse around an object which it has itself excommunicated. For Lacan, the object of phantasy is merely the ungraspable coherence of the chain of signifiers, and desire itself is nothing other than this sequence, the 'metonymy of a want-to-be'. Desire cannot act as a force upon language, as the wind and the pattern of strengthening compress and transform the text of the banner.

The disagreement between Lacan and Lyotard focuses many of the most crucial questions about the nature of, and relation between, the conscious and the unconscious. In Lacan it is the conscious and the perceptual which is described in terms of the passivity and stasis of the imaginary, while the unconscious is equated with the instability of the symbolic, whereas Lyotard sees stasis in the fixed intervals of the linguistic system, and links the unconscious with the fluidity and mobility of the perceived world. These opposed interpretations clearly bear also on the problems of archaism and regression in the unconscious. For Lyotard, there *is* a primacy – or at least a primitiveness – of perception: the figural is in a sense both more rudimentary and more forceful than speech: 'the first condition of discourse, which is discontinuity, the existence of *articuli*, is not satisfied by unconscious "discourse". Freud always characterizes the unconscious as *work*, as the other of discourse, and not as another discourse'.[52] Lacan, by contrast, repudiates any equation of the unconscious with 'the place of the divinities of night': there is nothing elementary about the unconscious except the elements of the signifier. This clash is most starkly illustrated by the differing interpretations of the third factor in Freud's account of the dreamwork: *Rücksicht auf Darstellbarkeit*. Since Freud's theory of the dream is inseparable from his distinction between a secondary process – the process of logical, waking thought – and a primary process which tends toward a reckless, hallucinatory fulfillment, the value of the dream as the 'royal road to the unconscious' appears to depend on its exemplification of the primary process, on its status as 'a substitute for an infantile scene modified by being transferred onto a recent experience'.[53] However, if what Freud terms 'the most striking psychological characteristic of the process of dreaming', the fact that 'a thought, and as a rule a thought of something that is wished, is objectified in the dream, is represented in a scene, or, as it seems to us, experienced'[54] is as essential an aspect of the dream-work as condensation and displacement, then Lacan's argument for a purely 'literal' understanding of dreams appears to be undermined.

Lacan parries this possible attack, in 'The Agency of the Letter in the Unconscious', by suggesting that what he terms 'regard for the means of staging' is a condition which 'constitutes a limitation operating *within* the system of writing'. He compares the dream with a game of charades, and suggests that the very ingenuity with which 'such logical articulations as causality, contradiction, hypothesis' are communicated despite this limitation, in both the dream and the game, demonstrates once again that 'the dreamwork follows the laws of the signifier'.[55] The attention of the analyst should be directed toward the proverb which the dumbshow is intended to convey, rather than toward the characteristic forms of mime and gesture by means of which the participants communicate their silent message. In so far as these forms have any interest, the questions which they raise are purely psychological. Elsewhere in the *Écrits* Lacan offers a list of such questions – 'little work of value has been done on space and time in the dream, on whether one dreams in colour or black and white, on whether smell, taste and touch occur, or the sense of vertigo, of the turgid and the heavy'[56] – but immediately goes on to suggest that these problems are remote from Freud's concern, which is with the 'elaboration of the dream' in the sense of its 'linguistic structure'. Questions of interpretation are therefore, for Lacan, entirely distinct from psychological explanations of the material of the dream; and the 'means of staging' are *not* part of the dream-work, in the sense of its linguistic elaboration. If the dream is the royal road to the unconscious, this is not because it operates in accordance with a primary process, but because it suspends the assertoric function of discourse, allowing the subject 'to be in a state of perhaps (*être à l'état de peut-être)'.*[57]

A similar relegation is apparent in Lacan's treatment of the fourth and final factor in the dream-work, secondary revision. Lacan pauses only to suggest that the phantasies or daydreams employed in secondary revision can be used either as signifying elements for the statement of unconscious thought, or in secondary revision in the true sense: this is a process which Lacan compares to the application of patches of whitewash to a stencil, in an effort to attenuate the rebarbative appearance of the rebus or hieroglyphs by transforming them into the semblance of a figurative painting. There are two important implications of this account. The first is that, although Lacan admits the 'rebarbative' appearance of the stencilled forms, he cannot admit any connection between this appearance and the nature of the unconscious: secondary revision is not a means of concealing a threatening disorder, since the unconscious is itself simply a hidden order. The second is that Lacan affirms a strict disjunction ('*ou bien/ou bien*') between the function of phantasy and daydream as a signifier of unconscious thought *within* the text of the dream, and the cosmetic operation of secondary revision carried out *on* the dream-text. For Lacan, the plastic transformation of a signifier cannot alter its function as a signifier, whereas for Freud – as Lyotard points out – no such disjunction can be said to apply. Lacan stresses a quotation in which Freud suggests that the activity of secondary revision is not to be distinguished from waking thought. But in his introductory essay 'On Dreams' Freud argues that 'one would be mistaken in seeing in the facade of the dream merely such actually uncomprehending and apparently arbitrary reworkings of the dream-content by the conscious agency of our psychic life'. Since the wish-phantasies which are employed in the manufacture of this facade of illusory coherence are of the same kind as unconscious phantasy, it can be argued that 'in many dreams the facade of the dream shows us directly the kernel of the dream, distorted through its mixture with other material'.[58] For Lyotard this ambiguous status, midway between the centre and the surface of the dream, torn between the discursive and the figural, is characteristic of phantasy.

Although Lyotard's view of phantasy as 'a word lost in a hallucinatory scenography, an initial violence'[59] does not erase the distinction between the conscious and the unconscious, between primary and secondary process, the very fact that it bridges the two in this way prohibits any simple equation between the expression of phantasy and liberation from discursive constraints. It seems that there is an implicit conflict in *Discours, Figure*, which Lyotard is increasingly forced to confront, between desire as striving for fulfilment and as the forceful means of this fulfilment. Thus the book contains an extended discussion of Freud's paper on the phantasy, 'A Child is being Beaten', in which Lyotard remarks that, despite its heterogeneity with the order of discourse, the phantasy is itself already a kind of ' "writing", a repetitive configuration, a sieve within which will be caught and made to "signify" everything which chance encounters, the days residues, episodes from daily life, will bring the way of the subject'.[60] In his articles and interviews dating from the immediate post-'68 period, this static quality of phantasy, its ability to immobilize desire, begins to take on a political significance for Lyotard; he argues that, in many forms of cultural production – religion, advertizing, cinema, political propaganda – the transgressions of the order of discourse required for the realization of the figural nature of phantasy are subordinated to the aim of producing a representation within which desire can be captured and enticed to an illusory fulfilment. In waking life the excessive disorder of the dream would generate anxiety, and must therefore be mitigated by the imposition of a 'good form'; the work of desire is concealed by its product. On this basis Lyotard can suggest that the co-operation of the pleasure principle and the reality principle, of Eros and Logos, represents the fundamental operation of ideology, an operation in which desire is made to overlook its own disruptive radicality.

In fact, the central concern of *Discours, Figure* is to establish a theory of art which can take account of Freud's crucial insight into the relation between artistic creation and unconscious phantasy, while at the same time providing a means of demarcating the work of art from forms of ideological representation. To this end Lyotard introduces the concept of 'reversal' (*renversement*). His argument is that the work of art reveals its continuity with the dream in so far as it disjoints the discursive in order to embody the figural, but that – at the same time – the work of art has a 'critical' function which goes beyond such an embodiment. The invasion of the discursive by the figural in the dream does not pose a threat, since the subject is no longer 'on the side of consciousness', and can enjoy the representation of phantasy. The work of art, however, stresses the gap between the discursive and the figural, laying bare the disorder of the unconscious rather than absorbing this disorder into an hallucinatory fulfilment. 'The artist', Lyotard suggests, 'does not produce outside the systems of internal figures, but is someone who tries to struggle in order to deliver *in* the phantasy, *in* the matrix of figures of which he is the location and the inheritor, that which is in the proper sense primary process and not repetition, "writing".'[61] The 'reversal' to which Lyotard refers therefore consists in the process whereby the work of art 'turns back' on the process of its own production and disrupts the world of illusion which it is its own deepest tendency to generate. 'Poetic reversal', Lyotard writes, 'concerns both "form" and "content" . . . while the phantasy fills the space of dispossession' – that is, the space in which the conscious subject is no longer in control – 'the work of art dispossesses the space of fulfilment. The phantasy makes opposition out of difference; poetics remakes difference with *this* opposition.'[62]

Clearly, this view of the work of art as constantly 'on the edge of its own rupture'[63] implies not only a critique of previous psychoanalytical approaches to art, in so far as these remain oriented towards the phantasy content of the work, or lay stress upon its reconciliatory function; concomitantly, it implies a strongly normative conception of artistic activity, and in particular a fundamental commitment to the deconstructive techniques of modernism. In his writings of the late sixties and early seventies Lyotard backs up this commitment with a historical sketch of the transformed situation of the artist under capitalism. In traditional societies the function of art is 'religious' in the etymological sense: art belongs to the domain of the sacred, of the symbolic expression of social integration, its forms and rhythms serve as a vehicle and reinforcement of the unquestioned understandings and beliefs which form the basis of collective existence. Since the consolidation of capitalism during the 19th century, however, the relentless expansion of commodity relations has deprived artistic expression of this collective foundation. Indeed, the artist now finds him- or herself in the contrary position of disrupting the illusion of integration, by refusing the attempt to constitute a pseudo-collectivity, even at the level of a stable artistic *style*, and of revealing the incompatibility between the social order and the disorder of desire. In Freudian terms, Lyotard expresses this position by denying that the modernist work achieves its critical task of reversal through a triumph of the secondary process over the primary process. Rather, in its denunciation of any complicity of Eros and Logos, of primary and secondary, the position of the modernist work can only be mapped with the aid of Freud's final theory of drives, in which the concept of the death-drive is introduced. In attempting to confront, to 'stare down', the chaos of the primary process – even at the cost of its own coherence – the critical work reveals the death-drive – the mark, in the final phase of Freud's work, according to Lyotard, of 'the limit of representation and of theory'[64] – as the fundamental tendency of every drive, of desire itself.

The Politics of Desire

Although *Discours, Figure* is concerned almost exclusively with the elaboration of a figural-energetic theory of the unconscious, and its application to poetry and the visual arts, there is a sense – throughout the book – that political concerns are never far away. Lyotard wrote the work during a two-year period of political reclusion, between the collapse of the newspaper *Pouvoir Ouvrier* in 1966 and the student rebellion at Nanterre, feeling that 'it was necessary to start thinking afresh without knowing, hence to begin philosophy afresh';[65] yet its theoretical assumptions accurately foreshadow the political practice of the 22 March Movement. How a work of philosophical aesthetics could function in this way as 'a detour intended to lead to the practical critique of ideology'[66] will perhaps become clearer if we consider Lyotard's most extended discussion of Marx, an article on 'La place de l'aliénation dans le retournement marxiste', which was written a year after the May Events, and which attempts to reformulate Marx's theory in the light of the political practice of the *22 Mars*. Like Althusser, Lyotard wishes to strip Marx's thought of its Hegelian residues, and in particular of the unacceptably 'dialectical' and historicist assumptions that the proletariat is the predestined grave-digger of capitalism, the locus of a negativity which brings the system to a critical consciousness of itself, and that Marxism itself is no more than the theoretical expression of this consciousness. Yet, at the same time, the motives of Althusser and Lyotard in their opposition to historicism are radically divergent. Althusser insists upon an ontological separation of knowledge and the real in order to preserve a positivist conception of Marxism as a science, but at the same time downgrades the lived experience of capitalism, so that a gulf opens up between the enlightened Marxist theoretician and the ideologically ensnared proletariat. Lyotard, on the other hand, wishes to retain the concept of alienation, which Althusser discards, as forming the crucial hinge between the theoretical explanation and the 'lived experience' of capitalism, while equally rejecting the notion of Marxist theory as simply the recovery of the reality hidden within this alienation, since such a notion inevitably encourages the speculative self-confirmation of a political elite. In Lyotard's view, 'Every dialectical philosophy of the relations of knowledge and experience provides the subject-matter for a bureaucracy of the spirit, which presents itself as the organ, both visible and mysterious, in whose name this dialectic operates.'[67] Thus Lyotard is seeking for a form of 'critical reversal' which will emphatically not be simply a 'negation of the negation', a theory which will describe the mechanisms behind the experience of capitalist alienation, rather than simply express the implicit truth of that experience, and a type of political intervention which will disrupt the very forms of political activity, rather than simply filling them with a new content.

It is the aesthetic reversal which Lyotard describes in *Discours, Figure* which provides the model for this political reversal. Lyotard's retrospective remark that 'the latent problematic of the *22 Mars*, after and with that of situationism, was the critique of representation, of the externalisation of activity and of the fruits of activity, of the *mise en spectacle* which places agents in the position of passive interpreters'[68] indicates how this parallelism will function. Just as, in the libidinal sphere, the illusory fulfilment made possible by representations of phantasy depends upon a binding of the energy of the primary process, so, in the social sphere, labour-power, creativity, individuality is absorbed into the ever-expanding circuits of the reproduction of capital. Indeed, for reasons we shall shortly discover, Lyotard increasingly tends to claim that the libidinal and the social are simply two perspectives on the same process. Just as the aesthetic reversal of modernism does not attempt to replace a no-longer-viable phantasy content with a more adequate form of fulfilment, but turns back to attack the collective function of art itself, so the forms of practical political intervention which Lyotard advocates eschew all mediation. When workers climb onto their own production line and travel along conversing with their workmates – visibly supplanting the product with the labour-power through which it is produced – or when students invade a metro station to urge passengers not to have their tickets punched, these actions are not aimed towards a transformation or democratization of political power: they reveal the factitious, constructed, 'secondary' nature of the social scene, but do not propose an alternative scene. What Lyotard, in an article on Nanterre, calls the 'attitude of the here-now' is not part of a strategy, a step towards a new system, but rather intends to provoke 'a mutation of desire in relation to the system',[69] to exacerbate rather than to heal the disjunction between ends and means, abstract and concrete, product and production characteristic of capitalism. In this way Lyotard's Freudian aesthetic provides the basis for a theorization 'from the inside' of what numerous commentators have noted as the fundamental characteristics of *enragé* politics: a determination to 'intensify contradictions rather than to resolve them' and the refusal of 'any knowledge which would permit (the movement) to say in advance what it wants and what will happen'.[70]

Inevitably, with the ebbing of the post-'68 upsurge, Lyotard quickly began to grasp the impasse of this form of political activity, an impasse which is identical with that of the modernist avant-gardes to which he looks for inspiration. As we have seen, the central attraction of Freud's thought for Lyotard is its anti-dialectical dualism, a dualism which is figured (rather than signified) in the very title *Discours, Figure*. Since the primary process is not constitutive of the secondary process, but is revealed only privatively through its disruptions of the secondary process, any philosophy, aesthetics or politics of mediation and reconciliation is rendered impossible. But the consequence of this position in the aesthetic domain is that, since the 'critical' work of art is dependent for its impact upon the violation of an order, and since the repetition of such violations weakens the order and therefore the effect of the transgression, artistic activity must be caught up in a perpetual *fuite en avant*. Lyotard himself draws attention to this process – 'the "artists" are pushed forward, they are chased away from the deconstructed forms they propose, at a given moment they are literally chased out, and must continually seek something different'[71] – but provides it with a favourable gloss:

'I believe that there is no other motor for their research than that.'[72] In the political domain, however, this problem cannot be so easily dispatched, since a form of 'critical' activity which is dependent for its effect upon the order which it transgresses not only risks rapidly losing its effectivity, but demonstrates an elementary bad faith with regard to its own political status in refusing to outline any intended alternative order. Lyotard's rejection of any determinate goal of struggle ultimately confronts him with the prospect of an 'indefinite, inexhaustible' 'task of demystification',[73] which is not so different from the Derridean deconstruction which he initially opposed in the name of the figural, non-discursive nature of desire. Lyotard's problem therefore becomes one of how to avoid any Hegelian philosophy of mediation, without lapsing in the tragic posture of finitude, irreconcilability, and the endless recession of the object of desire. In the quest for a solution, his 'drift starting from Marx and Freud' becomes a headlong race towards the characteristic 1970s terminus of Nietzsche.

Lyotard's fundamental move is to transform the nature of the dualism which had characterized his work around the time of *Discours, Figure*, and whose roots may be traced back to the distinction between the reflexive and the pre-reflexive, consciousness and world, which marked his Merleau-Pontyan account of phenomenology. In *Discours, Figure* it is the discursive and the figural, language and desire, which are ontologically opposed, and this contrast provides the framework for Lyotard's political conclusions. Even here, however, the opposition becomes more ramified on closer inspection. The figuration of phantasy requires a disruption of the order of discourse, but this disruption is not inherently critical, since desire invested in phantasy is already held in thrall. The crucial opposition is therefore almost imperceptibly displaced until – rather than contrasting language with desire – it contrasts two aspects of desire: desire as a longing for the lost object represented in phantasy, as 'forbidden in its very depths',[74] as negativity, and desire as the positive energy which disrupts discourse in order to embody the figurality of phantasy. Since, in *Discours, Figure*, Lyotard's primary target is the imperialism of semiology, these two conceptions of desire are obliged to cohabit uneasily. If 'desire does not speak' but 'violates the order of speech', then both the figural and the energetic are equally forms of this violation. But, confronted with the impasse of his libidinal politics, Lyotard begins to stress this dualism of desire as present in the work of Freud himself, and to stress one side of this dualism as a means of avoiding self-defeating orientation towards an impossible future: 'Desire thought under the category of lack, of the negative; and desire produced in words, sounds, colours, volumes, under the idea of positive processes. Desire as that which models in the void the double (phantasy, counterpart, replica, hologram) *of* that which it lacks, desire as work, metamorphosis without aim, play without memory. Both senses are there in Freud: the *Wunsch*, the primary process.'[75] From this standpoint the solution to Lyotard's dilemma appears to be simple; it is the solution attempted by Deleuze and Guattari in *Anti-Oedipus*: one abandons every negative, nostalgic interpretation of desire, and espouses a conception of desire as that which is exclusively positive, affirmative and productive.[76]

The difficulty with this position, as semiologists, deconstructionists, and Lacanians were quick to point out, is that it is founded upon a naive naturalism. The *désirants* appear to be guilty of searching for a 'primaeval state where we could and would be *ourselves*, subjects . . . unalienated and integral, prior to all fault and every prohibition', of attempting to relegate the reality principle 'to the obsolescent arsenal of the metaphysical police force'.[77] This critique, aimed by a Derridean at Lyotard, is in fact more appropriate to Deleuze and Guattari, since Lyotard was always careful not to claim that one could reach the pre-reflexive, the figural, the primary process in itself, and in the early seventies rapidly abandons the residual, ambiguous naturalism which had marked his concepts of 'alienation' and of 'critique'. This is both because, where the natural is unattainable, critique turns into perpetual negativity, and because Lyotard comes increasingly to believe that any theory of alienation – of a unity, innocence, creativity, dispersed in the fragmentation and indifference of capitalism – will lead to a totalitarian politics, an attempt to impose an illusory wholeness upon the social body. But if political action no longer expresses the return of the repressed, and no longer embodies the promise of a transformed future, then it ceases to possess any privileged status at all. The 'attitude of the here-now', the intensity which Lyotard had prized in the interventions of the *22 Mars*, becomes a possible dimension of any action, any experience. It is no longer a matter of political choice between discourse and figure or between two distinct systems of desire, but rather of an 'existential' choice between two possible attitudes towards desire: desire '*thought under the category* of lack', desire '*under the idea* of positive processes'. Lyotard's question now becomes a Nietzschean one: how must one imagine the world to be if pure affirmation is to be possible?

Nietzsche finds his answer to this question in the thought of the 'eternal return of the same'. His vision of cyclical time, his view of the world as 'a monster of energy without beginning, without end . . . a play of forces and waves of forces'[78] enables him to reject any teleology, the notion of any moment being for the sake of another, and to open up a 'vertical' dimension of time in which every moment contains its own justification. In *The Will to Power* Nietzsche asks: 'Can we remove the idea of purpose from the process and *still* affirm the process? – That would be the case if something within the process were *attained* in every moment – and always the Same'.[79] In *Économie Libidinale* Lyotard presents his own attempt to 'remove the idea of purpose from the process and still affirm the process', to consecrate the singularity and intensity of the event, rather than subordinate it to some broader meaning or goal. Accordingly, the book opens with its own more modest – and more Freudian – version of the Eternal Return, with what Lyotard terms the '*grande pellicule éphémère*', a labyrinthine ribbon composed by the continuous deployment – in the form of a moebius strip – of the surfaces, both inner and outer, of the body, and swept by incessantly mobile libidinal cathexes. Lyotard imagines the focus of cathexis as the continually displaced centre of gravity of a bar which rotates in all three dimensions – thereby tracing out the libidinal band – and whose function, essential to consciousness and conceptual thought, is the separation of a 'this' from a 'not-this'. Like the gateway labelled 'Moment' in Nietzsche's *Zarathustra*, the rotating bar is therefore the contradiction of past and future, of exterior and interior, of self and other: a point of pure intensity.

On the basis of this vision of a 'place which one must imagine without being able to conceive it',[80] Lyotard can now launch an attack on all those forms of thought which are dominated by the idea of absence, negativity, of an unattainable Other; he can bring to a conclusion his critique of the thought of Lacan, since it is here that the presuppositions of any semiology are most clearly articulated. The most crucial of these is the assumption that a mark can only become a sign, a vehicle of meaning, against a backdrop of absence. In the work of Saussure and the structural linguists this assumption takes the modest form of an argument for the differential nature of the sign, but – as the first wave of post-structuralism was quick to point out – this characterization leaves unanswered the question of the origin of difference itself.

In a sense, as Derrida tirelessly repeats, there cannot be an 'origin' of difference, since difference is the ground of all determinate meaning and all determinate being, and therefore cannot itself be made present. But this train of thought leaves difference in the position of a first principle and achieves no more than a draining of the realm of signs of any stable meaning, so that even the compensations of 'scientific' semiology are lost. Lacan resolves this dilemma, and brings the argument to its conclusion, by suggesting that it is precisely the perpetual flight of meaning which convinces us that *différance* – in the form of the Other – speaks to us in everything which we say. He therefore reveals that semiology is a 'religious science because haunted by the hypothesis that someone is talking to us in what is given and, at the same time, that their language, their competence, or in any event their performance ability, transcends us'.[81] The question which arises, however, is whether the here-now, the intensity and singularity of the given, must inevitably be transmuted into the pale token of a perpetually absent meaning, must be seen against the background of what Lyotard terms the 'great totalizing Zero'. 'The real question,' Lyotard suggests, 'which Lacan avoids on account of his Hegelianism, is that of knowing why it is necessary for the drives scattered across the polymorphic body to unite themselves in an object.'[82] Why must the mirror reflect back the prototypical image of an identity rather than its surface remaining a patchwork of intensities?

Fundamentally, this difference between Lyotard and Lacan concerns the status of consciousness. To be conscious of an object is to be conscious – even if implicitly – of consciousness itself as consciousness *of* that object. Hence a distance from the object is built into the very concept of consciousness. Consciousness presupposes an initial distinction between a this and a not-this, and representation of the this to the not-this. Naturally, Lyotard does not wish to deny the experience of self-consciousness, but he does wish to oppose the ontological primacy of negativity, the suggestion that there is, from the very beginning, a 'great totalizing Zero' into which the intensity of the moment is absorbed. In defending this position Lyotard returns to the Nietzschean – and Freudian – view that consciousness itself is already a form of exclusion and repression. 'Theatricality and representation,' Lyotard writes, 'far from having the status of a libidinal – and *a fortiori* – metaphysical given, result from a certain labour carried out on the moebian and labyrinthian band, a labour which imprints these special creases and folds whose effect is a box closed in on itself, filtering impulses, and only allowing to appear on the stage those which, arriving from what will now be called the exterior, satisfy the conditions of interiority. The representative chamber is an energetic system.'[83] In this connexion Lyotard recalls the mirror-animals of Borges, banished back to their mirrors by the Yellow Emperor, as punishment for their revolt, and condemned to 'the task of repeating, as in a kind of dream, all the acts of men'.[84] In Borges' story, Lyotard argues, the surface of the mirror cannot be equated with the Lacanian bar between signifier and signified, with the gap which is 'an effect of the Signifier, of the Father or the Name-of-the-Father, of the No, of writing, of language as a power of retreat and staging'.[85] Desire, in Lacan, is not *held in check* by language, and a system of representation is therefore not a system of power. Borges, by contrast, 'imagines these beings as forces, and this bar as a barrier; he imagines that the Emperor, the Despot in general, can only maintain his position on condition that he represses these monsters and keeps them on the other side of the transparent wall. The existence of the subject depends entirely on this wall, on the subjugation of these fluid and lethal powers repressed on the other side, on the function which represents them.'[86]

As has already been suggested, Lyotard's response to this situation is not to advocate a 'revolt of things represented' which would be 'a world without mirrors, without theatre and without painting'.[87] One of the persistent themes of *Économie Libidinale* is the impossibility of simply abolishing or jumping outside of the domain of signs, representations and meanings. However, if one wishes to retain the libidinal standpoint, while also asserting the inescapability of representation, yet not interpreting this in terms of negativity and alienation, the only option becomes a theory of 'dissimulation' in which there would be 'no notable difference between a discursive and libidinal formation'.[88] In the elaboration of this standpoint, Lyotard makes frequent reference to the new dualism introduced by Freud in *Beyond the Pleasure Principle*, and which persists throughout the last phase of his work. With the new opposition of Eros and the death-drive, Lyotard contends, Freud himself becomes conscious of, and attempts to theorize, the relation between 'negative' desire – desire as wish, as lack, as striving – and 'positive' desire – desire as energy, libido, primary process – which had been left unconsidered in his earlier work. Eros is the force which strives to maintain the unity and narcissistic uniqueness of the individual, which is concerned with homeostasis, the conservation of order, and the constitution of ever more complex wholes. The death-drive, on the other hand, is energy in his disruptive, unbound, anxiety-generating state: its ultimate aim – in a sense, the fundamental aim of every drive – is a total discharge of energy, a rejection of the tension and complexity of life itself in favour of the peace of the inorganic. For Lyotard the crucial aspect of this new dualism is that it does not at all operate like Freud's former dualism of ego-drives and object-drives, which in fact continues to be central to his aetiology of the neuroses. This is because, as Freud himself stresses, the task of determining what is the work of Eros and what expresses the death-drive is a highly problematic one, comparable to juggling with 'an equation with two unknown quantities'.[89] In the case of the celebrated *fort/da* game with which *Beyond the Pleasure Principle* opens, Freud admits that the compulsive repetition of the throwing away of the bobbin cannot be interpreted unequivocally as exemplifying an inertia counter to the pleasure principle; the purpose of the game could equally be to master the experience of the loss of the mother, and even to enact a symbolic revenge against her. And, in general, throughout his late work, Freud argues that 'there can be no question of confining one or other of the fundamental drives to one of the provinces of the psyche. They must both be discoverable everywhere.'[90]

The dissimulation of the death-drive in the activity of Eros, the persistence of its 'unobtrusive work' beneath the clamour of life, provides Lyotard with his model of the relation between 'sign' and 'tensor', idea and affect, during the phase of his work dominated by the notion of a libidinal economy. He now concludes that there is 'no need for declarations, manifestos, organizations, provocations, not even any need for *exemplary actions*',[91] since 'disorder, deconstruction, the figure, do not offer any guarantee of good conduction [of intensities]'.[92] Indeed, Lyotard now goes so far as to suggest that – as in the case of the Japanese *No* Theatre – coldness, classicism, order may function as an incitement to, rather than as a brake on, intensity. Even the sign can function as such a spur if it is taken as the *proper name* of a singularity. In itself, perhaps, this search for the incandescence of the moment, without origin, without purpose, without intention, could be dismissed as an unconvincing and self-defeating attempt to revive the ecstatic vision of Nietzsche: *Économie Libidinale* would be of interest chiefly as a case study, as the *reductio ad absurdum* of the concern of post-structuralism with the ineffably singular. But what gives the book its weight is its historical and political dimension, its treatment of the problem of the appropriate reaction to the erosion of the traditional, the meaningful, the sacred, entailed by the incessant expansion of capitalist economic relations. It raises the question of how one should respond to the anonymity, exchangeability, and indifference implied by the commodity form. Lyotard's answer to this question is now unequivocal: 'there is no exteriority, no other of Kapital, which would be Nature, Socialism, Carnival, or what have you . . . '.[93] Indeed, any attempt to restore a new sense of wholeness, a new relation to nature, a new collective meaning beyond the social fragmentation of capitalism betrays a 'furious concentrationary impulse'.[94] The world of capitalism, therefore, is not an alienated world. Rather, the cynicism and polymorphous perversity of an economy which can absorb any object, any capacity, any experience into the circuit of commodity exchange parallels the aimless voyage of intensities on the libidinal band, indeed – because forms of order are now themselves seen as merely stases of energy – is indistinguishable from the great ephemeral pellicule itself. Admittedly, in this respect capitalism, like every system of signification and exchange, dissimulates. The capitalist is concerned not with the product as such, but only with the constant augmentation of production, so that capital as a whole functions as a 'great totalizing Zero' which neutralizes the singularity of the object into the indifferently exchangeable sign of a value. Yet an almost imperceptible shift can transform this 'return to the Eternal' into an Eternal Return, into a 'production as consumption, consumption as production, that is to say a *metamorphosis* without end and without aim'.[95] The moment in which this shift is inaugurated would be the moment in which the anonymity and indifference of the commodity form is itself employed as an intensifier of pleasure, in which the 'bar of disjunction' which traces the libidinal ribbon is made to turn upon itself. Such a 'libidinal economy' may be found, Lyotard suggests, in the 'dandyism' of Baudelaire, or in the work of the neo-realist painter Jacques Monory, where the romanticism of theme and motif is both held in check and heightened by the fragmentation of the picture space and the impersonality of the painting technique. *Économie Libidinale* concludes with the attempt to adopt a similar position: 'Our fear of the system of signs, and thus our investment in it, must still be immense if we continue to seek for these positions of purity . . . What would be interesting would be to stay where we are, but at the same time silently to seize every opportunity to function as good conductors of intensities.'[96]

The Impasse of Libidinal Economy

In many ways *Économie Libidinale* must be considered as one of
the termini of post-structuralist thought. Beginning with a challenge to the supremacy of semiology in *Discours, Figure*, Lyotard is led to abandon the founding dualism of that book in favour
of a metaphysics of libido, and then to think this metaphysics
through consistently to the point of appreciating the futility of pit-
ting 'good' desire against 'bad' desire, 'revolutionary' desire
against 'fascist' desire, as Deleuze and Guattari still attempt to do in
Anti-Oedipus.[97] The result is a text which is bereft of any political or
moral orientation. In some of his essays from around this period,
Lyotard continues to speak as though it might be possible to base a
politics upon a pure libidinal economy, yet – beneath the reckless-
ness and bravado – he has already grasped that this is impossible:
any action, any discourse, any aesthetic structure can serve as an
equally good, or equally bad, conveyor of intensity. It is scarcely
surprising, therefore, that not long after *Économie Libidinale*,
Lyotard set off in new directions, abandoning what he now freely
admits was a metaphysics of force, in order to pose the question of
the 'post-modern', and more specifically of a post-modern concept of justice, a concept *between* critique and affirmation.
Indeed, Lyotard's turn towards the question of justice can, in one
respect, be seen as an attempt to 'make amends' for the implicit
amoralism of *Économie Libidinale*, whose standpoint of total
affirmation he begins to portray as a clearing operation which was
necessary before any new construction could begin.[98]

Yet it is difficult not to feel that, in abandoning the perspective
of libidinal economy, Lyotard has jettisoned too hastily a position
which should be preserved as a *moment* of any theory whose aim
is a philosophical diagnosis of the present. Lyotard's critiques of
semiology and its offshoots, of Derrida and above all of Lacan,
have genuine power, yet this power is dissipated by the very
attempt to totalize the libidinal standpoint. This self-defeating
dynamic therefore raises the question of whether it might be possible to accommodate simultaneously the logical and hermeneutic
insights of the 'first phase' of post-structuralism, and the insistence on the clash between discourse and extra-discursive forces
characteristic of the French thought of the early 1970s. In fact,
as we have already seen, a project of this kind is precisely that of
the first generation Frankfurt School, and in particular of
Adorno. For Adorno's philosophy establishes an *internal relation* between logical incoherence and the repression of what he

terms 'inner nature'. The fundamental theme of the *Dialectic of Enlightenment* is that the conscious self can only emerge through a separation from nature and a denial of its own natural basis. However, the cost of this separation and denial is the perpetuation of the blind coercion of nature within the self. The ego which imagines itself to be fully autonomous, free from any contamination by natural contingency, will repeatedly run up against contradictions in attempting to explicate this autonomy. And these contradictions in turn betray a self divided against itself, subjected to an internalized form of the compulsion which it originally attempted to evade. Thus, for Adorno, 'The antithesis of thought to whatever is heterogeneous to thought is reproduced in thought itself, as its immanent contradiction.'[99]

As we have found, Derrida's critique of transcendental philosophy takes a very different direction from this, since he attempts to derive the tension and antagonism between facticity and the transcendental from an ulterior *différance*, rather than perceiving in this antagonism the limit of any discourse claiming a priori validity. In this respect, despite the many debts which he owes to Nietzsche, Derrida is profoundly un-Nietzschean. The critique of 'philosophy of origins' which Nietzsche develops in *Twilight of the Idols*, and which was such an important influence on Adorno, could easily be directed against the role which Derrida allots to concepts such as '*différance*', and against a standpoint which Derrida himself admits to be entwined with that of 'negative theology': 'The other idiosyncrasy of the philosophers is no less dangerous; it consists in confusing the last and the first. They place that which comes at the end – unfortunately! for it ought not to come at all! – namely the 'highest concepts', which means the most general, the emptiest concepts, the last smoke of evaporating reality, in the beginning, as the beginning . . . That which is last, thinnest, and emptiest is put first as cause in itself, as *ens realissimum*.'[100] Derrida's appeals to Nietzsche in playing off difference against identity cannot disguise the fact that his work bears no trace of the deep naturalistic strain in Nietzsche, which repeatedly counters the tendency to hypostatize concepts with reminders of their biological and social functions. Similarly, although Lacan has a far more sophisticated account than Derrida of the dialectics of identity and difference, he has no sympathy for naturalism – not even in the work of Freud, let alone that of Nietzsche.

By contrast, it is precisely this aspect of Nietzsche's thought which Lyotard takes up. In *Économie Libidinale*, conceptual thought only becomes possible through a cooling of energy, through a slowing down of the rotation of the bar which constitutes the libidinal band. In consequence, the ideal identity forged by concepts entails the 'denial of disparities, of heterogeneities, of transits and stases of energy . . . the denial of polymorphy.'[101] Lyotard's work of the early to mid seventies can be seen as a prolonged protest against the inherent instrumentality of concepts, and against the sacrifice of the moment for the future which their use entails. He is constantly in search of the non-calculable and the unpredictable, of what he has sometimes termed the 'beside' (*l'à-côté*), and it is this which lies behind his interest in the vagaries of sexual experience.[102] Yet, taken to its logical consequence, his position would seem to require a total dissolution of consciousness into the chaos of impulse, and an abandonment of concepts in favour of the intensity of singularities. Recognizing the impossibility of this, Lyotard has no choice but to accept the affirmative conclusion that intensity is already everywhere: in other words, to abandon the very concept of discursive repression from which he began.

Lyotard's difficulty here can be seen as the opposite of that of Derrida. In Derrida's work, the contradictions inherent in the concept of pure self-identity are not connected with an account of the natural-historical genesis of the self, with the consequence that Derrida can only escape these contradictions by a shift to a higher principle of non-identity. In Lyotard, by contrast, the emphasis on the repression of inner nature, of desire or libido, is not developed in terms of a tracing of the contradictory structure of consciousness. Because of this, he is led to suppose an inevitable conflict between the 'unity' of consciousness and the diffuseness and disorder of desire. As early as *Discours, Figure* Lyotard had reached the conclusion that 'there is no ego whose function it would be to lift, to reverse repression'.[103]

The advantage of Adorno's position, against these two alternatives, is that it links the internal incoherence of the ego to the repression of inner nature. A self which can secure its identity only by what the *Dialectic of Enlightenment* terms an 'introversion of sacrifice', an exclusion and forgetting of its own natural basis, will necessarily be divided against itself: as Adorno declares in *Negative Dialectics*, 'Unity is division (*Einheit ist Spaltung*)'.[104] In contrast to Lyotard, who can only equate the ego with repression and the disorder of the drives with liberation, an equation which leads to the *impasse* which we have already observed, Adorno's argument allows him to give an account of the ambivalent status of both consciousness and the unconscious. For Adorno, the forging of the ego, as the form of organization of the drives, contains a moment of freedom, insofar as it is only through this process that human beings acquire the ability to foresee, calculate and withhold which frees them from the contingencies of inner and outer nature (significantly, Lyotard can give no account of the forging of the ego, but is obliged to attribute it to an inexplicable cooling and retroversion of energy). At the same time, however, the dialectic of Enlightenment consists in the fact that ever-intensifying self-restraint leads to the abolition of that very spontaneity of the self which calculating rationality was intended to preserve. Similarly, in one respect the unconscious drives can be seen as embodying the demand for a happiness which, for Adorno, is inseparable from sensuous contentment, and which is crushed by the pressure of instrumental rationality. While in another respect, the archaic features of the unconscious suggest the ever-present possibility of regression: a total dissolution of the self into impulse could not be construed as a liberation, since there would no longer be a self to enjoy the lifting of the barriers. Lyotard's interpretation of the death-drive as the chaotic limit of order wilfully flies in the face of the very meaning of the term: the death-drive is the inertial drag towards ultimate stasis, while concepts are *also* the preservers of life.

The opposition of a rigid consciousness and a spontaneous unconscious, in other words, is a perilous simplification. For Adorno, that spontaneity which Lyotard seeks is a potential of subjectivity – as that which both emerges from and *goes beyond* nature – which can never be entirely crushed, while the unconscious – as Lyotard begins to realize, when he reflects on the static quality of phantasy – is also characterized by abstraction and endless repetition. Furthermore, if the unity of the self is in fact a splitting, then there exists a tension of contradiction within the self, which is experienced as suffering, and which, however faintly, must push towards its own resolution. In such a resolution, it would become apparent that consciousness and the drives, in their antagonism, are themselves abstract moments of a divided self. This does not mean, however, that the overcoming of antagonism would produce a homogenous unity. If unity is splitting, then, paradoxically, this is only because unity fails to recognize itself as such. For Adorno, it is the deepest need and impulse of the self to open itself to its other – indeed, only by doing so can it truly become a self, by acknowledging the moment of non-identity in its own identity.

Adorno's argument also helps to highlight the political ambivalence of Lyotard's position. For it makes clear that the simple prioritization of the unconscious over the conscious can not only scarcely be seen as a liberation, but is also – in one sense – in conformity with the deepest requirements of what he terms the 'total socialized society', insofar as, in such a society, the mediating instance of the ego – which retains a kernel of spontaneity and autonomy – is no longer required. Adorno considers post-liberal capitalism to be characterized by a progressive liquidation of the distinction between the ego and the unconscious in a narcissistic personality type. It is the very concern for the preservation of the self above all else which leads to the dissolution of the self. The predominant social character becomes a 'subjectless subject', which is marked by a 'scattered, disconnected, interchangeable and ephemeral state of "informedness", which one can see will be erased the very next moment to be replaced by new information.'[105] Under such circumstances social psychology ceases to be essentially ego-psychology, and becomes 'libido psychology'.[106]

It can readily be seen that Lyotard's position, at the period of *Economie Libidinale*, simply gives a positive valorization to this collapse of the distinction between the individual and the social: indeed, Lyotard explicitly states that 'the dissolution of forms and individuals in the so-called "consumer society" should be *affirmed*.'[107] Part of Lyotard's reason for reaching this position, which endorses the most pulverizing tendencies of commodification, is that he assumes the only alternative to be a nostalgia for a pristine nature, outside – before or beyond – capitalism. Thus, he suggests that 'Marx-Adorno is obliged to produce the antibody [of exchange value], naturality, as that which *goes missing* in capitalism. One thinks the latter from a nihilist position, relative to a natural subject.'[108] But, of course, this is not at all Adorno's position. From his early lecture on 'The Idea of Natural History' onwards, Adorno always insisted that the natural and the social are inextricably intertwined within a history which – *up till now* – has been dominated by natural compulsion. It is for this reason that Adorno argues – contrary to Freud – that there is no purely timeless unconscious, since 'concrete historical components enter even into the experiences of early childhood', while the archaic and compulsive features of the historically formed ego are manifested in its own unconscious component – the mechanisms of defence.[109] For Adorno there was never a prelapsarian harmony of society and nature, but always from the first antagonism.

However, as we have seen, this antagonism also generates contradictions internal to society and the psyche – resistance to total socialization can never be entirely eliminated, so long as the self-reproduction of society is mediated by the activity of living individuals. Consequently, Lyotard is also mistaken to attribute the horizon of reconciliation in Adorno's work solely to a continued adherence to theological motifs, while overlooking its logical dimension. For if antagonism is characterized by logical contradiction – as in the case of a unity which is splitting, of a self divided against itself – then there must be, at the very least, a *logical* possibility of its overcoming. It is this which provides the basis for Adorno's critical perspective. And the need for such a critical conception of identity, rather than an abstract opposition between repressive order and 'emancipatory' disorder, is something which Lyotard himself implicitly acknowledges, as he moves into a new phase of his work beyond the dead-end of *Économie Libidinale*.

5

Michel Foucault:
Power and Subjectivity

The 'philosophy of desire' developed by Jean-François Lyotard in the period from the late 1960s to the mid 70s can be seen as the attempt, within post-structuralism, to affirm the independent force of an 'inner nature' – that 'transitivism of a spontaneous aesthetic' to which *Discours, Figure* refers[1] – against the assumption of both classical structuralism and Lacanian psychoanalysis that no genuine struggle is required, involving the repression of corporeal impulses and drives, in order for linguistic and social rules to be established and perpetuated. This line of argument, and the aestheticized conception of politics which accompanied it, evidently stands in a close relation to the flowering of self-expression, the assertion of physical and erotic spontaneity against the ascetic routines of the modern working world, which characterized the events of May '68. But this revelation of the potentially explosive force of individual 'desire' was not the only way in which the May revolt represented a fundamental challenge to the view of the social as consisting in systems of communication or symbolic exchange upon which the structuralism of the early 1960s had relied. It also made clear that symbolic structures, far from unfolding in accordance with an immanent logic, were determined by and served to mask relations of power. Theoretically, the concepts of desire and power, each considered as a 'dimension of force which escapes the logic of the signifier',[2] imply one another. Lyotard's – or Deleuze's – account of the production of the self-conscious subject through the containment of libidinal energy requires a theory of the power which enforces this containment, since without this, as the evolution of their thought demonstrates, desire comes to be seen as self-repressing and the basis of political critique is undermined.[3] Correspondingly, a theory of power with radical intent requires an account of that which power dominates or represses, since without such an account relations of power must cease to appear objectionable.

It is Michel Foucault who, during the 1970s, turns away from the more narrowly methodological concerns which preoccupied him during the late 1960s, and begins to develop the theory of power which disillusionment with the political inadequacy of structuralism required. It would be a mistake, however, to understand Foucault's concern with the problem of power during the seventies simply as the theoretical complement to the philosophy of desire developed by Deleuze and Lyotard. It is true that Foucault often appears to be producing theoretical generalizations about the nature of power. But, in a manner which has no parallel in the work of the *désirants*, Foucault's thought is rooted in a highly individual historical vision, which centres on the transition from traditional to modern, industrial societies, and is specifically concerned with the forms of knowledge and modes of social organization characteristic of capitalist modernity; his theoretical formulations on the nature of power can often only be fully comprehended when set in the context of this vision. Indeed, it can be argued that it is the persistence with which Foucault has held to and elaborated his understanding of the historical foundations of the modern West, and the strikingness of the image and allegory through which he has expressed his stance towards the process of modernization, which have been central to his force and his appeal, rather than his modishly fluctuating, and often inconsistent, theoretical and philosophical pronouncements. A consideration of Foucault's historical views is therefore an essential preliminary for an examination of his account of power.

From the very beginnings of his work, although more explicitly at some periods than at others, Foucault has been concerned with the emergence, expansion and consolidation of apparatuses of administrative intervention in, and control over, the social world, with what he has termed 'pastoral power'.[4] This theme is first broached – in a manner which sets the tone for many of Foucault's later discussions – in the chapter of *Madness and Civilization* devoted to the 'Great Confinement', where Foucault describes the springing up of institutions of segregation and forced labour, the workhouse, *Zuchthaus*, and *Hôpital Général*, across Europe during the seventeenth century. Foucault suggests that these institutions mark a qualitative transformation in the relations between the state and its citizens: madness, along with poverty, unemployment and the inability to work, is for the first time perceived as a 'social problem' which falls within the ambit of responsibility of the state. Foucault does not deny the economic dimension of the process of confinement, as a measure intended to reduce social pressures during a period of inflation and unemployment, but is far more concerned with the effects and implications of what he considers to be a new conception of the state as preserver and augmenter of the general welfare, and with the manner in which this conception intersects with a project of homogenization and moralization of the populace. The workhouses, whose task of instilling a new 'ethical consciousness of labour' – Foucault suggests – as more fundamental than their contradictory economic role, testify to 'the bourgeoisie's great dream and great preoccupation of the Classical Age: the laws of the state and the laws of the heart are at last identical'.[5] This account of the Great Confinement will then provide the model for Foucault's discussion of the emergence of 'humanitarian' attitudes towards the insane at the end of the eighteenth century. The opening of Tuke's York Retreat and Pinel's liberation of the insane at Bicêtre are portrayed as leading to a 'gigantic moral imprisonment'[6] which is more oppressive than the former practices of brute incarceration, since it operates on the mind rather than merely the body. Modern forms of public provision and welfare, Foucault implies, are inseparable from ever-tighter forms of social and psychological control.

A distinctive facet of Foucault's approach to historical analysis, which *Madness and Civilization* clearly introduces, is his tendency to condense a general historical argument into a tracing of the emergence of specific institutions. In Foucault's next historical work this concentration becomes even more evident, indeed is made explicit in the title of the book: *The Birth of the Clinic*. At the same time, however, Foucault's analysis of the debates on the status of medicine and on appropriate forms of medical provision which took place at the height of the French Revolution, and his presentation of the policies which ensued, make clearer the broad foundations of his account of modernity. *The Birth of the Clinic* can be seen as an oblique polemic against the Marxist view that, in the initial phases of industrial capitalism, the role of the bourgeois state was characteristically limited to upholding the order of private law which secures economic activity and providing corresponding general guarantees of order. According to this view, the bourgeois state has been driven into increasing intervention by the functional inadequacies of the market, whereas Foucault wishes to show that – from the very beginning – intervention and administrative control have defined the modern state. In the debates which Foucault follows, the dictates of economic liberalism, which would have entailed an entirely deregulated, freelance status for medicine, are shown to have been defeated by the demand for surveillance of the health of the nation, a demand which had already made itself felt before the Revolution in the setting up of the *Société Royale de Médicine* to function as 'a point of centralization of knowledge, an authority for the recording and assessment of all medical activity'.[7] From this perspective the 'birth of the clinic' may be explained as resulting from the need for a type of medical institution which would make possible a systematic observation of the nation's health, achieving the compromise of assigning to medicine 'a closed domain reserved for it alone, without either resorting to the corporate structures of the *ancien régime*, or lapsing into forms of state control reminiscent of the period of the convention'.[8] The 'medical gaze' referred to in the subtitle of the book is formed by the new, untrammelled type of observation made possible for the doctor at the bedside of the hospitalized patient intersecting with a system of monitoring of health and hygiene established at the level of the state. Thus, although Foucault's concern is here with physical rather than moral disorder, *The Birth of the Clinic* reiterates the view, already expressed in *Madness and Civilization*, that supervision of, and intervention in, the social domain by agencies of welfare and control is a more fundamental characteristic of modern societies than an economy released from directly political relations of domination.

In Foucault's two subsequent books, *The Order of Things* and *The Archaeology of Knowledge*, this concern with the emergence of modern forms of administration of the social world is barely present at all, and Foucault's attention shifts almost entirely towards the internal structure of scientific discourses, in particular the discourse of the 'human sciences', whose origins he believes to be closely intertwined with these forms of administration. In this respect Foucault may be said to have been moving away during the 1960s, in accordance with the objectivism of the structuralist movement as a whole, from any form of politically oriented analysis. Already, in the preface to *The Birth of the Clinic*, Foucault had proclaimed: 'This book has not been written in favour of one kind of medicine as against another kind of medicine, or against medicine and in favour of an absence of medicine. It is a structural study that sets out to disentangle the conditions of its history from the density of discourse, as do others of my works.'[9] There was, nevertheless, an evident overlap between the political question of institutions of social control, which was given a new immediacy by the events of May '68, and Foucault's longstanding concern with procedures of surveillance and confinement, so that although – in common with the other prominent figures associated with structuralism – Foucault played no direct part in the uprising, it was a comparatively simple matter for him to rework his position and to emerge as a major theoretician of *gauchisme* around the turn of the decade.[10] During the early seventies Foucault was active in various far-left debates and interventions, the most publicized of which was his participation in the setting up of a Group for Information on Prisons (GIP) after a hunger strike which began amongst leftist detainees in 1971. And in 1975, after a gap of six years since his previous book, this experience of political militancy bore theoretical fruit in the form of *Discipline and Punish*, a history of the emergence of the modern prison system.

Discipline and Punish clearly takes up again the historical analysis begun by Foucault in *Madness and Civilization* and *The Birth of the Clinic*, and partially abandoned during the structuralist euphoria of the mid sixties. Like its predecessors, it employs the organizational device of focusing on the emergence of a specific institution. Yet it is also the work in which Foucault introduces and begins to elaborate his theory of power, thereby taking his distance from many of his basic theoretical assumptions of the 1960s. The introduction of the concept of power enables Foucault to formulate far more systematically than hitherto his view of the transformation in forms of social organization and relations of domination which characterizes the transition from the *ancien régime* to the post-revolutionary society of the nineteenth century, a transformation which he describes, in a concise formula, as a 'reversal of the political axis of individualization'.[11] Under a feudal and monarchical system, Foucault suggests, individualization is greatest at the summit of society. Power is visibly embodied in the person of the king, yet in its operation it forms 'a discontinuous, rambling, global system with little hold on detail'.[12] Under this type of regime the notion of crime is still not fully distinguished from that of sacrilege, so that punishment takes the form of a ritual intended not to 'reform' the offender but to express and restore the sanctity of the law which has been broken, a principle spectacularly illustrated by the description of the execution of the regicide Damiens with which *Discipline and Punish* begins. Such forms of retribution, Foucault suggests, are intended to make manifest the unlimited, incomparable power (*surpuissance*) of the king over a more or less anonymous body of subjects. In modern societies, however, the agencies of punishment become part of a pervasive, impersonal system of surveillance and correction which pays an ever-increasing attention to the idiosyncrasies of the particular case, and above all to the 'psychology' of the individual, since intention rather than transgression now becomes the central criterion of culpability. In general, power in feudal societies tends to be haphazard and imprecise, whereas in modern societies effects of power 'circulate through progressively finer channels, gaining access to individuals themselves, to their bodies, their gestures, and all their daily actions'.[13]

With his characteristic flair for the arresting image, Foucault summarizes this transformation in the 'economy of power' in his description of the Panopticon, an architectural device advocated by Bentham towards the end of the eighteenth century. The device consists of a central elevated watch-tower surrounded by a circular disposition of cells, each of which traverses the entire thickness of the building, and thereby permits its single inmate to be caught, silhouetted, in the light which passes through the cell from the outside. This arrangement makes it possible for a lone observer in the central tower to supervise a multitude of individuals, each of whom is cut off from any lateral contact with his or her fellow inmates. Furthermore, since the guard, although unable literally to observe every inmate at once, cannot be perceived from outside the tower, an *effect* of constant, omniscient surveillance is obtained. Since no prisoner can be certain of when he or she is not being observed, the prisoners are obliged constantly to police their own behaviour for fear of possible detection: the Panopticon makes possible a new, radically more effective exercise of power, 'without any physical constraint other than architecture and geometry'.[14] As Foucault's references, in *Discipline and Punish*, to 'this panoptic society of which incarceration is the omnipresent armature'[15] suggest, the description of the Panopticon is intended as far more than an account of one form of the exercise of power. It not only condenses the argument of *Discipline and Punish*, but may be seen as a summation of the analysis of modern forms of social administration which Foucault had been conducting ever since *Madness and Civilization*, combining the themes of a centralization, and an increasing efficiency of power with the theme of the replacement of overt violence by moralization. Power in modern societies is portrayed as essentially oriented towards the production of regimented, isolated, and self-policing subjects.

Foucault and the Frankfurt School

As Foucault himself noted towards the end of his life, a historical-philosophical analysis in some respects very close to his own may be found – despite the evident disparity of intellectual traditions – in the work of the Frankfurt School.[16] Although the attention of Critical Theory is not directed as exclusively as that of Foucault towards modern systems of administration of the social world, and even less towards the genesis of specific institutions, the tendency of Critical Theory, both in the 'classical' phase represented by the thought of Horkheimer and Adorno, and in the work of its leading contemporary representative, Jürgen Habermas, has been to shift the emphasis away from the relations of production as the determining institutional framework of modern capitalist societies and, under the influence of Weber, to analyse the capitalist economy as merely one form of the unleashing of the autonomous dynamic of a means–end rationality. This makes possible not only an unprecedented increase in the forces of production, and therefore in the domination of external nature, but also in the domination of human beings, who are adapted to the system of production through social engineering and psychological manipulation. In Weber's original formulation of the theory of 'rationalization', the structures of consciousness which made possible modern bureaucratic forms of administration and the systematic profit-seeking of the capitalist enterprise are progressively set loose from the 'protestant ethic' which had nurtured them and given them their transcendent meaning. Regularity, asceticism, and relentlessly self-interested calculation are transformed into an 'iron cage', a system of behaviour to which individuals are now obliged to adapt in order to survive. In the thought of Horkheimer and Adorno these developments are transformed into a world-historical process of reification, in which the calculating, instrumental rationality required of the subject in its struggle to gain independence from the overwhelming powers of external nature requires a corresponding repression of the spontaneity of inner nature. The culmination of this process is an empty, adapted subjectivity which has lost that very autonomy for whose sake the conquest of nature was initiated.

It has already been suggested that what, in Foucault's work, often appear as abstract generalizations on the nature of power, are best understood if related back to his account of the transition from traditional to modern societies. A comparison with the Weber-Frankfurt School tradition tends to confirm this suggestion, since it reveals characteristics which Foucault attributes to power *per se* as historically specific. During the 1970s Foucault lays considerable stress on a critique of conceptions of power as fundamentally prohibitive, arguing that, 'We must cease once and for all to describe the effects of power in negative terms: it "excludes", it "represses", it "censors", it "abstracts", it "masks", it "conceals". In fact power produces; it produces realities; it produces domains of objects and rituals of truth.'[17] As commentators have been quick to point out, such formulations ignore many all-too-evident features of the exercise of power in contemporary societies, features which Foucault himself has on other occasions noted.[18] The argument becomes acceptable, however, if Foucault is taken as describing not power *tout court*, but the productivity and efficiency of those purposive-rational forms of organization which Weber detected in modern bureaucracies and in the capitalist organization of the labour process. Similarly, Foucault's repeated denials that power can be considered as a possession of groups or individuals becomes comprehensible in the light of Weber's account of the transition from 'charismatic' and 'traditional' to 'legal-rational' forms of domination: in modern societies power does not depend upon the prowess and prestige of individuals but is exercised through an impersonal administrative machinery operating in accordance with abstract rules. Foucault's juxtaposition of a spectacular public execution and the timetable of a 'House for young prisoners in Paris' at the beginning of *Discipline and Punish* highlights precisely this transition. This concern with the anonymity of modern forms of administration also helps to explain Foucault's neglect of class domination, and his presentation of power as 'a machine in which everyone is caught, those who exercise power just as much as those over whom it is exercised'.[19] For Weber, as for the classical Frankfurt School, it is the social forms engendered by purposive or instrumental rationality, with their indifference to personal ties, and their crushing of idiosyncrasy and spontaneity, which represent a profounder threat to human freedom than the class oppression specific to capitalist society.

Although it cannot be doubted that Foucault is attempting to theorize historical developments which were also a central concern of Weber and of the Frankfurt School, the framework within which he has carried out his analyses – summarized, during the 1970s, by the Nietzschean term 'geneaology' – is constituted by a very different set of philosophical assumptions. The differences centre on contrasting conceptions of the human subject, since in modern philosophy it is a view of the status and capacities of the subject which defines the content of concepts of domination and freedom. In the thought of the classical Frankfurt School the forging of a self-identical subject capable of restraining the spontaneity of impulse and acting in accordance with rational calculations of utility is not an arbitrary event, but is a necessary outcome of the drive for self-preservation, the need of human beings for control over the threatening, uncomprehended powers of nature which initially appear in mythical form. Yet, under capitalism, the rise of instrumental reason culminates in a social order which thwarts its own original purpose, the preservation of the subject. 'Through the mediation of the total society which embraces all relations and emotions, men are once again made to be that against which the evolutionary law of society, the principle of self, had turned: mere species beings, exactly like one another through isolation in the forcibly united collectivity.'[20] Yet, despite this fateful dialectic, in which 'the subjective moment becomes, as it were, enclosed by the objective, is itself, as a limit imposed upon the subject, objective',[21] classical Critical Theory firmly refuses the conclusion that subjectivity itself must be denounced as a principle of domination. The conditions of material coercion and struggle under which the identical self was formed have necessarily led to this identity taking on a compulsive character, yet these conditions could not be overcome by a simple renunciation of self-identity. In one of his last essays Adorno reminded his readers that 'the undifferentiated state before the subject's formation was the dread of the blind web of nature, of myth'; that 'if the subject were liquidated rather than sublated in a higher form, the effect would be regression – not just of consciousness, but a regression to real barbarism.'[22] For Adorno, such a sublation could only be actualized by breaking through the facade of identity to a mode of subjectivity which would preserve the reflective unity of the self in a form no longer inimical to the diffuseness and spontaneity of impulse. His fundamental philosophical assumptions, however, debar him from formulating such a transformation theoretically: a future state of 'reconciliation' – of difference without domination and affinity without identity – can only be evoked through a virtuoso exploration of the aporias of 'identity-thinking'.

In the contemporary Critical Theory of Habermas this dialectical *impasse* of the classical Frankfurt School is no longer considered inevitable, but is rather attributed to the failure of Horkheimer and Adorno fully to break with the presuppositions of modern philosophies of consciousness. The fundamental concepts of the theory of consciousness as developed from Descartes to Kant, Habermas suggests, do not permit the notion of reconciliation to be formulated at all, while in the concepts of objective idealism, from Spinoza and Leibniz to Schelling and Hegel, the notion can only be expressed in an extravagant form.[23] Habermas's innovative break with the earlier Frankfurt School tradition consists in his argument that the cognitive and instrumental relation between subject and object, and the accompanying form of rationality, which have been a central preoccupation of modern philosophy, must be seen as embedded in a broader communicative reason which is implicit in the intersubjectivity of dialogue, and to which subjects must conform in order to achieve mutual understanding and coordinate courses of action. Instrumental rationality cannot be pragmatically reduced to a moment in the cycle of self-preservation, but involves claims for the validity of cognitions and the effectivity of actions which can ultimately only be settled through intersubjective debate and testing.[24] In addition, Habermas's shift from a philosophy centred on consciousness to a communicatively-broadened philosophy of language allows him to argue that there are forms of rationality besides that which governs the cognitive-instrumental relation between subject and object. This type of rationality is related to the cognitive dimension of language, which is brought to the fore in constative speech-acts. But every speech-act also possesses an interactive and an expressive dimension – it establishes a relation between speaking subjects, and reveals an intention of the speaker. These distinct 'modes of communication' can also be highlighted in 'regulative' and 'representative' speech-acts, and form the foundation of types of rationality which Habermas terms the 'moral-practical' and 'aesthetic-practical'. This expanded conception of rationality implies that it is possible to raise claims to normative rightness and subjective sincerity which are no less capable of discursive thematization than are cognitive claims, although Habermas admits that, in the latter case, conclusive judgements cannot be reached purely through argument, but only by observing the continuing course of interaction.[25]

By means of this theory Habermas aspires to continue the critique of the primacy of instrumental reason while avoiding the blind alley into which Horkheimer and Adorno were led by their conflation of instrumental reason and domination. Instrumental reason cannot be transformed into the agent of a world-historical process of reification, whose origins are projected back before the beginnings of capitalist modernization into pre-history. The failure of Adorno and Horkheimer, Habermas suggests, consists in not distinguishing between the rationalization of the social life-world, and the particular, pathological form of the process of capitalist modernization which, despite its non-class-specific effects, must ultimately be rooted in the dynamics of class conflict.[26] By the 'rationalization of the life-world' Habermas understands the process in which claims to cognitive truth, to normative rightness, and to expressive sincerity cease to be inextricably interwoven in the fabric of religious and metaphysical world-views, and become increasingly separated out into three distinct spheres of value: science, morality and art. From this standpoint, the phenomena which Horkheimer and Adorno denounced as the seamless domination of technical reason cannot be simply attributed to the fact that, in the modern period, the rationality of cognition and effective action is no longer interwoven with moral and aesthetic considerations. What Horkheimer and Adorno perceive as a 'totalized purposive-rationality' is better characterized as a 'colonization' of this rationalized life-world by economic and administrative systems guided by purely functional imperatives, which can themselves only emerge on the basis of a rationalized life-world, and yet which impede the unfolding of the full potential of its communicative infrastructure. In contrast to Adorno's evocation of a state of reconciliation, the idea of which 'forbids irreconcilably its affirmation in the concept',[27] Habermas can point to possibilities of self-expression and collective self-determination which are ravaged by the hypertrophy of a one-sided instrumental rationality, and yet remain implicit in our cultural modernity.

Habermas's theory naturally implies a different attitude towards the modern subject from that of Horkheimer and Adorno. In the thought of the classical Frankfurt School even the space for individual responsibility and initiative which was opened during the early phases of capitalism is now closed by the administered society. If, in the era of free enterprise, 'the idea of individuality seemed to shake itself loose from metaphysical trappings and to become merely a synthesis of the individual's material interests',[28] the immanent logic of a society based upon the pursuit of private interest leads to the totalitarian extinction of that very individuality which originally set this logic in motion. For Habermas, however, the liberation of purposive rationality from the braking context of traditional norms, and its embodiment in the 'norm-free sociality' of the market, is only one dimension in which post-traditional structures of consciousness reveal themselves. Habermas characterizes this transition as a whole as one from 'role-identity' to 'ego-identity', understanding by the latter a form of personal identity which is no longer determined by contents unreflectively inherited from the cultural tradition, but is defined by the mastery of procedures of critical examination and argumentative grounding employed in the acquisition of cognitive and moral beliefs. From this standpoint Adorno's argument – parallel to that of the *désirants* – that the very form of the identical self represents a repression of the spontaneity of 'inner nature' can be seen as mesmerized by a Kantian conception of the moral subject as divided between an autonomous – but impersonally rational – and an individual – but heteronomous – self. Adorno overlooks the possibility that the culturally predetermined interpretations of human needs on which moral norms are based could be opened up to revision in the medium of norm- and value-building communication. In this way the contents of the cultural tradition would no longer function as a pattern imposed upon needs, but could offer expressive resources for needs in search of their appropriate formulation, thereby retrieving aesthetic experience from the marginalized position it occupies in bourgeois culture. Thus, although Habermas would dissent from Adorno's view that 'the diffuseness of nature . . . resembles the lineaments of an intelligible creature, of that self which would be delivered from the ego',[29] since he believes that it is only the increasing formalism of modern identity which makes possible its greater richness of content, he does argue that inner nature could be rendered 'communicatively fluid and transparent' in a non-repressive form of ego-identity.[30] The possibility of a form of selfhood which would combine the cognitive, moral and aesthetic dimensions of rationality in more equal measure, and allow their less constrained interaction, can be theoretically formulated, and need not be merely negatively evoked in terms of a quasi-eschatological 'reconciliation'.

If Habermas's work represents a shift towards a more optimistic evaluation of the potential of modern subjectivity than is to be found in the work of the first-generation Frankfurt School, then Foucault – in common with the majority of post-structuralists – moves in the opposite direction, to a position which eliminates the dialectical character of Enlightenment altogether, and proposes that subjects are entirely constituted by the operaton of power. Foucault's philosophical model for this process is to be found in the second essay of *On the Genealogy of Morals*, where Nietzsche recounts 'the long story of how responsibility originated'. Nietzsche's central argument is that a reflexive relation to the self, and in particular an internalized moral control of behaviour, can only be inculcated through threats and violence. In order for the breeding of 'an animal with the right to make promises' – and therefore able to guarantee the constancy of its own future conduct – to take place, the coercive task must be carried out of 'rendering man up to a certain point regular, uniform, equal among equals, calculable'.[31] This task is accomplished by enforcing a block on the spontaneous expression of instinct, since 'all instincts that do not discharge themselves outwardly turn inward – this is what I call the internalization of man: thus it was that man first developed what was later called his "soul"'.[32] The energy of the reversed instinct is transformed into the hostility towards self which is the foundation of moral consciousness, the torment of which Nietzsche contrasts unfavourably with the 'naive joy and innocence of the animal': 'This instinct for freedom forcibly made latent . . . pushed back and repressed, incarcerated within and finally able to discharge and vent itself only on itself: that, and that alone, is what *bad conscience* is in its beginnings.'[33]

In Foucault's first major work, *Madness and Civilization*, his account of the procedures employed in the early asylums becomes the occasion for the description of a similar process of repression of spontaneity and the introversion of impulse. The notion of madness functions throughout the book to suggest a fusion of the super- and the infra-human: it evokes those mythological powers of an untamed nature, whose disappearance Horkheimer and Adorno ambiguously lament in *Dialectic of Enlightenment*, but it also implies something of Nietzsche's arch equation of liberation with the untrammelled expression of instinct. If, up till the time of the Renaissance, madness had functioned as 'the sign of another world' to the consciousness of the Classical Age, Foucault argues, it 'revealed a freedom raging in the monstrous forms of animality'.[34] Like Nietzsche, Foucault analyses the transition from a state of overt violence and brutality to a condition of internalized restraint, although in his version this process is not projected into an imaginary past, but concerns the replacement of the bedlam and the prison by the prototypes of the modern asylum. And like Nietzsche, he reverses the conventional 'humanist' verdict on this transition. The central suggestion of his chapter on 'The Birth of the Asylum' is that the directly physical confinement and repression characteristic of the Classical Age left a greater power and freedom to madness than modern methods of treatment which aim to transform the consciousness of the insane. 'In classical confinement,' Foucault argues, 'the madman was also vulnerable to observation, but such observation did not, basically, involve him; it involved only his monstrous surface, his visible animality; and it included at least one form of reciprocity, since the sane man could read in the madman, as in a mirror, the imminent movement of his own downfall.'[35] By contrast, in the establishments of Tuke and Pinel, bodily constraint is no longer the principal means of control, but this 'liberation' is more than offset by the 'internalization of the juridical instance': where formerly there had been the 'free terror of madness', there now reigns the 'stifling anguish of responsibility'.[36] The philosophical resonances of Foucault's account make clear that his fundamental target is not the specific regime of the modern asylum, but modern self-reflective subjectivity as such: 'Freed from the chains that make it purely an observed object, madness lost, paradoxically, the essence of its freedom, which was solitary exaltation; it became responsible for what it knew of its truth; it imprisoned itself in an infinitely self-referring observation; it was finally chained to the humiliation of being its own object.'[37]

Although Foucault shares the Nietzschean critique of bad conscience – the asylum institutes 'a trial which has no outcome but in a perpetual recommencement in the internalized form of remorse'[38] – he differs from Nietzsche in his understanding of the fact that a reflexive relation to self cannot be produced simply through the limitation and introversion of instinct. Simple violence, as we have seen, fails to conquer madness for Foucault, who is closer to Sartre than Nietzsche in suggesting that it is only concrete exposure to the gaze of the other which makes possible the corresponding self-surveillance. In his account of the asylum Foucault repeatedly stresses that it is a regime of incessant observation and judgement which forms the condition for the internalization of morality. 'At the Retreat,' he writes, 'the partial suppression of physical constraints was part of an ensemble of which the essential element was the constitution of a self-restraint in which the freedom of the sick person, engaged in work and in the gaze of others, is continually threatened by the recognition of guilt.'[39] Again Foucault draws up a balance unfavourable to the modern age, introducing a contrast – which echoes through his later work – between the semi-protective darkness of the 'unenlightened' bedlam or dungeon, and an ineluctable surveillance which becomes more detailed as its source becomes ever more remote: 'The proximity instituted by the asylum, an intimacy neither chains nor bars would ever violate again, does not allow reciprocity: only the nearness of observation that watches, that spies, that comes closer in order to see better, but moves farther away, since it accepts and acknowledges only the values of the Stranger.'[40]

In *The Birth of the Clinic* the process of moralization does not figure, since Foucault is here concerned with the regulation of bodies rather than the control of minds. Nevertheless, the image of the gaze is central to the structure of the book, to the extent of featuring in its subtitle: 'Une archéologie du regard médical'. Here, however – although it does not lose its implications of surveillance – the predominant function of the gaze is epistemic. Foucault perceives a convergence between the institutional preconditions for the formation of a new mode of medical knowledge – modern clinical medicine – and for a centralized monitoring of the health of the nation, in the form of the new teaching hospital. He suggests an internal link between the 'implicit geometry' of the theme of pristine observation as the support of medical knowledge and the 'social space dreamt of by the Revolution' ('a space of free communication in which the relationship of the parts to the whole was always transposable and reversible'),[41] and argues that both are fundamentally illusory or ideological, since the apparent purity and transparency of the gaze can in fact only be established within new institutional structures which are, if anything, more confining than those which preceded them. 'The medical gaze', Foucault suggests, will be 'given its technological structure in the clinical organization';[42] the revolutionary theme of the 'majestic violence of light', which 'brings to an end the bounded, dark kingdom of privileged knowledge', is seen to lead to an intensified administration of individuals.[43]

The depth at which the image of the gaze is implanted in Foucault's work is revealed by its return, nearly a decade and a half after *Madness and Civilization*, in the discussion of 'Panopticism' in *Discipline and Punish*. In this work Foucault unites the three functions of the gaze which we have so far distinguished: the moral, the epistemic and the political. In terms more explicitly Nietzschean than those of *Madness and Civilization*, Foucault now highlights his concern with the formation of the modern subject, with a 'genealogy of the modern soul', and – like Nietzsche –

he presents the constitution of 'psyche, subjectivity, personality, consciousness' as the result of 'methods of punishment, supervision and constraint'.[44] Even more paradigmatically than the asylum or the hospital, the panoptic system institutes a unidirectional gaze whose effect is to generate morally self-monitoring subjects: 'The efficiency of power, its constraining force have, in a sense, passed over to the other side – to the surface of its application. He who is subjected to a field of visibility, and who knows it, assumes responsibility for the constraints of power; he makes them play spontaneously upon himself, he inscribes himself in a power relation in which he simultaneously plays both roles; he becomes the principle of his own subjection.'[45] *Discipline and Punish* also lays greater stress than earlier works on the manner in which the epistemic function of the gaze interweaves with its moralizing function. Panoptic power isolates and individualizes, transforming its targets into possible objects of cognition. 'The moment when the sciences of men became possible,' Foucault suggests, 'is the moment when a new technology of power and a new political anatomy of the body were implemented.'[46] Lastly the notion of panoptic power is generalized to provide an account of the overall structuring of social relations in modern societies. The unidirectional link which the gaze establishes between the unity of the observer and the multiplicity of the observed provides a metaphor for the anonymous centralization of modern power.

If both *Madness and Civilization* and *Discipline and Punish*, despite the chronological and theoretical gap which separates them, are in part concerned with the formation of the moral-practical relation to self, just as *The Birth of the Clinic* and *The Order of Things* are concerned with the formation and self-relation of the knowing subject, then Foucault's next book, *The History of Sexuality*, may be seen as concerned with the formation of Habermas's third dimension: the aesthetic relation to the inner world of passion and impulse.[47] In *The History of Sexuality* Foucault draws attention to the dissolution of the forms of group-identity characteristic of traditional societies, and their replacement by a form of identity which depends increasingly upon the capacity of the individual to reflect upon and articulate the domain of private experience, suggesting that this transition is epitomized by the change in meaning of the word *avowal*: 'For a long time, the individual was vouched for by the reference to others and the demonstration of his ties to the commonweal (family, allegiance, protection); then he was authenticated by the discourse of truth he was obliged to pronounce concerning himself.'[48] Foucault correlates this transition with the shift from epic narrative to the modern literature of introspection, and with the rise of philosophies of consciousness, 'the long discussions concerning the possibility of constituting a science of the subject, the validity of introspection, lived experience as evidence of the presence of consciousness to itself'.[49] Yet, as is the case with his account of the formation of moral consciousness, Foucault wishes to suggest – in genealogical fashion – that our broadened access to an 'inner world' distinct from the external worlds of both nature and the social is the result of a forgotten coercion: 'One confesses – or is forced to confess. When it is not spontaneous or dictated by some internal imperative, the confession is wrung from a person by violence or threat; it is driven from its hiding place in the soul or extracted from the body.'[50] By linking the capacity for avowal to the inquisitions of the confessional, Foucault is able to argue that 'the obligation to confess is now relayed through so many different points, is so deeply ingrained in us, that we no longer perceive it as the effect of a power which constrains us; on the contrary, it seems to us that truth, lodged in our most secret nature, "demands" only to surface'.[51]

There can be no doubt that the central intention of this form of genealogy, as it is developed in Foucault's work from *Madness and Civilization* to *The History of Sexuality*, is to dissolve the philosophical link – inherited by the Marxist tradition from German Idealism – between consciousness, self-reflection and freedom, and to deny that there remains any progressive political potential in the ideal of the autonomous subject. Moving beyond Horkheimer and Adorno's reluctant deciphering of the paradox of an autonomy which leads to its own abolition, Foucault seeks to establish a direct, unequivocal relation between 'subjectification' and 'subjection'. During the 1970s he spells out the political implications of this argument in terms of the relations between the operation of 'discipline' and the principle of 'sovereignty'. In Foucault's view, the use of the concept of sovereignty implies the assumption that power resides essentially in the capacity to enact and enforce legislation, the theory of sovereignty being concerned with the justification of possession of this capacity. He then points out that, in the transition from feudal or absolutist monarchy to the modern bourgeois state, the concept of sovereignty itself is not abandoned. 'It is this same theory of sovereignty,' Foucault writes, 're-activated through the doctrine of Roman Law, that we find in Rousseau and his contemporaries . . . now it is concerned with the construction, in opposition to the administrative, authoritarian and absolutist monarchies, of an alternative model, that of parliamentary democracy.'[52] Yet this continued concern with the problem of sovereignty, Foucault argues, serves only to mask the real transformation in the operation of power which takes place with the emergence of the bourgeois state: it conceals the expansion and consolidation of a disciplinary power, of an ever-tightening coercive control of the body and of normalizing 'technologies of behaviour'.

It should not be assumed that Foucault is here simply pointing – in quasi-Marxist fashion – to the discrepancy between bourgeois principles of juridical equality and democratic sovereignty, and the continued material inequality and oppression of class rule, or between 'the general juridical form that guaranteed a system of rights that were egalitarian in principle' and 'all those systems of micro-power that are essentially non-egalitarian and asymmetrical that we call disciplines'.[53] For such a critique functions by counterposing to the limitations of existing democratic sovereignty a more adequate conception of self-determination which would promote the elimination of these discrepancies, whereas Foucault's argument is that any theory of sovereignty or self-determination must be abandoned, since the 'free subject' upon which such theories rely is in fact intrinsically heteronomous, constituted by power. For Foucault the 'real, corporeal disciplines' do not constitute a *limitation* on, but rather the '*foundation* of the formal, juridical liberties';[54] so that *Discipline and Punish* repeatedly returns to the contrast between the illusion of a social order grounded in the will of all, and the grim reality of a technology of power which constantly enforces conformity to norms and secures 'the submission of forces and bodies'. Furthermore, in contrast to the Frankfurt School, for whom this contradiction between the illusory autonomy of the subject and its real enslavement betrays 'a preponderance of the objectified in subjects which prevents them from becoming subjects',[55] for Foucault it suggests the desirability of a 'destruction of the subject as pseudo-sovereign'.[56] 'The man described for us,' he writes, 'whom we are invited to free, is already in himself the effect of a subjection much more profound than himself.'[57]

Power and Resistance

Foucault's genealogy of the modern soul evidently raises a series of political problems. As we have seen, during the 1970s Foucault's inclination is to play down the repressive and negative aspects of power and to present the operation of power as primarily positive and productive. This is a matter not simply of stressing – in Weberian fashion – the efficiency of modern forms of economic and administrative organization, but of underlining the fact that power constitutes the individuals on whom and through whom it subsequently operates. 'The individual', Foucault writes, 'is not to be conceived as a sort of elementary nucleus, a primitive atom, a multiple and inert material on which power comes to fasten or against which it happens to strike, and in so doing subdues or crushes individuals. In fact, it is already one of the prime effects of power that certain bodies, certain gestures, certain discourses, certain desires, come to be identified and constituted as individuals.'[58] Yet, if the concept of power is to have any critical political import, there must be *some* principle, force or entity which power 'crushes' or 'subdues', and whose release from this repression is considered desirable. A *purely* positive account of power would no longer be an account of power at all, but simply of the constitutive operation of social systems. At many points, Foucault appears to believe it possible to adopt such a neutral stance – indeed this may be described as his standard fall-back position – while at others he continues to use the concept of power in a critical sense. His work must therefore contain, even if only implicitly, an account of that which modern power, and hence the self-reflexive subject formed by such power, represses.

In *Madness and Civilization* this role is played by the notion of 'madness'. Despite its initiation of Foucault's enquiries into systems of confinement and social control, it can be argued that *Madness and Civilization* is as much concerned with the plight of everyday consciousness in the modern world as with the specific fate of those labelled insane. The real object of Foucault's investigation, as he states in the 'Preface' to the original French edition, is the moment of partition, the point at which the reciprocal, participatory relation between reason and folly was severed, ultimately leaving on one side a rational certainty of self closed off from any experience of the numinous or the transcendent, and on the other such an experience trivialized as illness, reduced to the mechanisms of a psychological determinism.[59] The fundamental theme of *Madness and Civilization*, therefore, is 'disenchantment' in the Weberian sense, and the elegiac ground-bass of the book places Foucault implicitly but insistently in the camp of the critics of Enlightenment. For Foucault it is not the freedom of the rational self which is impaired by the irruption of madness, but rather madness which is stripped of its 'powers and prestige' through the formation of rational awareness: 'Instead of submitting to a simple negative operation that loosened bonds and delivered one's deepest nature from madness, it must be recognized that one was in the grip of a positive operation that confined madness in a system of rewards and punishments, and included it in the movement of moral consciousness.'[60] Hence the importance taken on in this work by writers such as Nietzsche and Artaud, prepared to pursue the critique of modern consciousness even at the cost of their own lapse into silence, who give madness 'for the first time an expression, a *droit de cité*, and a hold on Western culture which makes all contestations, and total contestation, possible.'[61]

Foucault never entirely abandons his concern with the dissolution of rational consciousness. Even during the late sixties, when Foucault was at his most 'structuralist', it returns in a discussion of the use of psychotropic drugs.[62] But during the 1970s, when he takes up again the political – as opposed to structuralist-methodological – critique of the subject, he shifts the emphasis from the disenchanted nature of modern consciousness, to the processes of corporeal regulation and control by means of which a stable self is produced. In his discussion of the emergence of disciplinary power in *Discipline and Punish*, Foucault's suggestion is that new techniques of a minute parcellization and ordering of time, space and gesture which originated in a military context were progressively transferred to the process of production. This transfer involves the elaboration of new types of knowledge of human behaviour which mould the 'objects' to which they are applied, so that the soul may be seen as 'the present correlative of a certain technology of power over the body', indeed as the 'prison of the body'.[63] Yet, despite this verbal insistence, the notion of the body remains little more than a cipher in Foucault's work of this period. Although it is logically required in order for Foucault to restage – in more readily identifiable period costume – the drama of the production of interiority recounted by Nietzsche in *On the Genealogy of Morals*, Foucault's discussions of the body are curiously anodyne, devoid of any hint of Nietzsche's celebration of the 'strength, joy and terribleness' of the 'old instincts' which were crippled by the emergence of self-consciousness – a celebration on which the critique of bad conscience is dependent for its polemical charge. Without some evocation of the intrinsic forces of the body, without some theory which makes the corporeal more than a malleable *tabula rasa*, it is impossible to reckon the costs imposed by 'an infinitesimal power over the active body', or the sacrifice involved in the 'individualizing fragmentation of labour power'.[64]

Foucault's caution in this respect, his reluctance to participate in the wilder celebrations of unleashed libido engaged in by his contemporaries, should not be taken to imply his possession of a more adequate framework for the theorization of the relations between power, subjectivity and the control of the body. Foucault's lack of any theory of drives or of any interest in the internal complexity of the psyche – a lack undoubtedly conditioned by his hostility of psychoanalysis – is a lacuna in, not a virtue of, his work, since in his recorded political discussions of the 1970s he gravitates towards a position in which the very aim of political action appears to be abrogation of reflection and the cancellation of self-consciousness. Since the autonomous subject is, for Foucault, already the product of subjection to power, the aim of political actions cannot be to enhance or expand this autonomy. Indeed, he goes so far as to suggest that 'political struggle in the context of class warfare' can function as a ' "desubjectification" of the will- to-power', and that 'consciousness as the basis of subjectivity is a prerogative of the bourgeoisie'.[65] Even when expressed less extravagantly, Foucault's position implies at the very least an extreme spontaneism, exemplified by his argument, in a debate with Maoists, that 'popular justice' should take the form of on-the-spot retribution without the mediation of a court, or even of a revolutionary tribunal.[66] In many of these discussions, furthermore, two perspectives overlap in a never adequately clarified way. On the one hand, Foucault continues to speak as if political struggle were a matter of a context between classes and social groups with irreconcilable aims and interests. On the other, his theoretically unelaborated notion of 'resistance', a corporeally grounded opposition to the power which – at the most fundamental level – moulds human beings into self-identical subjects, implies a hostility to any form of conscious formulation of aims or strategic calculation. This incoherence did not pass unnoticed, since in a discussion of Bentham's Panopticon one interlocutor pertinently enquired: 'Are resistances to power, then, essentially physical in character? What about the content of struggles, the aspirations that manifest themselves in them?'[67] In his reply, Foucault took refuge in a series of evasions.

In a sense, Foucault's political embarrassment was resolved for him by the ebbing of the post-'68 wave of militancy. *Discipline and Punish* remains very much the testament of Foucault's *gauchisme*, its argument buoyed up by an indignation whose complement is a belief – however tenuous – in the positive value of rebellion. By the second half of the 1970s, however, the momentum of *gauchisme* was largely spent, and spontaneist doctrines of liberation began to appear increasingly ingenuous, if not positively dangerous. Foucault's work, after *Discipline and Punish*, reflects this shift in political consciousness. He begins to take his distance from the *gauchiste* celebration of madness, childhood, delinquency, sexuality, retreating once more into an olympian objectivity: 'It is necessary to pass over to the other side – the other side from the "good side" – in order to try to free oneself from these mechanisms which made two sides appear, in order to dissolve the false unity of this other side whose part one has taken. That's where the real work begins, the work of the historian of the present.'[68] Foucault's engagement in this work, in *The History of Sexuality*, takes the form of an attack upon what he calls the 'repressive hypothesis', the assumption that the asceticism and work-discipline of bourgeois society demanded a repression of sexuality, culminating in the nineteenth century, from which we are still struggling to emerge. Foucault does not deny that there may have been a Victorian puritanism which enforced a deeper reticence and a stricter decorum in the discussion of sexual matters, and in certain areas of sexual life, but he suggests that such puritanism must be seen as 'a digression, a refinement, a tactical diversion' within what was in fact an incessant expansion in the 'great process of transforming sex into discourse'.[69] The fundamental argument of the book is that sexuality is not a natural reality, but the product of a *dispositif*, a system of discourses and practices which forms part of the intensifying surveillance and control of the individual which is Foucault's central historical theme. From this standpoint the notion of sex as a 'rebellious energy', as a 'specific and irreducible urge', which had formed the basis of theories of sexual liberation from D.H. Lawrence to Wilhelm Reich, can be seen as 'the most speculative, most ideal, and most internal element in a deployment of sexuality organized by power'.[70] The very notion of such a liberation is part of our system of servitude.

There is an unmistakable parallel between the shift in the position of Foucault – the leading theorist of power – after *Discipline and Punish*, and the evolution of the thought of Jean-François Lyotard – as 'philosopher of desire' – during the first half of the 1970s. In Lyotard's work the process of social modernization is viewed entirely in terms of the expansion of the market economy, to the extent that he is obliged to present even such obviously interventionist remedying of the inadequacies of the market as universal compulsory education – although utterly implausibly – as a form of capitalist enterprise.[71] Initially, Lyotard portrays commodification as an ambivalent, double-edged process. Because it continuously overthrows and desacralizes tradition, the expansion of the commodity form has a liberating, 'revolutionary' effect, which for Lyotard is most tangible in the ceaseless experimentation of modernist art. Yet the capitalist labour process also abstracts from the living individual, absorbing libidinal energy into the indifferent circuits of commodity exchange. If Lyotard's historical account were less lopsided, if he possessed a theory of power as well as a theory of desire, he would be able to explain what is oppressive about this process, what is pathological in this abstraction from the sensuous self. Without such a theory, as we have seen, he is ultimately obliged to abandon the supposition that this abstraction is enforced at all. In an essay on the painter Jacques Monory, Lyotard begins to argue that culture, and in particular the postponement of satisfaction demanded by the labour process, functions as an intensification – rather than demanding the reunciation – of pleasure.[72] By the time of *Économie Libidinale* (1974) there is no longer any conflict between the discursive and the figural, sign and tensor, exchange-value and use-value, since the sign – whether word or commodity – is portrayed as always already invested with libido. Thus, just as Foucault concludes that liberation is a form of servitude, since our apparently 'natural' sexuality is in fact a product of power, so Lyotard discovers that servitude is a form of liberation, since even the anonymity and indifference of the commodity form can function as a conductor of libidinal 'intensity'.

If Lyotard places an exclusive emphasis on the revolutionizing effects of the 'norm-free sociality' of the market in his account of capitalist modernity, then Foucault's work espouses an equally one-sided view, in its unrelenting stress on the expansion of rationalized system of administration and social control. Foucault has no difficulty, therefore in describing the functioning of modern societies as determined by systems of power, but he does have difficulty in defining what this power operates again, since – unlike the *désirants* – he has no positive theory of the libidinal body. The result is this simplification, however, is that power, like the desire of the *désirants*, having nothing determinate to which it could be opposed, loses all explanatory content and becomes a ubiquitous, metaphysical principle. For only if we can produce a counterfactual, specifying how a situation would change if an operation of power were cancelled or a repressed desire made conscious, can these concepts be empirically applied. In the chapter on 'Method' in *The History of Sexuality*, Foucault excludes the possibility of such a counterfactual since he speaks of the 'omnipresence of power: not because it would have the privilege of gathering everything under its invincible unity, but because it is produced at every moment, at every point, or rather in every relation between points. Power is everywhere; not because it englobes everything, but because it comes from everywhere. And "power", in so far as it is repetitive, inert, self-reproducing, is merely the general effect which is outlined on the basis of all these mobilities, the concatenation which is based on each of them and which seeks in turn to fix them.'[73] This image of an originary, all-pervading force which reacts back on itself and regiments itself could apply equally well to the desire of the *désirants* as to Foucault's 'power'. Just as desire turns back on itself from above, so power filters up from below: the adoption of a monism of one 'dimension of force which escapes the logic of the signifier' dissolves the link between power and oppression and desire and liberation, and therefore the political content of the concepts themselves.

However, just as Lyotard, around the time of *Économie Libidinale*, cannot entirely relinquish the idea that there might be privileged aesthetic and political sites of intensity, and continues to advocate an assault upon the self-identity of the subject as a means of liberating the disorder of the drives, so Foucault cannot rest content with his critique of naturalism, his attempt to transcend the notion that there are 'two sides'. *The History of Sexuality* is concerned, as we have seen, to debunk the notion of sexuality as 'a stubborn drive, by nature alien and of necessity disobedient to power, which exhausts itself trying to subdue it and often fails to control it entirely.'[74] Foucault suggests, on the contrary, that 'sex' – as the core of sexuality – must be viewed as the product of an apparatus or *dispositif*, as the illusory vanishing point of a system of discourses and practices, thereby apparently overcoming the naturalism which he believes to have vitiated his earlier works. In fact, this achievement is only apparent. Foucault mocks the notion of sex as 'an unbearable, too hazardous truth',[75] not primarily because of its naturalism, but because of the role which he believes sexuality to play in determining the concrete identity of modern subjects. Yet in order for his account of such identity as coercive to succeed, Foucault cannot avoid invoking his own 'unbearable, too hazardous truth' which sexuality itself occludes: the 'repressive hypothesis', therefore, is not abolished, but simply displaced. This is made clear by Foucault's persistent though unfocused references, throughout *The History of Sexuality*, to 'the body and its pleasures' and to an *ars erotica* which would be fundamentally opposed to occidental rationality and its *scientia sexualis*, an art in which 'pleasure is not considered in relation to an absolute law of the permitted and the forbidden, nor by reference to a criterion of utility, but first and foremost in relation to itself.'[76] Foucault is here clearly gesturing towards that experience of intensity, hostile both to the calculations of purposive rationality and to moral deliberation, which Lyotard seeks to evoke in *Économie Libidinale*, and Deleuze and Guattari in *Anti-Oedipus*. As is the case with Lyotard's account of the 'labyrinthine libidinal band', or Deleuze and Guattari's theory of 'desiring machines', Foucault's argument depends upon an implicit rejection of the Lacanian view that the 'fragmented body' is no more than a retrospective mirage, a phantasy which expresses the fear of losing an identity already acquired. For Foucault, as for the *desirants*, self-identity is only formed through the *coercive* unification of the fragmented body. It is the 'deployment of sexuality', Foucault maintains, which generates the llusion that there exists 'something other than bodies, organs, somatic localisation functions, anatomo-physiological systems, sensations and pleasures'.[77] Thus the theoretical outcome of *The History of Sexuality* is not a refutation of naturalism, or the dissipation of the illusion of liberation. It is rather a restatement of the fundamental 'second phase' post-structuralist critique of the prison of self-identity and of the concomitant repression of the corporeal other.

This interpretation is confirmed by Foucault's 'Introduction' to the memoirs of Herculine Barbin, which appeared two years after *The History of Sexuality*. Here Foucault evokes the 'happy limbo of non-identity' in which his hermaphrodite hero-heroine dwelled before the brutal, classificatory intervention of the medical authorities, and suggests that modern Western societies have 'obstinately brought into play this question of a "true sex" in an order of things where one might have imagined that all that counted was the reality of the body and the intensity of its pleasures.'[78] Yet because Foucault is also sensitive to the difficulties of appealing to any supposedly natural force as the basis of resistance to power, even the covert instatement of 'the reality of the body and the intensity of its pleasures' as the 'repressed' of the *dispositif* of sexuality cannot be allowed to pass entirely unqualified. There are passages of *The History of Sexuality* which appear to repeat the pattern of the philosophies of desire, since the 'pleasure' – which elsewhere Foucault opposes to sex and sexuality – is portrayed as turning back on itself in the form of the *dispositif* of sexuality. The operations of power are themselves eroticized, so that the opposition which Foucault requires in order for his account to function as a theory of power at all, is once more dissolved: 'The power which thus took charge of sexuality set about contacting bodies, caressing them with its eyes, intensifying areas, electrifying surfaces, dramatizing troubled moments. It wrapped the sexual body in its embrace . . . Pleasure spread to the power that harried it; power anchored the pleasure it uncovered.'[79] Thus the 'perpetual spirals of power and pleasure' which Foucault detects are matched by the theoretical spirals of his own work, torn – as it is – between the political necessity of some form of naturalism, of an appeal to a 'general economy of pleasure not based on sexual norms',[80] and an awareness that even the apparatus of sexuality must be grounded on a 'positive economy of the body and of pleasure'.[81]

In one sense, the spiralling of Foucault's work between naturalism and anti-naturalism is a testimony to his awareness of theoretical and political difficulties which Lyotard attempts to abolish through a libidinal monism. Lyotard, beginning from the conviction that consciousness and desire stand in a necessarily antagonistic relation to each other, yet wishing to avoid the standpoint of perpetual negativity, is eventually driven – in *Économie Libidinale* – to suppress the antagonism, to supplant critique with unreserved affirmation. By contrast, Foucault, in his unwillingness to abandon entirely his critical stance towards power, and his simultaneous suspicion of any normative standpoint, is obliged to cling to an elusive, residual naturalism, which he himself realizes is philosophically untenable. Once again, an important corrective to the discursive idealism of Derrida or – in a different sense – of Lacan, is undermined by its own theoretical incoherence: the emphasis upon power as a former and transformer of discourse, in its Foucauldian form, can simply be dismissed as dependent upon a pre-critical metaphysics. However, as we shall see, the difficulty does not lie with the concepts of power or desire *as such*, but rather with the failure to appreciate that the only manner in which these concepts can be employed, without falling into naturalism, is within a *normative* horizon. Once again, the characteristic dialectic of post-structuralist thought has played itself out. The rejection of any normative standpoint as complicit with the coercive imposition of identity, eventually leads to the malfunctioning and breakdown of the very concepts which were intended to expose the intrinsically coercive character of normativity, as Foucault's late abandonment of the concept of power suggests. In order to escape this dialectic the fundamental poststructuralist assumption that identity can never be anything other than the suppression of difference must be challenged. But, before we turn to explore this question more fully, we must first examine how the central oscillation of Foucault's work is reproduced in his theorizations of knowledge.

6

Michel Foucault:
Power and Knowledge

As is the case with the general theory of power, it is in Foucault's work of the 1970s that the relation between forms of power and forms of knowledge, the functioning of what he terms 'regimes of truth', is most explicitly proposed as an object of enquiry. But again, as with the general theory of power, the apparent level of abstraction of Foucault's discussions of what is frequently fused together as a single entity, 'power-knowledge', belies the extent to which his work is concerned with the status of scientific discourse, and in particular the administrative role of the human sciences, in modern industrial societies. In this regard, also, comparison with the Frankfurt School tradition can prove illuminating. Already, in *Economy and Society*, Weber had noted that 'Bureaucratic administration means fundamentally the exercise of control on the basis of knowledge. This is the feature which makes it specifically rational.'[1] Weber's epistemology, however, does not allow for an intrinsic relation between knowledge and power; indeed, the concept of value-freedom implies their categorial separation. It is only in the work of the Frankfurt School that the internal connection between scientific knowledge and the capacity for technical intervention and control, first over nature, then over society, and lastly even over inner nature, becomes a central philosophical theme. The first generation of Critical Theorists is often tempted by the view that, to employ a phrase of Marcuse's, the 'political content of technical reason' is – intrinsically – domination. This is a theme which came very much alive during the student protests of the late 1960s. One of the major detonators of the French student uprising – as Foucault himself has noted[2] – was the transformation of the university from a site for the transmission of liberal culture to a self-perpetuating elite to a 'mass-university' producing the scientists and social engineers required by an advanced capitalist society. The rebellion was directed not only against the antiquated and hierarchical structure and teaching practices of the university, but also against the content of what was taught: there was a pervasive awareness amongst the protesters that, as students of psychology, sociology, political science, they were being trained for menial tasks of information-gathering and social control. In a pamphlet entitled 'Why sociologists?' a number of student militants, including Daniel Cohn-Bendit, a leading figure in the uprising, argued that 'The practice of organizing capitalism creates a mass of contradictions; and for each particular case a sociologist is put to work. One studies juvenile delinquency, another racism, a third slums. Each seeks an explanation of his partial problem and elaborates a "theory" proposing solutions to the limited conflict he is studying. Thus, while serving as a "watchdog" our sociologist will at the same time make his contribution to the mosaic of sociological "theories".'[3]

It seems unlikely that these arguments were influenced by structuralism in its positivist phase, or by the work of Foucault who, during the mid sixties, adopted an apolitical and even technocratic stance; the Frankfurt School, via the thought of Marcuse, plus the native influence of *Socialisme ou Barbarie* and of the veteran Marxist philosopher Henri Lefebvre – then teaching at Nanterre – probably played a greater role in their elaboration. Yet Foucault could claim, in retrospect, and not without justification, that there existed a considerable overlap between the concern of his earlier work with the politics of psychiatry and medicine and the themes of May '68. Certainly, the *Évènements* gave a new stimulus to his own investigations. Yet despite the fact that both the Frankfurt School and Foucault have addressed themselves to the same socio-historical developments, the gulf between their theoretical approaches remains immense. Horkheimer and Adorno envisage a genuine dialectic of Enlightenment: the ability to co-ordinate means and ends with a view to the maximum efficiency of action does indeed characterize one type of reason, and the development of this ability is rooted in the ineluctable demands of self-preservation. The immense increase in human power both over nature and over other human beings which takes place under capitalism – and the correlative decline of belief in an intrinsically meaningful world order – must therefore be attributed to a cognitive process which – although disastrously one-sided – cannot be considered as reversible or contingent. 'The transition from objective to subjective reason was not an accident,' Horkheimer notes, 'and the process of development of ideas cannot arbitrarily at any given moment be reversed.'[4] There *is* an element in Foucault's work of the 1970s, as we have seen, which stresses the contrast between the haphazard and costly nature of feudal power, its extravagance and excess, and the 'productivity' and systematicity of disciplinary power, 'the gentle efficacy of total surveillance'.[5] *Discipline and Punish* draws an explicit parallel between the emergence of technologies of power and other contemporary technical innovations, and argues for the interdependence of 'the economic take-off of the West', and 'a political take-off in relation to the traditional, ritual, costly, violent forms of power, which soon fell into disuse and were superseded by a subtle, calculated technology of subjection'.[6] Yet Foucault is unwilling to attribute this economic and administrative take-off to an advance in rationality: the notion of the progress of reason remains throughout one of the prime targets of Foucault's historiography of the sciences. Yet, by taking the view that rationality and cognitive validity are always relative to a historically specific system of discourses and practices, Foucault deprives himself of the most obvious means of accounting for the connection between power and knowledge: that modern scientific knowledge enhances the effectiveness of action, and in so doing more adequately fulfils one of the aims with which knowledge has always been elaborated. In *Discipline and Punish* Foucault explicitly distances himself from this view, suggesting that if 'power produces knowledge' this is 'not simply by encouraging it because it serves power or by applying it because it is useful'.[7] The problem is raised, therefore, of what relation – other than instrumental – Foucault perceives between knowledge and power.

Foucault's most straightforward answer to this question is limited to the human sciences, and presents power as a precondition of knowledge, rather than knowledge as a precondition of power. In *Madness and Civilization* Foucault is concerned with a transformation of the 'fundamental structures of experience' through which human beings become able to think of themselves as the subjects of a purely procedural rationality of enquiry, and to consider other 'irrational' human beings as the possible objects of such an enquiry. This transformation involves a severing of the reciprocal, participatory relation between reason and unreason which remained in force, so Foucault believes, up to the time of the Renaissance, and the installation of self-certainty as the foundation of all knowledge, a process which is summarised in Foucault's well-known analysis of a passage from Descartes's first *Meditation*.[8] Already in *Madness and Civilization* the effect of Nietzsche's allegorical materialism upon Foucault is evident, however, since the book argues that the separating out of the subject and object of the science of madness is not the result merely of a transformation of consciousness, but requires institutional – and even specifically architectural – preconditions. During the Classical Age, Foucault suggests, the subjective certainty of not being mad stood in a tense and criss-cross relation to a system of confinement which still tended not to discriminate between madness and other forms of disorder. It is only with the emergence of the asylum, where 'a system of social protection' could be 'interiorized in the forms of consciousness' and a recognition of the specificity of madness could be made manifest 'on the surface of institutions',[9] that the new science of psychiatry became possible. If 'the knowledge of madness presupposes, in the one who possesses it, the ability to escape from its grasp, to disengage oneself from its perils and prestige', then 'this disengagement was in fact only made possible by a whole architecture of protection, designed and constructed successively by Colombier, Tenon, Cabanis, Bellart . . . '.[10] To make human beings available as potential objects of science, Foucault suggests, presupposes a system of procedures for their confinement and control.

In *The Birth of the Clinic* a similar stress is laid upon the institutional, and political, preconditions for the elaboration of a form of knowledge, although in this case the science in question is one of the body rather than that of the mind. Foucault argues that it was on the basis of what he terms – after describing the abstract space of the classificatory table, and the concrete space of the perceived body – the 'tertiary spatialisation' of disease ('all the gestures by which, in a given society, disease is circumscribed, medically invested, isolated, divided up into closed, privileged regions, or distributed throughout cure centres, arranged in the most favourable way'[11]) that 'the whole of medical experience was overturned and defined for its most concrete perceptions new dimensions and a new foundation'.[12] With the construction of the new teaching hospitals, the outcome of the Revolutionary debates on medical reform, an institutional space was created in which disease could be exposed to the systematic, unimpeded gaze of the physician. A new knowledge of illness was made possible, no longer clouded by the opaque lore of feudal corporatism, but grounded in the pellucid evidence of observation: 'In the hospital disease meets, as it were, the forced residence of its truth.'[13] The internal link between constraint and the veridical sealed by this final phrase may be said to form one of the fundamental themes of Foucault's work as a whole. Even in the later 1960s, when Foucault's concern is primarily with immanent rules of formation of scientific discourse, he does not entirely neglect the institutional preconditions of knowledge, although not yet – and no longer – prepared to suggest that these preconditions form a system of power. Thus *The Archaeology of Knowledge* refers to objects of knowledge as only emerging 'under the positive conditions of a complex bundle of relations. These relations are established between institutions, economic and social processes, forms of behaviour, systems of norms, techniques, types of classification, modes of characterisation.'[14]

It is in *Discipline and Punish* that the delineations of the connection between procedures of confinement and control and the emergence of the human sciences to be found in Foucault's earlier works achieve their definitive expression. It is true that, in the opening chapter of the book, Foucault argues that there exists a relation of mutual dependence and reinforcement between power and knowledge, that 'power and knowledge directly imply one another; that there is no power relation without the correlative constitution of a field of knowledge, nor any knowledge that does not presuppose and constitute at the same time power relations'.[15] Yet even this formulation appears to attribute a certain ontological priority to power, and this priority is confirmed by Foucault's central image of the Panopticon, where an architectural mechanism which renders human beings available to continuous observation forms the precondition for the elaboration of knowledge. Many other statements by Foucault, both in *Discipline and Punish* and in essays and interviews from around the same period, suggest that the relation between power and knowledge which he has in mind concerns the repressive institutions which make the formation of certain kinds of knowledge possible: 'If it has been possible to constitute a knowledge of the body, this has been by way of an ensemble of military and educational disciplines. It was on the basis of power over the body that a physiological, organic knowledge of it became possible';[16] 'The archaeology of the human sciences has to be established through studying the mechanisms of power which have invested human bodies, acts and forms of behaviour. And this investigation enables us to rediscover one of the conditions of the emergence of the human sciences: the great 19th-century effort in discipline and normalisation';[17] 'that moment when the sciences of man become possible is the moment when a new technology of power and a new political anatomy of the body were implemented'.[18]

Despite its frequency in Foucault's writings of the 1970s, this argument based on the institutional preconditions of forms of knowledge does not establish the intimacy of relation between power and knowledge which Foucault requires. Foucault's fundamental contention is that knowledge and power cannot – even analytically – be separated, that 'it is not the activity of the subject of knowledge that produces a corpus of knowledge, useful or resistant to power, but power-knowledge, the processes and struggles that traverse it and of which it is made up, that determines the forms and possible domains of knowledge.'[19] It is perfectly possible, however, to take account of social and institutional preconditions of knowledge without denying that knowledge also possesses its own immanent, rational historicity, as the work of Foucault's former teacher, philosopher and historian of science Georges Canguilhem makes clear. In his essay on 'L'Objet de l'histoire des sciences', for example, Canguilhem points out that 'biometry and psychometry can only be constituted by Quêtelet, Galton, Catell and Binet when non-scientific practices have had the effect of providing to observation a homogeneous subject-matter capable of mathematical treatment. The stature of human beings, Quêtelet's object of study, presupposes the institution of national armies and of conscription, and an interest in criteria of reform. Intellectual aptitudes, Binet's object of study, presupposes the institution of obligatory primary education, and an interest in criteria of backwardness.'[20] For Canguilhem, however, the question of scientific truth cannot be reduced to the question of the preconditions of, and interests served by, scientific knowledge: the history of science is a history of concepts and their transformations, of questions and answers, and not simply of powers and social practices.[21] One result of this view is that, though a form of knowledge may require a coercive relation between subject and object as a condition of its formation, this knowledge itself is not intrinsically coercive, but may be appropriated for a critical purpose. Information on the relative stature of members of different social classes – to continue Canguilhem's example – may become part of a critique of social inequalities. The fact that Foucault implicitly denies such a possibility, arguing that struggles do not take place between power and resistance over the *use* of knowledge, but traverse 'power-knowledge' itself, suggests that his reasons for portraying an intrinsic relation between power and knowledge lie deeper than any consideration of institutional and social preconditions. For Foucault, the mere fact of becoming an object of knowledge represents a kind of enslavement. Cognition is itself a form of domination. In order to follow the ramifications of this argument in Foucault's work, however, we must return to its origins in Nietzsche.

Foucault and Nietzsche

From the very beginning of his work Nietzsche is concerned to combat conceptions of knowledge as the disinterested reproduction of an objective reality, believing that such conceptions impose an unacceptable limitation upon the range of human thought and experience. The argument is already central to *The Birth of Tragedy*, where Nietzsche draws an unfavourable contrast between Greek tragedy at the height of its powers, a form of artistic creation which – through its blending of Dionysiac insight and Apollonian order – was able to confront the chaos and horror of existence, and yet draw an affirmative conclusion from this confrontation, and the Socratic dialectic – and its scientific offspring – with its naively optimistic belief that reality can be exhaustively grasped in concepts. *The Birth of Tragedy* is directed against 'the illusion that thought, guided by the thread of causation, might plumb the furthest abysses of being, and even correct it.'[22] Throughout his work Nietzsche will stress the aversion of the human intellect to chaos, its fear of unmediated intuition, and its resultant attempts to simplify the world by reducing diversity to identity. There is, however, an equally strong pragmatic tendency in Nietzsche, which suggests that this process of ordering and simplification takes place not simply because of an 'existential' need for security, but in the interests of sheer survival: 'In order for a particular species to maintain itself and increase its power, its conception of reality must comprehend enough of the calculable and constant for it to base a scheme of behaviour on it. The utility of preservation – not some abstract-theoretical need not to be deceived – stands as the motive behind the development of the organs of knowledge . . . '.[23] It is on such considerations that Nietzsche bases his many paradoxical pronouncements on the nature of knowledge and truth: that truth is 'the kind of error without which a certain species of life could not live'; that knowledge is merely 'a measuring of earlier and later errors by one another'.[24]

Many commentators have attempted to moderate the perplexing and scandalous effect of these formulations by suggesting that Nietzsche has two kinds of truth in mind. His attack is directed against 'correspondence' theories of truth, the failure to consider the extent to which our language and our concepts shape our world, but does not exclude a deeper kind of insight into the nature of reality which would merit the title 'truth'.[25] Such elucidations are not without textual support, but they also have a tendency to overlook the extent to which Nietzsche's paradoxical formulations betray a genuine dilemma in his thought. For there is a strong positivist element in Nietzsche's outlook, which sees modern science as having decisively undermined the validity of any specifically philosophical enquiry, or the possibility of any non-scientific path to truth. One important consequence of this viewpoint is a denial that there could be a philosophical assessment of the adequacy of knowledge. 'The intellect cannot criticise itself,' Nietzsche writes in *The Will to Power*, 'simply because it cannot be compared with other species of intellect and because its capacity to know would be revealed only in the presence of "true reality" .... This presupposes that, distinct from every perspective kind of outlook or sensual spiritual appropriation, something exists, an "in-itself". – But the psychological derivation of the belief in things forbids us to speak of "things-in-themselves".'[26] Yet, despite his own strictures, from *The Birth of Tragedy* onward, where he contrasts the shallow optimism of science to an alternative Dionysiac insight into the nature of things, Nietzsche will repeatedly counterpose a vision of ultimate reality to accepted truths. Indeed, in *The Birth of Tragedy*, he employs the Kantian concept of a noumenal world to illustrate precisely this opposition: 'The contrast of this authentic nature-truth and the lies of culture which present themselves as the sole reality is similar to that between the eternal core of things, the thing-in-itself and the entire world of appearance.'[27] Nietzsche's critique of philosophy, therefore, of the 'knowledge of knowledge' drives him towards a perspectivism which equates what is real with what is given in a form of knowledge, while his critique of all perspectives which see through their own 'illusory' nature pushes him towards a reinstatement of the distinction between appearance and reality.

This oscillation continues throughout Nietzsche's thought, even into the final phase, where he begins to move towards a more systematic metaphysics. Aware of the circle involved in proposing a biological or psychological theory of the drives which lie behind the formation of human knowledge, Nietzsche transforms his naturalism into a *metaphysical* theory of evaluations, a 'perspective theory of affects', which are seen as ramifications of a single underlying principle, the will to power. According to this view, knowledge no longer primarily functions as a means of survival; the process of ordering characteristic of knowledge is an expression of a more fundamental principle: 'To impose upon becoming the character of being,' Nietzsche remarks, 'that is the supreme will to power.'[28] Even this formulation, however, betrays the dilemma at the heart of Nietzsche's thought. On the one hand Nietzsche, by means of his perspectivism, wishes to attack the denigration of the world of the senses by priests and philosophers, a denigration which relies on the positing of a 'true' world of static purity beyond the realm of flux and change. 'The "real world",' Nietzsche writes, 'however one has hitherto conceived it – it has always been the apparent world *once again*.'[29]

Yet, if there are indeed nothing but appearances determined by perspectives, then the viewpoint of the 'backworldsmen' which posits a real world behind appearances would be no less valid than any other perspective. Hence Nietzsche is obliged to develop his own conception of ultimate reality in order to possess a means of judging the adequacy of perspectives. It is the doctrine of the 'eternal return of the same' which fulfils this task in Nietzsche's later thought. 'The antithesis of this phenomenal world,' Nietzsche argues, 'is not "the true world", but the formless unformulable world of the chaos of sensations – *another kind* of phenomenal world, a kind "unknowable" for us.'[30] Nietzsche would not admit, of course, that the eternal return is simply another version of the true world, but this is because of the residues of an ontological conception of truth in his work, which lead him to assume that the 'true world' must necessarily possess the characteristics of ideality and immutability, as is made clear by his evocation of the 'character of the world in a state of becoming as "false", as self-contradictory".'[31] Nietzsche's confession of the unknowability of chaos, bizarrely clashing with his stress of its phenomenality, reveals that the world of incessant flux and becoming, upon which the will to power imposes the identity of being, is no less a true world than any other. For it is only in the light of this definitive vision of the world as 'a monster of energy, without beginning, without end',[32] that Nietzsche is able to criticize the illusions of perspectives which posit a stable being, despite the fact that the possibility of such a vision has already contradicted his argument that perspectives are constitutive of reality. Thus, not only does Nietzsche's work oscillate between the need for a critical reflection on knowledge and a disbelief in the possibility of such reflection: it culminates in two opposed and irreconcilable metaphysical conceptions – the perspectivism of the will to power, and the true world of the eternal return – which canonize this very oscillation.

Despite the fact that all the major thinkers of post-structuralism – with the significant exception of Lacan – owe a considerable intellectual debt to Nietzsche, it is arguable that Foucault's relation to his 19th-century mentor is more intimate than that of any of his contemporaries. For, throughout the 1960s and seventies, Foucault's thought, rather than simply taking up Nietzschean themes or adopting a Nietzschean stance, can be seen as repeatedly re-enacting the tensions, dilemmas and inconsistencies of Nietzsche's work. As with Nietzsche, there is a strong positivist strand in Foucault's thought, inherited – via structuralism – from Comte and Durkheim. Because of this heritage, Foucault has persistently shied away from the disreputably philosophical enterprise of developing a critical conception of knowledge, and has adopted the view that cognitive validity is always relative to a specific system of discourses and practices, and that therefore the history of knowledge can be nothing other than the history of what has been taken for knowledge in any particular epoch. This assumption of the impossibility of distinguishing between the greater or lesser rationality or validity of different epistemic frameworks is accompanied by the view that the constitution of such frameworks must in all cases be susceptible to the same type of explanation. In Nietzsche's case, one major type of explanation employed tends towards naturalism and pragmatism, while another views the will-to-truth as the expression of the asceticism of a moral imperative which eventually sees through itself as incapable of any ultimate justification. By contrast, Foucault eschews naturalism or psychologism. In his early work, the emergence of forms of scientific knowledge is explained in historical and political terms; in his writings of the later 1960s this dimension is screened out in favour of an immanent systematicity of discursive formations; while in the 1970s Foucault adopts an explanation in terms of strategies of power. Like the modes of experience or discursive formations which Foucault had earlier discussed, the 'regimes of truth' of the 1970s are not susceptible – as their name implies – to any external assessment of their truth or falsity. ' "Truth"', Foucault suggests, 'is to be understood as a system of ordered procedures for the production, regulation, distribution, circulation and operation of statements.'[33]

From the very beginning, however, the positivism of Foucault's work – just like that of Nietzsche – has vied with an equally strong conviction that forms of knowledge do not simply constitute, but can also obscure and obliterate reality. In Foucault's first book, *Maladie Mentale et Psychologie*, there is an explicit reflection on the relative adequacy of different cognitive frameworks: Foucault argues that forms of psychiatry which model their conception of mental illness on that of physical illness generate a '*préjugé d'essence*', the assumption that there is some pathogenic agency which lies behind the multiplicity of symptoms and which defines the fundamental nature of the disorder.[34] In this early work, published in 1955, Foucault suggests that Freudian psychoanalysis and – to a greater extent – existential psychoanalysis may offer a more adequate account of the nature of mental disorder. By the time of *Madness and Civilization*, however, despite a continued qualified preference for Freud over conventional psychiatry, the whole of Foucault's argument has radically shifted. As the original Preface unequivocally suggests ('the tragic structure on the basis of which the history of the Western world takes place is nothing other than the refusal, the forgetfulness, the lapse into silence of tragedy'[35]), the intellectual groundplan of *Madness and Civilization* is provided by Nietzsche's *The Birth of Tragedy*; Foucault's central concern is the loss of a sense of the horror and mystery of existence, its obliteration by the neutrality of the concept and the naive optimism of science. Up until the time of Shakespeare and Cervantes, Foucault suggests, reason and unreason were relatively permeable to each other: reason remained conscious of its precariousness and dependency, while folly continued to harbour the possibility of a wisdom beyond the sagacity of the wise. Even during the Classical Age the very rigidity and ferocity with which the separation between sanity and madness was maintained suggests a continued sense of the awesome powers of unreason, which was perceived as 'a subterranean danger', as 'the threatening space of an absolute freedom'.[36] From this historical standpoint, the coercion implicit in the new science of psychiatry no longer consists primarily in the fact that human beings must be confined and exposed to surveillance in order for psychiatric knowledge to be produced. Rather it consists in the fact that any modern scientific account of madness robs the phenomenon of its grandeur and tragic force, of its power of 'contesting suddenly and without recourse everything which is most essential in man and truest in truth'.[37]

The elevation of madness to this status of contestant of truth itself, however, now raises for Foucault the difficulties and dilemmas which we have already encountered in Nietzsche. If there is indeed 'an experience of unreason which it has been the function of psychology in the modern world to mask',[38] then Foucault cannot be simply a perspectivist, for whom each viewpoint generates its own truth, and cannot therefore be assessed by any external standard. Indeed, beneath the ostensible claim of *Madness and Civilization* that the history of madness consists simply in a sequence of 'fundamental structures of experience', none of which is closer to the ultimate truth about madness than any other, lies the story of an increasing obliteration of the experience of unreason, a progressive stripping away of its significance. In his chapter on 'Doctors and Patients', for example, Foucault describes, and implicitly laments, 'the impoverishment of the meanings which had richly sustained the therapeutic methods throughout the entire classical period'.[39] During the Classical Age the therapeutic use of movement had involved horse-riding, sea-voyages, walks in the country; it sought to restore the patient, locked-up in the non-being of his or her own subjectivity, to 'the plenitude of the exterior world, the solid truth of being'.[40] There are overtones here, in Foucault's sympathetic presentation, of re-integration with an objective cosmic order. After the advent of the new psychiatry, however, with its 'rotatory machines' which subjected patients to violent artificial motion, 'movement no longer aimed at restoring the invalid to the truth of the external world, but only at producing a series of internal effects, purely mechanical and purely psychological. It was no longer the presence of the truth which determined the cure, but a functional norm'.[41] Although he is here describing what Horkheimer, in *The Eclipse of Reason*, refers to as the transition from objective to subjective or instrumental reason, Foucault – unlike Horkheimer – does not believe that the objectification of human beings, and the attendant withering of the symbolic content of therapy, was the result of genuine, although one-sided, cognitive progress, but rather the reverse. There are many passages in *Madness and Civilization* where modern psychiatry is denounced unequivocally as ideology. 'The objectivity of psychiatry', Foucault affirms, is 'from the beginning a reification of a magical kind'; 'What we call psychiatric practice is a certain moral tactic contemporary with the end of the eighteenth century, preserved in the rites of asylum life, and overlaid with the myths of positivism.'[42]

To denounce positivist psychiatry as a myth, however, implies a contrast between this myth and the reality which it conceals. And it is here that Foucault's difficulties begin, since such a contrast implies the possibility of access to madness as it is in itself, or at least of a more adequate standpoint, even if located in the past, which would clash with Foucault's fundamental commitment to a Nietzschean relativism. Foucault cannot go so far as to claim that there *is* no madness 'in itself', for then the force of his denunciation would be lost. But – at the same time – he must assert that no perspective can be anything more than *one* perspective, and that any such perspective will be an imposition of reason upon unreason, that 'the freedom of madness can only be understood from the heights of the fortress which holds it prisoner',[43] just as, for Nietzsche, the world of becoming can only be grasped in the clumsy categories of being. However, to be obliged to criticize a form of knowledge – modern psychiatry – from the standpoint of a reality which cannot itself be known is clearly an uncomfortable position to be forced into, too close to the kind of metaphysics which Foucault's relativism and historical objectivism are an attempt to escape. It is in order to avoid this dilemma that Foucault suggests: 'To write the history of madness therefore means: to carry out a structural study of the historical ensemble – notions, institutions, police and juridical measures, scientific concepts – which hold captive a madness whose wild state can never be restored in itself.'[44] Foucault, as if worried by this stipulation, immediately goes on to suggest that the aim of such a 'structural study' would be 'to return towards the decision which links and separates at the same time reason and madness', but he also admits that the 'perpetual exchange, the obscure common root' of the two can never be attained,[45] so that the very notion of a 'wild state' of madness begins to appear chimerical. Hence, under the impact of structuralism in the early 1960s, Foucault was led increasingly to pursue the concrete and apparently objective type of investigation presaged by his notion of an historical ensemble, and to dismiss the pursuit of a reality beyond the objects of knowledge constructed by specific historical ensembles – and the critical standpoint supported by this pursuit – as fruitless. For the 'structuralist' Foucault the notion of an object which is not constructed by the 'discursive formation' in which it is identified and described becomes theoretically and practically redundant.

It is important to bear in mind that the insistence that there are no naturally constituted objects of knowledge and no experience which is not entirely pre-formed by discourse, and that therefore the epistemological or political appeal to a reality or principle outside discourse has no force, is not simply a theoretical ploy on Foucault's part. This viewpoint follows inevitably from Foucault's conviction that it is impossible to 'climb outside' of discourse in order to compare discursive representations with something other than themselves; for Foucault, as for Nietzsche, knowledge can be said to consist in 'a measuring of earlier and later errors by one another'. The earnestness with which Foucault adopts this position during the 1960s can be gauged by the entire consistent position which he takes up on questions of technocracy and politics. Having rejected the view that the concept of the subject is central to the theory of knowledge, and therefore unable – from this positivist-structuralist position – to appeal to the capacity of the human subject to reflect critically on the categories through which it grasps itself, Foucault has no recourse but to adopt positions which are an impeccable embodiment of that technocratic functionalism which Marxist critics had accused structuralism of reflecting.[46] Thus, when Foucault is queried, in an interview given after the publication of *The Order of Things*, about the political aims of his critique of humanism ('in the name of who or what is the concept of Man criticized, if not of a more adequate conception of Man?'), he replies: 'I believe it is possible to define an optional social functioning, to be obtained by means of a certain relation between demographic increase, consumer goods, individual freedom, possibilities of happiness given to each person, without ever making use of the idea of man: an optimal functioning can be defined in an internal manner, without it being possible to say 'for whom it is better that things should be thus'.[47] In another interview from around the same period Foucault expresses a similar position: 'It is humanism which is abstract! All these heartfelt cries, all these claims for the human person and for existence are abstract: that is to say cut off from the scientific and technical world which is our real world.'[48] Foucault's positivism, combined with the abandonment of his attempts to evoke a reality beyond the reach of positive knowledge, leads him to endorse the nightmare of administration against which his earlier thought had rebelled.

Even during the heyday of structuralism, however, Foucault can never bring himself – despite the inconsistency – entirely to abandon the notion of a reality which is not constituted by the *episteme* or discursive formation. The 'blank region of self-implication where nothing is said'[49] haunts the margins of the discourse of reason. In the 'Preface' to *The Order of Things* Foucault explicitly describes his intellectual itinerary as a move from the 'history of the Other – of that which, for a culture, is simultaneously interior and alien', to a 'history of the Same – of that which is, for a culture, both dispersed and related, thus to be distinguished by marks and gathered up into identities',[50] and accordingly continues occasionally to evoke, although to no theoretical effect, 'the confused, indefinite, faceless, and, as it were, indifferent, backdrop of differences'[51] upon which the order of *episteme* is imposed. In *The Archaeology of Knowledge*, however, Foucault appears entirely to drop the notion that the identity of objects of knowledge is not only discursively constituted, but imposed upon a primal non-identity, to the extent of repudiating his own position in *Madness and Civilization*: 'We are not trying to reconstitute what madness itself might be, in the form in which it first presented itself to some primitive, fundamental, mute, scarcely articulated experience, and in the form in which it was later organised (translated, deformed, travestied, perhaps even repressed) by discourses, and the oblique, often twisted play of their operations.'[52] Yet, symptomatically, straight after this declaration, and in a work largely devoted to the critique of the notion of prediscursive experience, Foucault goes on to remark: 'Such a history of the referent is no doubt possible; and I have no wish to exclude at the outset any effort to uncover and free these "prediscursive" experiences from the tyranny of the text.'[53]

Foucault's dilemma is evident: his theoretical premises render unavoidable the assumption that modes of experience, systems of meaning and objects of knowledge are entirely determined by 'rules of formation' or – later – by operations of power. Yet, in order to function as a political critique of these rules or operations, Foucault's work must appeal to some form of meaning, experience or knowledge which is not so determined. The result – as in Nietzsche – is a perpetual oscillation. In a 1969 interview, for example, Foucault suggests that one of the distinctions between his own philosophical generation and its immediate predecessor consisted in the rejection of 'the Husserlian idea that there is meaning before anything else, which surrounds us and invests us even before we begin to open our eyes and to speak' in favour of an analysis of the 'formal conditions of appearance of meaning'.[54] Yet, within a few paragraphs, he is suggesting – as in his comparison of classical and modern therapies – that it is the formation of scientific objects which is subject to formal conditions, and which blots out an original meaning: 'In order for madness and illness to cease to be immediate significations and to become objects of a rational knowledge a certain number of conditions were necessary, which I have tried to analyse. It was a question, so to speak, of the ''interruption'' between meaning and the object of science, in sum of the formal conditions of appearance of an object in a context of meaning.'[55] When asked if this does not contradict his initial statement, Foucault revealingly affirms that he cannot be considered a structuralist, since he is concerned with 'the manner in which meaning disappeared, as if eclipsed, with the constitution of the object'.[56]

Genealogy and the Critique of Ideology

As this brief review of Foucault's itinerary in the 1960s makes clear, the oscillations characteristic of Nietzsche's view of knowledge are already well established in Foucault's work before the explicit introduction of a notion of 'power-knowledge'. Fundamentally, as both Foucault's work of the sixties and his later use of Nietzsche would lead one to expect, the domination implied by knowledge does not reside in its instrumental value, or in the coercive institutions which form the precondition for its elaboration, but rather simply in the fact that it imposes an order on disorder, reduces non-identity to identity. On closer inspection, it in fact becomes apparent that Foucault has always laid the greatest stress on the classificatory function of knowledge. Already, in *Madness and Civilization*, he remarks that, 'The science of mental disease, as it would develop in the asylum, would always be only of the order of observation and classification.'[57] And a similar point is made in *Discipline and Punish*, where Foucault stresses that the 'notions which have circulated between medicine and jurisprudence' – 'monsters', 'psychical anomalies', 'perverts', 'maladjusted' – are not primarily means of 'explaining an action', but are 'ways of defining an individual':[58] the danger of the human sicences consists in the manner in which their objects – human beings – are pinned down within an ever-more-tightly defined identity. Furthermore, like Nietzsche, Foucault suggests that this imposition of order is motivated, at the most fundamental level, by a fear of the chaotic and the unclassifiable. This *motif* appears perhaps most clearly at the beginning of the chapter on Panopticism in *Discipline and Punish*, where Foucault describes the plague regulations which he believes constitute a 'compact model of the disciplinary mechanism'. 'The plague as a form, at once real and imaginary, of disorder,' Foucault writes, 'had as its medical

and political correlative discipline. Behind the disciplinary mechanisms can be read the haunting memory of "contagions", of the
plague, of rebellions, crimes, vagabondage, desertions, people
who appear and disappear, live and die in disorder.'[59] Because of
his commitment to relativism, Foucault does not wish – as Nietzsche clearly does – to link the imposition of a conceptual order on
reality with increasing efficiency of control, since this would imply
a certain – even if only instrumental – adequacy or appropriateness
of concepts. Hence his only recourse is to propose the sheer
imposition of order as the irreducible motivation of modern
power-knowledge, a proposal often accompanied by fleeting, and
historically suspect, evocations of a prior state of felicitous
confusion. In a text dating from 1980, for example, Foucault
writes that 'Biological theories of sexuality, juridical conceptions
of the individual, forms of administrative control in modern
nations, led little by little to rejecting the idea of a mixture of the
two sexes in a single body, and consequently limiting the free choice
of indeterminate individuals. Henceforth everybody was to have
one and only one sex.'[60]

The proximity of Foucault's account of power-knowledge to
the Nietzschean conception of knowledge as a form of the will to
power is revealed in a second important way during the 1970s.
During the previous decade Foucault – in so far as he possessed a
theory of the social at all – tended to portray the social as constituted by systems independent of human consciousness and
agency, but did not link these systems specifically with the concept of power. In the 'Introduction' to *The Archaeology of
Knowledge*, for example, Foucault writes that 'the researches of
psychoanalysis, of linguistics, of ethnology, have decentred the
subject in relation to the laws of his desire, the forms of his language, the rules of his action, or the play of his mythical or fabul-
ous discourses.'[61] Here determination is not associated with
coercion. In the 1970s, however, it is the concept of power which
takes over this constitutive function. The shift to this concept has
the advantage of introducing a greater mobility into Foucault's
conception of the social, of dissolving any strict determinism, and
of allowing him to reintroduce notions of strategy and intentionality into historical analysis, without having to attach them to
individual subjects. 'Relations of power,' Foucault writes in *The
History of Sexuality*, 'are both intentional and non-subjective. If,
in fact, they are intelligible, it is not because they are the effect, in
terms of causality, of another instance which would explain them,
but, because they are entirely traversed by calculation.'[62] Yet this

use of the concept of power also has a major drawback. Because Foucault has argued for the intrinsic relation of knowledge and power, he is under a constant temptation to equate his socially constitutive power with Nietzsche's perspectival will to power, with a cognitive force which 'forms, simplifies, shapes, invents',[63] and this implicit equation produces the impression that forms of knowledge entirely constitute the social reality which they describe and analyse. On the model of what Habermas has termed the 'grandiose subjectivism' of Nietzsche's later work, power – often spoken of in the singular – becomes something like a constitutive subject in the Kantian or Husserlian sense, with the social as its constituted object.[64]

This is not, of course, a theory of society which Foucault formally develops or would consciously defend: there is no such theory in his work. Yet it is suggested by his work of the 1970s because there is no other constitutive principle which would provide the social domain with dynamic analytically separable from that of power. This inadequacy has been repeatedly indicated in criticisms of Foucault's historiography, and of that of his followers. In a discussion of *Discipline and Punish*, for example, Jacques Léonard notes that Foucault 'exaggerates the rationalization and normalization of French society in the first half of the nineteenth century. He minimises, in several domains, the resistance of customs inherited from the past, he underestimates the importance of disorder, of tolerance, of the jungle, in sum of common confusion.'[65] Similarly, in a perceptive critique of Foucault and Foucauldian historiography, Gianna Pomata has noted a 'fairly serious limitation' of works such as Donzelot's *La police des familles*: 'The tutelary ''police'' is here reconstructed and analysed through its ''knowledge'', that is to say, the texts of doctors and philanthropists; but the book lacks, by contrast, a reconstruction of the other ''knowledges'' which this police encountered and with which it came into conflict, above all the knowledge of popular traditions. In this manner the book privileges the image of social processes and of relations of power which emerges from texts linked to the ''police'', in relation to other possible images, other points of view. It limits its viewpoint to the image which the ''police'' provides of its own self-realization without taking account of other social processes with which it intersected.'[66] In reply Foucault could, of course, have pointed to his concept of resistance. Yet, as we have seen, Foucault cannot attribute to resistance determinate aims and intentions, or even portray it as capable of forming such intentions. This is because the whole capacity for strategy and calculation has passed over to the side of power, and is imprinted upon the modern subject – as are moral consciousness and aesthetic self-awareness – only through the operation of power, so that resistance can only confront this power as pure spontaneity, a spontaneity in which Foucault himself can scarcely believe.

This is the dilemma which we have already observed in examining *The History of Sexuality*. But, having traced the Nietzschean origins of Foucault's theory of knowledge-power, we can see that Foucault's political dilemma over naturalism is also an epistemological dilemma. For if objects of knowledge are always constituted within a specific form of power-knowledge, there cannot be 'other possible images', 'other points of view' – to employ Pomata's terms – on the *same* historical and social processes. Foucault's doctrine that it is only within a form of power-knowledge that statements can be candidates for truth or falsity has the paradoxical consequence that any critique of a form of power-knowledge as misrepresentation must already have accepted its fundamental assumptions: it is only within the *dispositif* of sexuality that arguments about the adequate representation of sexuality can take place. On the other hand, to argue that the concept of sexuality masks 'the reality of the body and the intensity of its pleasures' *is* to suggest that the concept of sexuality has an ideological as well as an epistemological function, yet Foucault wishes to abandon the concept of ideology, since he believes it to imply an unjustifiable claim to possess a privileged access to truth on the part of the critic. Hence, as was already apparent in *Madness and Civilization*, Foucault's relativism clashes with his political commitments. To deny that political critique possesses an epistemological dimension is to be condemned either to a self-defeating acceptance of the 'truth' of the contested perspective, or to resort to an appeal – of whose vulnerability Foucault is well aware – to some 'prediscursive experience', or natural reality outside all perspectives.

Perhaps the most consistent response to these difficulties, a response which Foucault frequently adopts, is to retreat from any political commitment, and simply to conduct a historical enquiry into the 'correlative formation of domains, of objects, and of verifiable and falsifiable discourses related to them'.[67] For, to the extent that Foucault wishes to take up a political position, he often finds himself obliged to dissolve the internal relation between power and knowledge, both by presenting power as supported by an illusory knowledge, and by describing a genuine knowledge which is on the side of resistance, rather than of power. Already, in *Madness and Civilization*, Foucault writes: 'It is thought that Tuke and Pinel opened the asylum to medical knowledge. They did not introduce science, but only a personality, whose powers borrowed from science only their disguise, or at most their justification.'[68] Similar remarks, indicating that a claim to scientific knowledge is in fact merely a pretext for a claim to authority are to be found throughout Foucault's work. In a discussion of *Discipline and Punish* he enquires: 'Have you ever read any criminological texts? They are staggering . . . I fail to comprehend how the discourse of criminology has been able to go on at this level. One has the impression that it is of such utility, is needed so urgently and rendered so vital for the working of the system, that it does not even need to seek a theoretical justification for itself, or even a coherent framework.'[69] It is clear from this statement that the application of the title 'knowledge' to criminology would be purely honorific. What Foucault here describes could more properly be described as ideology: a set of concepts and representations which are 'vital for the working' of a system, and yet can be shown to be epistemologically incoherent. Foucault avoids the concept of ideology because 'like it or not, it always stands in virtual opposition to something else which is supposed to count as truth', it requires 'drawing the line between that in a discourse which falls under the category of scientificity or truth and that which comes under some other category'.[70] Yet the result of this avoidance is that Foucault is simply obliged to draw the same distinction surreptitiously, by means of qualifications and sceptical inverted commas, remarking at the end of *Discipline and Punish*, for example, that 'the supervision of normality was firmly encased in a medicine or a psychiatry which provided it with a sort of "scientificity"'.[71]

Not only does Foucault break the link between power and knowledge by suggesting that forms of science which support relations of domination are – in some cases at least – merely pseudo-sciences, he also breaks the link in the other direction by theorizing forms of knowledge which are not forms of power. In a lecture dating from 1976 Foucault develops an account of what he terms 'subjugated knowledges'. There is, he suggests, 'a whole set of knowledges, located low down on the hierarchy, beneath the required level of cognition or scientificity . . . it is through the re-emergence of these low-ranking knowledges (such as that of the psychiatric patient, of the ill person, of the nurse, of the doctor – parallel and marginal as they are to the knowledge of medicine – that of the delinquent etc.), and which involve what I would call popular knowledge . . . that criticism performs its work.'[72] This evocation of an 'insurrection of knowledges' also permits Foucault to tackle the difficult problem of the status of his own discourse. For if, as Foucault claims, 'Truth is a thing of this world: it is produced only by virtue of multiple forms of constraint',[73] it appears that Foucault's own genealogies – as a form of knowledge – must be the expression of a relation of power. Nietzsche, faced with a similar theoretical situation, is prepared to admit this implication, since he employs the concept of power in an affirmative rather than a critical sense. For Nietzsche the genealogical philosopher strives to impose a perspective on reality whose 'truth' is dependent only on the vigour with which it is affirmed and enforced. Foucault, however, wishes to detach his genealogy from power, by portraying it as a combination of 'specialised areas of erudition' with 'disqualified popular knowledge', as entertaining the 'claims to attention of local, discontinuous, disqualified, illegitimate knowledges'.[74] This separating out from the supposedly unbreakable unity of power-knowledge of a false knowledge linked to power and authentic knowledge linked to resistance seems to imply the reinstatement of a form of *Ideologiekritik*. But in fact this logically required realignment does not take place, since this would imply the ability of subjects to reflect critically on the disjunction between their experience and the categories of power-knowledge, rather than the capacity for reflection being itself a product of power. Hence the critique of power-knowledge continues to lack an epistemological dimension: the experience of the oppressed, both directly expressed and relayed by genealogy, is not allowed to reveal the *inadequacy* of the representation of the social disseminated by power. Insurrectionary knowledges, Foucault suggests, 'are opposed primarily not to the contents, methods or concepts of a science, but to the effects of the centralizing powers which are linked to the institution and functioning of an organized scientific discourse within a society such as ours.'[75]

It will be apparent by now that Foucault's attempts to establish a non-contingent relation between power and knowledge on a Nietzschean basis cannot easily be squared with his political commitments. Foucault's strong, 'official' thesis is that power and knowledge directly imply one another; that 'there is no power relation without the correlative constitution of a field of knowledge, nor any knowledge that does not presuppose and constitute at the same time relations of power.'[76] Yet, in his specific historical and political discussions, the intimacy of this relation is not maintained. At times he defines this relation in terms of the institutional *preconditions* for the elaboration of a form of knowledge, at others in terms of the authority and prestige which accrue to the holder of a discourse *recognized* as true or scientific. On other occasions, as we have seen, Foucault severs the link between power and knowledge, and suggests either that the discourse of a specific human science is in fact delusive and incoherent, or that there can be forms of knowledge – including his own genealogy – which are on the side of resistance rather than that of power. The irony of this outcome is that what is, in itself, an important philosophical project – the attempt to decipher the relation between power and knowledge – risks discredit for lack of an adequate theoretical framework. The basic philosophical thrust of Foucault's position, that knowledge is not produced in the course of a disinterested quest for truth, and the core of his historical argument, that in modern societies a panoply of forms of information, theorization and analysis which are not *simply* ideological – and which he groups together as the 'human sciences' – are a central element in techniques of social management and social control, demand to be taken seriously. Yet what Foucault's work of the 1970s reveals is that a coherent account of the human sciences and their historical role cannot be developed if all problems of validity are bracketed. The *epoche* which Foucault attempts to perform with regard to the epistemological status of the forms of knowledge which he analyses cannot be consistently carried out, since without an assessment of the truth of the discourse studied, the very object of investigation remains ill-defined, and the possibility of a political critique is undermined.

Foucault and Habermas

We have already observed a complex interplay of similarities and differences between Foucault's thought and the work of the classical Frankfurt School. This interplay becomes apparent once more in the epistemological dilemmas which we have just examined. For Horkheimer and Adorno, the critical standpoint cannot help but lay claim to truth – this is the constant objection which the Frankfurt School make to a Mannheimian sociology of knowledge – yet, confronted with the totalization of instrumental reason, there appears to be no point within existing reality on which immanent critique could gain a purchase, no standard in

terms of which existing forms of knowledge and consciousness could be classified as ideological, as untrue. Following
Nietzsche, although a different aspect of Nietzsche from that
emphasized by Foucault, the foundations of the delusiveness of
identifying and objectifying thought are laid at such a deep
anthropological level, in the fundamental need for control over
nature, that even critical thought appears unable to escape from
the same delusion, to establish an autonomous basis. From the
early 1940s onwards this dilemma becomes a major preoccupation of the Frankfurt School, culminating in *Negative Dialectics*, where the problem of turning conceptual thought against
itself becomes a central concern. As Adorno writes: 'The utopia of
knowledge would be to open up the non-conceptual with concepts,
without making it equivalent to them.'[77] Within such a framework,
social science can at best play the role of an auxiliary discipline,
subservient to philosophical cognition, and under constant ideological suspicion.

Foucault could be said to react to a similar problem with a diametrically opposite solution. Rather than empirical science being
subordinated to a philosophical meditation on the *possibility* of
truth, social theory and historical investigation are liberated from
the philosophy's claims to truth and totality, which now rather
become part of the object to be investigated. Thus, Foucault is no
longer obliged to engage in the intricate operation of turning
concepts of truth and reason against themselves, in order to
salvage their clandestine emancipatory potential. Rather, he
believes it possible to write the history of truth without being
committed to a truth about history, to analyse historical structures
of rationality, without being committed to any normative
conception of what reason might be.[78] The result of this move is to
open up to Foucault a wide field of detailed historical investigations – the concreteness and specificity of Foucault's work is
often brought forward as a decisive advantage in comparisons
with the Frankfurt School. Yet, at the same time, it involves Foucault in the kinds of perpetual oscillations which we have just
examined – between subjectivism and objectivism, between the
critical and the normatively neutral.

One way of understanding Habermas's work is as an attempt to
steer between these two equally undesirable alternatives. Like
Foucault, he wishes to escape from the spiralling movement of a
perpetual reflexive critique, towards a concrete understanding of
society and history. Yet, unlike Foucault, he does not believe that
this escape can be secured by an arbitrary refusal of self-reflection,

and the adoption of a conscious perspectivism. Rather, Habermas's solution is to develop a more differentiated concept of knowledge, which will account for both its oppressive functioning and its emancipatory potential, while at the same time securing the legitimate function of empirical social science within a critical social theory. The basic strategy of differentiation which Habermas develops in his earlier work is most clearly presented in *Knowledge and Human Interests*. It is significant that, whereas Horkheimer and Adorno proceed by means of a philosophy of history, employing the concept of 'self-preservation' to illuminate the course of social development, and whereas Foucault proceeds dogmatically, treating power in the manner of a metaphysical substrate, Habermas proceeds quasi-transcendentally. All three positions share a common assumption that scientific knowledge is grounded in prescientific interests, yet Habermas seeks to justify this assumption by pushing the *immanent* exposition of the logic of the sciences to the point at which methodological distinctions are revealed as basic differences of world-orientation. As a result, while agreeing with both Foucault and the first generation Frankfurt School that an interest in technical control guides the formation of what he terms 'empirical-analytic knowledge', which is oriented towards the formulation of causal laws, he argues that there is also an interest in intersubjective understanding which constitutes a different categorial framework, defining knowledge which is 'hermeneutic' rather than 'empirical-analytic'. For Habermas, the relations of language, action and experience differ in principle in the two forms of knowledge: 'Empirical analysis discloses reality from the viewpoint of possible technical control over objectified processes, while hermeneutics maintains the intersubjectivity of possible action-orienting mutual understanding.'[79] Habermas, however, denies that this position entails a pragmatic relativism, since these interests cannot simply be set aside. Any society must both be able to reproduce itself materially through work, and to maintain structures of action coordinated through mutual understanding, so that for Habermas the term *interests* denotes 'the basic orientations rooted in specific fundamental conditions of the possible reproduction and self-constitution of the human species, namely *work* and *interaction*.'[80] The 'cognitive interests' may therefore be described as 'quasi-transcendental': they cannot be gone behind if we wish to acquire knowledge of nature or to understand other human beings via their symbolic expressions, yet they are, at the same time, rooted in the specific, contingent natural history of humankind.

On the basis of this distinction between work and interaction, and their respective cognitive interests, Habermas is able to develop, during the 1960s, an account of modern capitalist society which theorizes many of the features which Foucault also highlights, without falling into the philosophical contradictions of Foucault's account. In his well-known essay on 'Technology and Science as Ideology' Habermas registers the shift from ideological forms of legitimation to a 'technocratic consciousness' which is ' "less ideological" ' than all previous ideologies' since 'it does not have the opaque force of a delusion which only transfigures the implementation of interests', and which is therefore 'more irresistible and further reaching than ideologies of the old type'.[81] The pervasiveness of this technocratic consciousness may be compared with the pervasiveness of knowledge-power in Foucault's thought: both are signalled by the transformation of ever more domains of social life into objects of manipulation and control. Because of his awareness of this process Habermas – no less than Foucault – warns against a confusion of 'the democratisation of the forms and a growing anonymity of the exercise of political domination with the actual dismantling of repressive force'.[82]

Yet, at the same time, Habermas can avoid Foucault's dilemma – either power-knowledge constitutes the social, in which case there is no basis for resistance, or the social has an autonomous dynamic, in which case power-knowledge is neither power nor knowledge – by suggesting that the pervasive 'non-ideological' character of technocratic consciousness is grounded in a systematic *categorial* confusion, in a form of knowledge which is not illusory, but which misunderstands the validity-basis of its own propositions. Social technology depends upon the application of the methods of empirical-analytical sciences, oriented to prediction and control, to the social domain, and although the laws and regularities which it discovers are objective, this objectivity is the 'pseudo-objectivity' of social processes which remain opaque to the subjects by whom they are sustained. Social technologies transform human subjects into objects of manipulation, screening out their ability to reflect upon, to transform and collectively to determine their own situation. 'It is a singular achievement of this ideology', Habermas suggests, 'to detach society's self-understanding from the frame of reference of communicative action . . . and to replace it with a scientific model. Accordingly the culturally defined self-understanding of a social life-world is replaced by the self-reification of men under categories of purposive-rational action and adaptive behaviour.'[83]

During the 1970s, Habermas does make some substantial alterations to this model, culminating in his *Theory of Communicative Action* (1981). Although he continues to insist on the basic viability of the schema of cognitive interests, he now prefers to proceed by means of a closer analysis of linguistic intersubjectivity and its normative conditions, which reveals that there can be no monological validation of cognitive-instrumental thought: all validity-claims are referred to intersubjective agreement. A further development, which could in one respect be seen as a move towards Foucault's position, occurs with Habermas's conscious appropriation of systems theory. For Habermas's intention, here, is to correct the assumption, which has deep roots in the Marxist tradition, that in an emancipated society *all* social structures and relations could be brought back within the horizon of the life-world: his insistence of the necessary differentiation of system and life-world in modernity seems to parallel Foucault's suspicion of reconciliation, and his insistence of the ineliminability of relations of power. However, Habermas's distinction between the differentiation of aspects of reason in modernity and the differentiation of system and life-world also has anti-Foucauldian implications. For this distinction makes clear that there is no fatality of reason as such, which threatens to become total as instrumental reason in the manner which both Foucault and the first generation Frankfurt School suggest. Foucault, Habermas argues, is correct to emphasize the damaging effects of the bureaucratic administration of welfare and social justice. But what is at stake here is not the central organizing principle of modernity, opposed to the ramshackle systems of pre-modern power, but rather a *contradictory* attempt, the expression of a class-compromise, to bring forth new and more egalitarian life-forms by legal and bureaucratic means. This contradiction appears in the inherent resistance of social domains which are communicatively structured to commodification and bureaucratizaion. There is a dynamic of egalitarian solidarity which, although damaged and repressed, is no less central to modernity than the functional dynamic of money or power.[84]

Ultimately, of course, the strength of Habermas's position depends upon his ability to demonstrate the normative content of intersubjectivity – this is a question to which we shall be returning in conclusion. For the time being, it is sufficient to note that, for Foucault, the structure of intersubjectivity must be ruled out a priori as a principle of resistance, since he believes all subjectivity to be a product of power. Thus, in *Discipline and Punish*,

Foucault describes panoptic power as 'a technique of overlapping subjectification and objectification', as 'the subjection of those who are perceived as objects and the objectification of those who are subjected'.[85] Even later still, Foucault described his whole intellectual itinerary in terms of this correlation between the formation of object-domains and the constitution of subjects: 'My work has dealt with three modes of objectification which transform human beings into subjects. The first is the modes of enquiry which try to give themselves the status of sciences; for example, the objectivizing of the speaking subject in *grammaire générale*, philology and linguistics . . . In the second part of my work, I have studied the objectivizing of the subject in what I shall call "dividing practices". The subject is either divided inside himself or divided from others. This process objectivizes him. Examples are the mad and the sane, the sick and the healthy, the criminals and the "good boys". Finally I have sought to study . . . the way a human being turns him- or herself into a subject. For example, I have chosen the domain of sexuality – how men have learned to recognize themselves as subjects of "sexuality".'[86]

This retrospective, however, is fundamentally confused in its reliance on the notion of 'modes of objectification which transform human beings into subjects', since a domain of reality can only be objectified *for* a pre-existing subject. In his historical investigations Foucault sometimes appears to appreciate this. *Madness and Civilization*, for example, argues that it is only because the citizens of the bourgeois state acknowledge each other as possessors of a consciousness (and conscience) which is at once both 'private and universal', that the insane can become the targets of techniques designed to restore them to rational subjectivity, and the objects of the concomitant forms of knowledge. 'As the sole sovereign of the bourgeois state,' Foucault writes, 'the free man becomes the first judge of madness.'[87] The importance which Foucault attaches to the passage from the first *Meditation* in which doubt as to one's own sanity is excluded by Descartes from the procedure of hyperbolic doubt, makes clear that the self-reflection of the individual as epistemic subject is the *condition* for the objectification of the insane.[88] Indeed, one of the reasons why Foucault's panoptic gaze tends to take on the characteristics of a transcendent meta-subject is that Foucault implicitly appreciates that the totality of social individuals can only be objectified for a subject. Even if the panoptic metaphor were accepted, however, Foucault's contention that subjects can be forged through objectification, through a non-reciprocal operation of power, is incoherent. A human being can only acquire the competences which transform her or him into a speaking and acting subject through interaction with other subjects: the identity of the self is constituted through an entry into social roles, but these roles can themselves only be acquired through identifications, not with the actual behaviour of others, but with symbolically – above all linguistically – mediated models of behaviour. Foucault's account of a monstrously unidirectional surveillance, of a strict separation of seer and seen, fails to register the fact that socialization, the formation of subjects, depends upon a mutual recognition of subjects, however distorted. Thus, throughout his work, Foucault has correctly stressed the increasing individualization of subjects in modern society, yet is unable to explain this process except as the result of an ever-closer observation and tighter definition of the individual by power. In this respect Foucault's work reproduces, in a different form, the error of Horkheimer and Adorno, when – in *Dialectic of Enlightenment* – they attempt to explain the formation of the self entirely in terms of an instrumental encounter with nature. In neither case is the reciprocity specific to the social domain as such given adequate theoretical recognition.[89]

It is worth noting, however, that Foucault's work is not entirely without trace of a normatively weighted contrast between a state of reciprocity and a state of unilateral surveillance and control. As we have seen, *Madness and Civilization* recounts the history of a progressive distanciation of reason and folly, which culminates in the regime of observation of the modern asylum. For Foucault, this observation is 'deeper and less reciprocal' than that which occurred during the Classical Age, when 'the sane man could read in the madman, as in a mirror, the imminent moment of his downfall'.[90] Foucault's qualified approval of Freud, expressed towards the end of the same book, is based specifically upon the fact that psychoanalysis reintroduced a measure of reciprocity into the relation between sanity and madness – indeed, Foucault argues that Freud did not go far enough. In *Discipline and Punish*, nearly fifteen years later, a similar contrast appears between the 'ambiguous rituals' of the public execution and the regimentation of the prison. 'In these executions,' Foucault writes, 'which ought to show only the terrorizing power of the prince, there was a whole aspect of the carnival, in which rules were inverted, authority mocked and criminals transformed into heroes.'[91] Foucault's very tone clearly betrays his preference for 'the ceremony of the public execution . . . that uncertain festival in which violence was instantaneously reversible' over the 'gentle efficacy of total surveillance';[92] indeed, most tellingly, he remarks that the prisoner within the panoptic system 'is seen, but he does not see; he is the object of information, never a subject in communication'.[93] In general, however, the reciprocity which Foucault evokes is not a reciprocity of communication between equal subjects, but a reciprocity of force which remains embedded within a hierarchy. 'Confinement, prisons, dungeons, even tortures,' Foucault remarks in *Madness and Civilization*, 'engaged in a mute dialogue between reason and unreason – the dialogue of struggle. With the advent of the asylum, however, this dialogue itself was now disengaged; silence was absolute.'[94] Thus, although the concept of reciprocity does play an implicitly critical role in Foucault's work, this is not a non-coercive reciprocity which could be made the goal of political struggle. Rather, it is a reciprocity of struggle which has now been replaced by an enforced tranquility; its effect is to make the social order of the present appear even more hopelessly unilateral and oppressive. Foucault's critique of modernity is essentially a backward-looking one.

7

Foucault and Lyotard:
The Politics of Truth

In our discussions of the work of Lyotard and Foucault, we have
traced the fate of two attempts to introduce a more explicitly political dimension into post-structuralist thought, through a challenge to the primacy of language or the 'symoblic order'. Yet, in
both cases, this attempt – indispensable in itself – was seen to lead
to intractable difficulties. Lyotard begins from an insistence on
the heterogeneity – and incompatibility – of figure and discourse,
as a means of countering the Lacanian conception of the unconscious as 'structured like a language', yet his very stress on the
irreconcilability of the two orders leads, in a series of apparently
ineluctable stages, to the total displacement of critique by affirmation in *Économie Libidinale*. Similarly, Foucault introduces the
concept of power as an explicit counter to semiological models of
the social, arguing that 'the history which bears and determines us
has the form of a war rather than that of a language: relations of
power, not relations of meaning.'[1] Although Foucault is never
tempted even to experiment with an 'affirmative' position – always
preserving, even if in an oblique and inexplicit manner, an antagonism between power and its other – he is nevertheless driven into
inconsistency, as we have seen, in his attempts to prevent this
political antagonism from becoming also an epistemological one.
Foucault resists the suggestion that the 'untruth' of power-
knowledge is revealed from the standpoint of resistance, insisting
rather that all regimes of power are also regimes of truth.

In both cases, the deepest motivation for these lines of argument
is undoubtedly a political resistance to the standpoint of critical
totalization, which is understood as involving an attempt to reveal
the determinations, and in so doing appropriate the truth-content,

of all other partial standpoints, on the basis of an anticipation of a future, non-antagonistic society. This resistance – which can justly be described as one of the *leitmotifs* of post-structuralism – is grounded in the conviction that the standpoint of totalization is inherently oppressive. In Foucault's case, this conviction is made manifest in the assumption that the standpoint of totalization is necessarily that of the Panopticon. Throughout his work, he connects the revolutionary ideal of a 'transparent' society, a society whose mechanisms are comprehensible to its members, with programmes of total surveillance. Thus, in a discussion of the political themes of the French Revolution, Foucault suggests that 'the reign of "opinion", so often invoked at this time, represents a mode of operation through which power will be exercised by virtue of the mere fact of things being known and people seen in a sort of immediate, collective and anonymous gaze . . . If Bentham's project aroused interest, this was because it provided a formula applicable to many domains, the formula of "power through transparency", subjection by "illumination".'[2] It is this conviction which leads Foucault to disagree with a young interlocutor in a political conversation dating from 1971. In response to Foucault's stress on the 'amazing efficacy of discontinuous, particular and local criticism', Foucault's partner replies that: 'I can't believe that the movement must remain in its present phase, in this vague, disjointed ideology of the *underground* . . . At this level, the groups remain incapable of taking on the whole of society and, ultimately of conceiving it as a whole.' Foucault rejects this argument, however: 'We readily believe that the least we can expect of our experiences, actions and strategies are projects which take account of the "whole of society"; this would be the minimum required for their existence. I think on the contrary that this would be to ask the maximum of them; that it would thus be to impose on them an impossible condition; since the "whole of society" functions precisely in such a way that these actions can neither take place, nor succeed, nor perpetuate themselves. The "whole of society" is that which we need not take account of, except as an objective to be destroyed.'[3] Consequently, Foucault repeatedly denies any intention of providing a comprehensive theory of history or society, and lays stress on the contrast between the 'disordered and fragmentary' character of his own genealogies and the 'tyranny of globalizing discourses with their hierarchy and all their privileges of a theoretical *avant-garde* . . . '[4]

In Lyotard's work, a similar suspicion of totalizing critique develops from his article on the concept of alienation in Marxism onwards, although here opposition can be said to focus on the problems of critique, rather than of totalization. In his final 'Marxist' essay, Lyotard continues to advocate a 'practical critique' of capitalist society, while arguing that no theoretical critique has the right to serve as a basis for the organization and direction of political tasks, and rejecting any conception of Marxist theory as the coming-to-consciousness of objective contradictions.[5] However, having rejected this dialectical account of the status of Marxism, Lyotard is directly confronted with the problem of what the theoretical superiority of the Marxist standpoint could be based on. It is not surprising, therefore, that by 1972 he has concluded that the very concept of critique implies an unjustifiable claim to pre-eminence over what is criticized: 'critical activity is an activity of selection: a certain experience, a certain declaration, a certain work, a certain libidinal position is displayed in its insufficiency, denied therefore, seen from the standpoint of its limit and not of its affirmativity, challenged to match up to the object of desire of the critic, in other words, to infinity, to universality, to necessity . . . from where does the critic draw his power over what is criticized? he *knows* better? he is the professor, the educator? so he is universality, the university, the state, the city, leaning over childhood, nature, singularity, the dubious, in order to raise it to his own level? the confessor and God helping the sinner to be saved?'[6] In the text from which this quotation is taken, Lyotard has also already formulated the argument which will be central to *Économie Libidinale*, that the critical standpoint, concerned only with the limits of a perspective, robs that perspective of its intrinsic force: 'it is not true that a political, philosophical or artistic position is abandoned because it is ''superseded'', it is not true that the experience of a position signifies ineluctably the development of its entire content to the point of exhaustion, and thus of its growing over into another position in which it is conserved and suppressed . . .'[7] Lyotard wishes to prevent an irreducible plurality of perspectives from being seen against the background of the 'great totalizing Zero'.

In both Lyotard's thought and that of Foucault, it is clear that the fundamental objects of attack are the political and philosophical positions of the Hegelianized Marxism which was a powerful influence on French intellectual life throughout the 1950s and into the 1960s. In Lyotard's case, the break with this form of Marxism came much later than in that of Foucault, since Lyotard – as we have seen – does not truly move into the mainstream of post-structuralist thought until the early 1970s. Nevertheless, the difficulties encountered, and the types of solution proposed, are broadly similar. Furthermore, in both cases, it is Nietzsche who provides the inspiration for a post-Hegelian and post-Marxist position. In an interview dating from 1969, Foucault remarks that 'As regards the influence which Nietzsche has had on me, it would be difficult to be specific, precisely because I realize how deep it has been. I will just say that, ideologically, I remained a "historicist" and Hegelian until I read Nietzsche.'[8] Similarly, Lyotard moves toward Nietzsche as he beings to suspect Marxism of an inevitable complicity with power, in search of the 'attitude of powerlessness' which – he believes – 'Nietzsche tries to maintain in the face of all powers, and which puts him in a position to detect them.'[9] In both cases, what Nietzsche is assumed to have made possible is a critical standpoint which does not rely on a conception of the meaningfulness, rationality and unity of a process within which the criticized object can be situated, and the extent and limits of its truth thereby determined. Rather, Nietzsche shows any conception of an immanent order of the world to be a creation of the will to power. We must therefore turn once again to Nietzsche in order to understand the basis of post-structuralist attempts to establish an oppositional position which does not depend upon an anticipation of harmony, or a 'metaphysical' interpretation of the totality.

Nietzsche on Truth

During what is sometimes referred to as the 'positivist' phase of his work, which stretches from *Human, All too Human* until the concluding sections of *The Gay Science*, Nietzsche's thought is basically sympathetic to the attitude of scientific Enlightenment. Religious and metaphysical systems, all concepts of the world as the 'epitome of an eternal rationality',[10] are to be traced back to their origins in human drives, fears and aspirations, and their historical transformations. The ideal of science plays a dual role in this conception. Firstly, the meticulousness and caution of the scientific attitude, the refusal to be seduced into belief by considerations of human happiness, and the abandonment of unanswerable questions concerned with the overall purpose and meaning of the world, provides a means of exposing the illusions of traditional world-views. 'It is the mark of a higher culture', Nietzsche suggests in *Human, All Too Human*, 'to prize small, inapparent truths discovered by strict method more highly than the gladdening, blinding errors which stem from metaphysical and artistic ages and men.'[11] And secondly, scientific procedure offers a means of explaining the origins of these age-long illusions, on the basis of a thorough-going naturalism. Even after the 'positivist' phase of his work, this attitude remains a permanent strand in Nietzsche's thought, so that – as late as *Beyond Good and Evil* – he can present his task as being 'to confront man henceforth with man in the way in which, hardened by the discipline of science, man today confronts the rest of nature, with dauntless Oedipus eyes and stopped up Odysseus ears, deaf to the siren songs of the old metaphysical birdcatchers who have all too long been piping to him "you are more! you are higher! you are of a different origin!"'.'[12]

But although Nietzsche is prepared to employ science as a weapon against religion and metaphysics, he cannot accept the assumption of nineteenth-century positivism that science alone can provide an answer to the problem of the aims and meaning of human existence. Towards the end of *The Gay Science*, Nietzsche suggests that 'It follows from the laws of hierarchy that scholars, in so far as they belong to the middle rank, may not even come into view of the truly great problems and questions.'[13] Nietzsche's own problems are problems of the totality, of the ultimate nature and purpose of the world and of the place of human life within it, and he is thus obliged to condemn the myopia of science, while unable to ignore the undermining by modern science of traditional claims to knowledge of the whole. Already in the *Philosophenbuch*, written – though not published – in the wake of *The Birth of Tragedy*, Nietzsche is centrally concerned with this dilemma, conscious that 'absolute and unconditional knowledge is wishing to know without knowledge',[14] while unable to deny the immense power and value – indeed the necessity – of philosophical systems. And already he outlines his characteristic solution to this dilemma, in which the energy with which a viewpoint is affirmed becomes the criterion of its validity. 'The philosopher', he suggests, 'is filled with the highest pathos of truth: the value of his knowledge guarantees its truth for him. All fruitfulness and all driving forces reside in this gaze turned towards the future.'[15]

Ultimately, Nietzsche resolves the tension of his relation to science by suggesting that science itself is a continuation of metaphysics, in so far as it embodies the belief in the possibility of an exhaustive and uniquely true account of the world. The infinity of the world which Nietzsche – in his third phase – reasserts against the immodesty and naivety of science, is no longer the religious infinity of a transcendent reality, but the interminable proliferation of perspectives: 'The world has rather become "infinite" for us again, in so far as we cannot banish the possibility that it encloses endless interpretations within itself.'[16] Part of the basis of Nietzsche's attempt to overcome 'nihilism', the spiritual desolation resulting from the loss of a transcendent meaning of existence, is the acceptance that all cognition and all evaluation is perspectival, that the world as a whole cannot be appraised or known. The assumption is not novel in Nietzsche, of course, since it is expressed by the counterposition of the Dionysiac and Apollonian principles in *The Birth of Tragedy*. Here Nietzsche suggests that although it is only through the ordering and simplifying activity of the Apollonian principle that the world can be grasped at all, the result of this activity must always be accompanied by a marginal awareness of illusion. By its very nature, the Dionysian 'primal unity' (*Ureine*) which overflows all boundaries and erases all distinctions cannot be grasped in itself, yet it remains the backdrop against which the deceptive, dreamlike quality of Apollonian consciousness is revealed. For Nietzsche, this tension cannot be resolved by conceiving the task of philosophy as the comprehension of the inner logic of a succession of perspectives, considered as moments of truth to be integrated into an historical whole. The thrust of Nietzsche's invocation of the Dionysian – or of 'life' – as the ultimate principle of reality is to block any such cumulative ordering: life is inherently multifarious and contradictory, 'there would be no life at all if not on the basis of perspective evaluations and appearances'.[17] The notion of life implies contradictions that cannot be mediated.

If no perspective can claim ultimate validity, however, then the problem of the correct philosophical standpoint is raised for Nietzsche himself. Nietzsche has a two-stage answer to this problem, both aspects of which have been influential on poststructuralism. The lack of an ultimate perspective must first be compensated for by a tireless variation of perspectives, none of which lays claim to absolute validity. In *On the Genealogy of Morals*, Nietzsche argues that 'There is *only* a perspective seeing, *only* a perspective "knowing"; and the *more* affects we allow to speak of one thing, the *more* eyes, different eyes, we can use to observe one thing, the more complete will our "concept" of this thing, our "objectivity", be.'[18] Even this multiple approach to the object, however, is ultimately portrayed by Nietzsche as a training and preparation for the true philosophical task of commitment and creation. Throughout his work, art functions as a model for this task, since – in the absence of any ultimate truth – art is the form of representation which acknowledges its own illusory nature.

'Art treats appearance as appearance', Nietzsche remarks in the *Philosophenbuch*, 'therefore intends precisely *not* to deceive, is true . . .'[19] Accordingly, the task of the philospher is not to discover, but rather to decree, not to reveal truths, but rather to render true: 'Authentic philosophers . . . are commanders and law-givers: they say "thus it shall be!", it is they who determine the Wherefore and Wither of mankind . . . Their "knowing" is *creating*, their creating is a law-giving, their will to truth is – *will to power*.[20]

Perspectivism in Foucault and Lyotard

It is significant that, almost at the beginning of his career, in an essay called 'Nietzsche, Freud, Marx', Foucault takes up a position which stresses the irreducible pluralism of interpretation, and portrays Nietzsche as the most determined exponent of this pluralism. Foucault begins by contrasting the closed world of resonances and resemblances imagined by Renaissance science, with the open-endedness of modern hermeneutics, most clearly exemplified – he argues – in the work of Marx, Nietzsche and Freud. Since the work of these three thinkers, he suggests, 'There is nothing absolutely first to interpret, because, at bottom, everything is already interpretation, every sign is itself not the thing which is offered to interpretation, but an interpretation of other signs.'[21] But although Foucault discerns the same interpretation of interpretation in Marx, Freud and Nietzsche, it is clear that he considers Nietzsche's thought to be the most consistent in its following through of the implications of this view. Foucault contrasts semiology, which he defines as the belief that 'there are signs . . . which exist primarily, originally, and truly as coherent, pertinent and systematic marks' with a hermeneutics which believes that 'the life of interpretation . . . is to believe that there are only interpretations,'[22] and, foreshadowing the arguments of the 1970s, he goes on to claim that 'A hermeneutics which bases itself on a semiology believes in the absolute existence of signs: it abandons the violence, the incompleteness, the infinity of interpretations, in order to promote the reign of terror of the index, and to cast suspicion on language'.[23] This, he suggests, has been the fate of Marxism after Marx. However, Foucault is unwilling to go as far as Deleuze, who affirms in *Nietzsche and Philosophy* that 'To be walking with one's feet in the air is not something with which one dialectician can reproach another, it is the fundamental character of the dialectic itself.'[24] In a clear dissension from

Deleuze's view, Foucault denies that talk of setting the dialectic on its feet is meaningless, yet also wishes to eliminate any suggestion of an ultimate resolution of contradictions: 'If this expression has any meaning, it would be that of having put back into the density of the sign, into this open, endless, gaping space, into this space without real content or reconciliation, the entire play of negativity which the dialectic had – in the end – disarmed by giving it a positive meaning.'[25]

During the 1960s Foucault's insistence on the endlessness of the hermeneutic process, in 'Nietzsche, Freud, Marx' and elsewhere, cannot be easily squared with his claims for the objectivity of his own archaeologies: the tension here is similar to that in the work of Nietzsche himself, between commitment to a scientific study of the historical determination of forms of thought, and an awareness that science itself is simply one more form of illusion. Nietzsche attempts to escape from this dilemma, as we have seen, by arguing for the intrinsically perspectival character of 'life', which – in his later work – is theorized more systematically in terms of the conflicts and metamorphoses of the will to power. In the transformation which Foucault's thought undergoes between the 1960s and the 1970s, a similar move can be detected. During the 1960s Foucault had attempted to block evolutionary and teleological conceptions of history by arguing that objective investigation revealed history to be discontinuous, at least on the level of systems of thought. Already in *The Archaeology of Knowledge*, however, this strategy is clearly breaking down under the impact of criticism of the illusory coherence and independence of the *epistemai* analysed in *The Order of Things*, and, by the early 1970s, Foucault is attempting to evade these criticisms – while still blocking any concept of rational progress – by appealing to the notion of a play of forces which itself resists any ultimate interpretation.

The *locus classicus* of this argument, and the pace-setter for Foucault's work of the 1970s, is the essay on 'Nietzsche, Genealogy, History', first published in 1971. Here Foucault's aim is still to reveal the illusory nature of those 'transcendental teleologies' which he believes to be fraught with political perils; he denies that concepts can be said to have an implicit content whose unfolding can be historically traced, preferring Nietzsche's suggestion that meaning and its transformations are entirely determined by local relations of forces: 'The isolation of different points of emergence does not conform to the successive configurations of an identical meaning; rather, they result from substitutions, displacements, disguised conquests, and systematic reversals. If interpretation were the slow exposure of the meaning hidden in an origin, then only metaphysics could interpret the development of humanity. But if interpretation is the violent or surreptitious appropriation of a system of rules, which in itself has no essential meaning . . . then the development of humanity is a series of interpretations.'[26] By adopting Nietzsche's conception of the primacy of force over meaning Foucault can oppose 'the hazardous play of dominations', the 'exteriority of accidents',[27] not only to notions of the rationality of, but to any conception of an immanent direction of history. 'The traditional devices for constructing a comprehensive view of history and for retracing the past as a patient and continuous development must', Foucault suggests, 'be dismantled.'[28] In particular, since no social consensus can be the expression of a shared interpretation of the world, rather than the result of a temporary equilibrium of forces, it can be affirmed that 'Humanity does not gradually progress from combat to combat until it arrives at universal reciprocity, where the rule of law finally replaces warfare; humanity installs each of its violences in a system of rules and thus proceeds from domination to domination.'[29]

But while this committed exegesis of Nietzsche confirms Foucault's earlier repudiation of the possibility of reconciliation as envisaged by the Hegelian-Marxist tradition, it equally marks a distance from the objectivism and positivism of the 1960s. Foucault now endorses a form of historiography, modelled on Nietzsche's 'effective history', whose aim is not to systematize, but rather to disperse and fragment the past: 'History becomes "effective" to the degree that it introduces discontinuity into our very being – as it divides our emotions, dramatizes our instincts, multiplies our body and sets it against itself.'[30] Effective history, furthermore, recognizing the impossibility of historical objectivity, is characterized by its 'affirmation of knowledge as perspective'. Nietzsche's version of historical sense', according to Foucault, 'is explicit in its perspective and acknowledges its system of injustice. Its perception is slanted, being a deliberate appraisal, affirmation, or negation. . . . It is not given to a discreet effacement before the objects it observes and does not submit itself to their processes; nor does it seek laws, since it gives equal weight to its own sight and to its objects.'[31] This endorsement of a self-conscious perspectivism is already a long way from Foucault's claim, during the later 1960s, to be countering metaphysical and teleological histories with a 'pure description of the facts of discourse':[32] the standpoint of his own enquiries is a problem which

Foucault will not be able entirely to ignore during the 1970s.

Foucault's conceptualization of history as composed of discontinuous structures, or – later – as a 'hazardous play of dominations' is directed against the philosophy of history, and – primarily – against the Marxist aim of comprehending the totality of past and present from the standponit of a future yet to be realized. Here Foucault's underlying fear, one which he shares with many liberal critics of Marxism, is that a theory which believes itself to have deciphered the movement of history will tend to encourage an authoritarian political practice which overrides moral qualms by means of an appeal to the inevitability of progress. Yet there is a deeper strand in Foucault's thought during the 1970s which is opposed not simply to philosophies of history, but to any systematic theory, even in a comparatively restricted domain. 'Concretely,' Foucault argues, in a lecture dating from 1976, 'it is not a semiology of the life of the asylum, it is not even a sociology of delinquency, that has made it possible to produce an effective criticism of the asylum and likewise of the prison, but rather the immediate emergence of historical contents. And this is simply because only the historical contents allow us to rediscover the ruptural effects of conflict and struggle that the order imposed by functionalist or systematizing thought is designed to mask.'[33] Foucault's objections here are evidently based on the Nietzschean assumption that any systematic theory must inevitably simplify and falsify, with the corollary that such simplification – if taken as a guide for practical intervention – will encourage the attempt to force social reality to conform to its expectations. Thus Foucault speaks quite generally of 'the coercion of a theoretical, unitary, formal and scientific discourse',[34] and has no hesitation in including Marxism amongst those modes of thought which have 'the inhibiting effect of global, *totalitarian theories*', although he admits that it may provide 'useful tools for local research'.[35]

On an even more fundamental level, if Foucault refuses to draw any distinction between hermeneutic and objectifying, dialectical and positivist, social theory, whereas Critical Theory counterposes the former to the latter, this is because science, in modern societies, is considered as the pre-eminent vehicle of truth, and Foucault implies that any truth-claim – regardless of the theoretical status of the discourse involved – must embody a claim to power. This suggestion first appears in *The Order of Discourse*, where Foucault lists the *division* between the true and the false, along with the *prohibition* of discourses and the *separation* between reason and madness, as one of the three 'systems of exclusion'. Foucault admits that, at first sight, it appears inplausible to align the 'constraint of truth' with partitions which are 'arbitrary from the very beginning or which at the least are organized around historical contingencies';[36] yet he goes on to suggest that even the distinction between the true and the false must ultimately be considered as arbitrary and contingent, although its contingency has become ever more deeply obscured in the course of history. Foucault perceives the first step in this concealment in the emergence of philosophy from poetry and myth: 'Still, for the Greek poets of the sixth century, true discourse – in the strong and valorized sense of the word – the true discourse for which one had respect and terror, to which it was necessary to submit, because it reigned, was the discourse pronounced by whoever had the right and according to the stipulated ritual.'[37] Between Hesiod and Plato, however, this status is transformed: 'a century later the highest truth no longer resided in what discourse *was* or in what it *did*: the day arrived when truth was displaced from the ritualized efficacious and just act, from the utterance towards the statement itself: towards its meaning, its form, its object, its relation to its reference.'[38] For Foucault, however, this separation of criteria of truth from the recognition of an actual power and authority is merely apparent. Even in the case of modern science, which Foucault considers to be the result of the latest mutation in a 'will to knowledge' inaugurated by Greek philosophy, the very meaning of propositions is inseparable from the systems of practices with which scientific discourse is interwoven, so that to comprehend propositions as candidates for truth or falsity is already to have acquiesced in specific institutional arrangements, and – as we have seen – for Foucault such arrangements must always crystallize an unequal relation of forces. 'Truth', Foucault suggests, a few years after *The Order of Discourse*, 'is linked in a circular relation with systems of power which produce and sustain it, and to effects of power which it induces and which extend it. A "regime of truth".'[39]

As might be expected, given the symmetries which we have already noted between their philosophical positions, Foucault's account of the immanent connection between truth and power is paralleled, in Lyotard's work of the 1970s, by a similar link between truth and desire. In an essay on the painter René Guiffrey, Lyotard rehearses the classic Nietzschean argument for the impossibility of ultimate truth: 'In truth, there is no such thing as a lie, except measured by the standard of the desire for truth, but this desire is no truer than any other desire, and the paradox does not state what is really the vicious circle of the lie, but the circulation of masks which do not mask anything, beneath none of which can be discovered, at last, at first, the face itself.'[40] However, whereas Foucault is primarily concerned with the implications of the ultimate arbitrariness of criteria of truth for our view of the human sciences, Lyotard is much more concerned with the repercussions on philosophy itself. Thus, whereas Foucault takes science as the paradigmatic modern form of a discourse which conceals its own motivation ('the will to truth, as it has imposed itself on us for a long time, is such that the truth which it wills cannot help but mask it'[41]), Lyotard considers theory, by which he understands less the individual sciences than philosophical discourse claiming to provide an apodictic, universal, and systematic foundation for knowledge, as a form of fiction which denies its own fictive status, as a *dispositif pulsionnel* which refuses to acknowledge itself as such. Lyotard's initial task, therefore, is to reveal the structure of libidinal investment which characterizes theory, a task which he attempts to carry out in the concluding chapter of *Économie Libidinale*.

Here Lyotard suggests that theoretical discourse is characterized by the demand for clarity and consistency: whether an object falls under a particular concept, whether a judgment is true or false must be unambiguously decidable: 'every statement advances into pathos in order to separate the this and the not-this, advances therefore armed with a cutter, a double-edged blade, and cuts.'[42] However, because 'each segment of the libidinal band is absolutely singular', the attempt to divide up the band into conceptual identities 'implies the denial of disparities, of heterogeneities, of transits and stases of energy, it implies the denial of polymorphy.'[43] A theoretical text may therefore be described as an 'immobilized organic body'. Lyotard admits that a discourse which tells a story may form a similar unified body, but points out that theoretical discourse is distinguished from narrative-figurative discourse by the fact that the totality which it constitutes is not situated at the pole of reference, but becomes one with the theoretical text itself. Lyotard suggests that, between these two poles, abstract painting constitutes an intermediate case. But whereas, in the case of abstraction which has not degenerated into mere system, 'the apparent immobility, insignificant for an eye which takes no pleasure in it, of the patterns of points, lines, surfaces, colours, is precisely what desire makes movement out of' – a movement on the surface of the canvas which contrasts with the immobilization of the spectator – in theoretical discourse this

movement tends towards stasis and repeatability, and is comple-
mented by the disconnection and emotional neutrality of producer
and consumer.[44] Even this indifference, however, must be interpreted libidinally. 'The notorious *universality* of knowledge,'
Lyotard writes, 'generally interpreted as an *a priori* condition of
theoretical discourse in its communicablity, is, understood in
terms of drives, a mark of the destruction of personal identities.'[45]

If Lyotard is to be consistent, then the analysis of theoretical
discourse as a *dispositif pulsionnel* cannot provide him with the
means to criticize the theoretical mode. Theory is characterized
not by its detachment from libidinal investments, but by the distinctive configuration of those investments: the disjunctive bar
which traces the libidinal band is – according to Lyotard – both
immobile *and* in rapid rotation, a paradox which is explained by
the fact that 'as disjunctive, it suspends all passage of energy from
the body-client to the body-text and vice versa: as animated, it
opens a passage onto the disjunctive function itself . . . it makes a
connection out of this disconnection.'[46] In theory, therefore, 'the
libidinal band appears at the very point where it seems excluded',[47]
and Lyotard is obliged to admit that 'we do not claim that [theory]
is an error, a perversion, an illusion, an ideology. If mimesis gives
you a hard-on, gentlemen, what could we have against it?'[48] At
the same time, Lyotard cannot entirely prevent a note of disappro-
bation from colouring his conclusions. Indeed, from the standpoint of an ontology of singularities theory *is* illusory since it
demands an elimination of the inherent dissimulation of libidinal
reality: 'Every fixation of a standard is related to a demand for
appropriation, it invests the disjunctive bar in its exclusive function, and induces the confusion of intensities and identities.'[49]

The conclusion of *Économie Libidinale* is largely concerned
with an analysis of theory as a closed deductive system of propositions based upon a small set of axioms. Lyotard seems to ignore
the fact that dialectical thought is also opposed to the fixed conceptual identities which he arraigns. In the essays written after
Économie Libidinale, however, and collected as *Rudiments
païens*, Lyotard's attention turns towards theories of the dialectical type, and, since this brings him closer to questions of politics,
his antagonism to the claims of theory becomes even fiercer. In an
essay on historical interpretations of the dechristianizing movement of 1793, Lyotard offers an ontology of socio-historical reality which parallels Foucault's views in 'Nietzsche, Genealogy,
History'. Just as Foucault suggests that history consists of 'a complex of distinct and multiple events, incapable of being mastered

by the powers of synthesis',[50] so Lyotard suggests that 'the political "body" is a monster composed of a unified body and of a plurality of drives which are incompatible with it and with each other'.[51] In opposition to the interpretation of Daniel Guérin, who portrays the dechristianization movement as in part a diversionary manoeuvre on the part of the Hérbertists, a means of channelling popular energies, in part a cathartic release from the age-old oppressive structures of which the church was an integral part,[52] Lyotard sees in the carnival antics of the dechristianizers the pure disorder of the drives, a mockery of all – even Republican – order. Guérin's interpretation, which suggests that the 'abolition' of religion was premature, since the misery for which religious belief compensates could not be eliminated by a merely bourgeois revolution, itself depends on belief in a 'beyond' termed socialism. All historical interpretations must, in the same way, ultimately rely upon a priori assumptions, and will involve a coercion and defusing of intensities unknown to reasonable history.[53] 'History, like politics,' Lyotard writes, 'seems to have need of a unique point of perspective, a place of synthesis, a head or eye enveloping the diversity of movements in the unification of a single volume: a synthesizing eye, but also an evil eye which strikes dead everything which does not enter its field of visibility.'[54]

Despite the distinction between the vocabulary of forces and power and that of libido and drives, the homology between the arguments of Lyotard and Foucault is unmistakable, as is their common ancestry in Nietzsche's insistence that 'life' – 'changeable and untamed and in everything a woman, and no virtuous one'[55] – cannot be grasped from any single, comprehensive perspective. However, because of Lyotard's more detailed interest in the question of philosophical claims to truth, there can be found in his work both a logical and a historical reflection on the problems of foundational philosophy which are missing from Foucault's writings. Foucault's case for relativism is based upon the historical variation of systems of thought, whereas Lyotard's logical case takes up the paradoxes of self-reference exemplified by the celebrated declaration of Epimenides the Cretan, by certain arguments of the Sophists and, in a twentieth-century form, by the difficulties encountered by Russell in the theory of classes. In an essay on the arguments of the Sophists, Lyotard suggests that the Platonic and Aristotelian opposition to Sophism is directed against 'a logical ruse which is also moral, political, economic; it simply consists in placing what presents itself as absolute, as the last word, in placing that in relation with itself'.[56] Russell's attempted solution to the paradoxes of self-reflexive statement, in the form of the theory of types, is of particular interest to Lyotard, since he sees the very arbitrariness of the theory of types – a theory which other philosophers have found singularly *ad hoc* and unconvincing – as an involuntary betrayal of the *coup de force* on which all attempts to provide criterial accounts of truth and rationality must be based. Thus his conclusion converges with that of Foucault, even if his mode of reaching it is different: 'All discourse of knowledge rests on a *decision*, namely that the two statements *the soup is served* and *it is true that the soup is served* do not belong to the same class and must be distinguishd. But this decision is not itself demonstrable. In other words, what is called the "paradox" of the Liar is not refutable; and by the same token the decision constituting the discourse of knowledge, constitutive of the constituting order, appears as a fact of power and as the power of a fact.'[57]

The Reflexive Problem

There is one obvious difficulty which theories such as those of Foucault and Lyotard, which espouse a perspectivist account of truth, and – furthermore – attempt to ground a conception of political practice in this account, must confront: the problem of their own status and validity as theories. Although Foucault cannot be said to pay any systematic attention to this problem, he does not neglect it entirely. As we have seen, during the 1960s he tends to understand his work as an objective analysis of the history of forms of knowledge, doubtless on the model of Nietzsche's historical philosophy, the 'youngest of all philosophical methods', which can 'no longer be thought of in separation from the natural sciences'.[58] Nietzsche's own formulation points to the unease and ambiguity of the conception, and Foucault is not unaware of the problems which his enterprise raises; indeed, in the conclusion of *The Archaeology of Knowledge*, he puts the most obvious objections into the mouth of an imaginary interlocutor: if Foucault has done no more than carry out an empirical enquiry, then he cannot avoid the 'naivety of all positivisms', while if he raises the question of the subject of knowledge, he will become entangled in the 'transcendental thought' from which he wishes to escape. Is his work history or philosophy?[59] Foucault's response to his imaginary interrogator, however, is somewhat evasive. He reiterates the anti-hermeneutic principles of archaeology, stresses that archaeology is connected to the sciences both by its objects ad its methods, although he does not claim for it the status of a science, and concludes by suggesting that 'in so far as it is possible to constitute a general theory of productions, archaeology, as the analysis of the rules proper to different discursive practices, will find what could be called its *enveloping theory.*'[60]

What is perhaps most striking about these formulations at the end of *The Archaeology of Knowledge* is the absence of any consideration of the relation between theory and practice: for Foucault, at this period, a practical intention can only be attributed to his opponents, whom he suspects of bolstering their own political prejudices with a philosophy of history. In the aftermath of May '68, however, when Foucault's historical studies of institutions took on a new political relevance, it was no longer possible entirely to avoid the question of theory and practice, and – as we have seen – Foucault begins to back away from his former objectivist position. Firstly, because he suspects, on Nietzschean grounds, that any system must betray the complexity of reality, he begins to stress the 'disordered and fragmentary' nature of his own researches, and explicitly renounces the striving for systematic unity: 'It will be no part of our concern', Foucault remarks, 'to provide a solid and homogeneous theoretical terrain for all these dispersed genealogies, nor to descend upon them from on high with some kind of halo of theory that would unite them.'[61] Only a thought which is itself not systematic could 'entertain the claims to attention of local, discontinuous, disqualified, illegitimate knowledges against the claims of a unitary body of theory which would filter, hierarchize and order them in the name of some true knowledge . . . '[62] Secondly, Foucault opposes to the representative function of the 'universal' intellectual – the intellectual 'taken as the clear, individual figure of a universality whose obscure, collective form is embodied in the proletariat'[63] – the notion of the 'specific' intellectual engaged in particular struggles in his or her workplace, whether asylum, hospital, laboratory or university. Insofar as these struggles have any general import, and insofar as the intellectual does develop theory, Foucault suggests that its validity must be interpreted instrumentally. Theory is merely a 'tool-kit' in the service of a particular struggle, and may be discarded as soon as it loses its utility.'[64]

Even setting aside the intrinsic – and intractable – difficulties of an instrumentalist reduction of theoretical truth-claims, it is doubtful whether Foucault ever seriously espoused such a position, which would entitle anyone with different political aims to reject his arguments out of hand. Indeed, Foucault does not even appear to adopt the weaker, Weberian position, according to which explanatory theories can be tested for truth or falsity, although theory-formation is always determined by specific interests and values, since he seems to understand the relation between political commitment and theory-construction simply as a relation of empirical motivation. 'If one is interested in doing historical work that has a political meaning, utility and effectiveness,' Foucault suggests, 'then this is possible only if one has some kind of involvement with the struggles taking place in the area in question.'[65] Indeed, it is clear that, behind this activist stance, Foucault never abandons his fundamental objectivism, since he immediately goes on to *distinguish between* truth and effectivity: 'The problem and the stake was the possibility of a discourse which would be both true and strategically effective, the possibility of a historical truth which could have a political effect.'[66] But if Foucault is claiming truth for his historical theories, while insisting on an immanent connection between truth and power, he can only be claiming recognition for the particular system of power with which his own discourse is bound up. The fundamental question which emerges at this point, therefore, a question which is central to Nietzsche's thought, is whether it is possible to secure assent to a discourse by mobilizing a persuasive force entirely disconnected from considerations of veracity. It is a measure of the perfunctory nature of Foucault's formulations on truth and power that he fails to pay attention to this problem. At one point Foucault describes a reciprocal, hermeneutic relation between truth and fiction in historical investigation,[67] but, for the most part, he seems content to assume that the mere label 'genealogy' is sufficient to free his work from the power-contamination of the 'human sciences' which it denounces.

Because he takes more seriously than Foucault the reflexive paradoxes involved in any account of the nature of truth – even an account as iconoclastic as that of Nietzsche – Lyotard tends to be more concerned with the problem of the status of his own discourse. In the opening essay of *Rudiments païens* he takes Freud's *Beyond the Pleasure Principle* as the model for a form of discourse which openly admits its own lack of ultimate grounds. Since, according to Freud's final dualism, all events which can be attributed to Eros can equally be attributed to the death drive, Freud himself is obliged to stress the speculative and uncertain nature of his own thought: the 'dissimulation' of the drives excludes any conclusive determination of causes. For Lyotard, however, this uncertainty does not reveal a defect in Freud's thought: 'It is not a weak conviction, or a *lack* of conviction which the economist of 1920 experiences, but an undecidability of affect, a positive power of affirmation alien to the question of belief.'[68] Yet simply to abandon theoretical discourse in favour of fiction, or to develop a philosophical critique of theory, would not resolve the problem, since this would either be to leave the pretensions of theory untouched by abandoning the terrain, or to remain on that terrain, and it is the 'desire for truth' expressed in theoretical discourse, Lyotard affirms, which 'feeds terrorism in everyone'.[69] The solution to this problem is to produce *théorie-fiction*, a type of discourse which does not simply renounce the norms of theoretical discourse, but rather takes the form of a subversive parody of them. 'To destroy theory', Lyotard suggests, 'is to produce one, many pseudo-theories; the theoretical crime is to fabricate theoretical fictions.'[70] If such a form of discourse wishes to convince it must do so without any appeal to truth, just as in Nietzsche the will to truth of the authentic philosopher ultimately reveals itself as will to power. Lyotard's most sustained attempt to produce such a philosophical fiction is to be found in *Économie Libidinale*, a work in which deduction and denunciation, argument and anecdote are woven into a text of considerable rhetorical vehemence. The aim, as in Nietzsche, is to reveal 'the meaning hidden in emotion, the vertigo in reason', to confront the reader with a 'force of language beyond truth'.[71]

The Return to Truth

Économie Libidinale illustrates – perhaps more clearly than any other post-structuralist text – the fundamental dynamic of the shift towards Nietzsche during the 1970s. Far more consistently than Foucault, who continuously equivocates over the epistemological status of his own discourse, Lyotard appreciates that a pluralist ontology of forces cannot claim to be *true*, except at the cost of self-contradiction, but can rather only be *affirmed* – if we understand by affirmation, as Nietzsche does, a form of acceptance disconencted from the recognition of truth. However, although the discourse of *Économie Libidinale* is intended to sweep the reader along, disarming all critical consciousness, the question of why this vision, rather than some other, should be affirmed cannot be entirely sidestepped. In Nietzsche's work, as we have seen, the ultimate criterion – although debarred from explicitly functioning *as* a criterion – is the enhancement of life. In post-struturalism, it can be argued, the fundamental criterion is the fostering of an epistemic and evaluative pluralism. Unity and universality are inherently oppressive, and any philosophical move which promotes their disintegration is to be approved.

At this point, however, post-structuralist thought runs up against its internal political limit. Characteristically, Foucault and Lyotard conceptualize political conflict in terms of a clash between two kinds of forces – in Foucault these are '*pouvoir*' and '*résistance*', in Lyotard the 'white terror of truth' and the 'red cruelty of singularities' – on the assumption that an oppressive force is one which claims truth or universal validity for its standpoint. However, the deep naivety of this conception lies in the assumption that once the aspiration to universality – whether cognitive or moral – is abandoned, what will be left is a harmonious plurality of unmediated perspectives. Thus Lyotard writes that 'it is always a matter of minorities crushed in the name of the Empire. They are not necessarily critical (the Indians); they are much ''worse'', they *do not believe*. . . . In this sense they are polytheists, whatever they may have said and thought about themselves: to each nation its authorities, none endowed with universal value or a totalitarian vocation.'[72] But although the universality of a principle does not in itself guarantee absence of coercion, the rejection of universality is even less effective in this respect, since there is nothing to prevent the perspective of one minority from including its right to dominate others: the Empire which Lyotard so vehemently denounces is simply the minority which has fought its way to the top. Similarly, Foucault's position – according to which only power can be socially constitutive – implies that successful resistance will itself become simply another power, while Deleuze and Guattari, in a parallel development in *Anti-Oedipus*, become lost in interminable labyrinths in attempting to distinguish *désir molaire* from *désir moléculaire*. It is clear, therefore, that the distinction of qualities of force or violence upon which the post-structuralists of the 1970s attempt to base their politics cannot be upheld, since one is simply the triumphant version of the other. In this respect, Nietzsche is far more consistent than his emulators, since he accepts, and even celebrates, the fact that, if claims to universality can never be more than the mask of particular forces and interests, then 'life' cannot take the form of a harmonious plurality of standpoints, but is '*essentially* appropriation, injury, overpowering of the strange and weaker, suppression, severity, imposition of one's own forms, incorporation and, at the least and mildest, exploitation'.[73] 'Every drive is a kind of lust to rule,' Nietzsche writes in *The Will to Power*, 'each one has its perspective that it would like to compel all the other drives to accept as a norm.'[74]

By the later 1970s, the fundamental inconsistency of this Nietzschean pluralism had begun to seep into public consciousness in France. The first alarm bells were set ringing by the *Nouveaux Philosophes*, some of whom very rapidly evolved from an initial adherence to an incoherent fusion of Maoism and mysticism, toward a clear appreciation that a *right* to difference can only be upheld by universal principles.[75] From the beginning of the 1980s, the argument was increasingly heard that, far from Nietzschean pluralism providing a bulwark against the totalizations of Marxism, both Marx and Nietzsche are dangerously at fault in their attempts to dissolve moral and political principles into historical or natural determinations. Through an appreciation that, without an appeal to rules and norms which are not themselves the expression of particular interests, pluralism cannot be consistently defended, the implicitly liberal themes of post-structuralist discourse began to break out of their ill-adapted Nietzschean modes of presentation. This major shift of intellectual outlook, comparable only to the arrival of structuralism two decades earlier, could not fail to have its effect upon the work of the surviving representatives of post-structuralist thought.

This impact can be seen clearly in the final phase of Foucault's career, centred on the publication of the second and third volumes of the *History of Sexuality*. For example, in an interview given in 1984, Foucault introduces three major revisions to the account of truth which had informed his work – implicitly at least – ever since the beginning. Firstly, Foucault retreats from the historicist and relativist implications of his earlier work, arguing rather that his concern is with the difficult relation between temporality and truth: 'What I try to achieve is the history of the relations which thought maintains with truth; the history of thought insofar as it is the thought of truth. All those who say that truth does not exist for me are simple-minded.'[76] Secondly, Foucault denies that he had ever suggetsed the equivalence of power and knowledge (despite his use, during the 1970s, of the hyphenated term 'pouvoir-savoir'), arguing instead that his concern has always been with the complex relations between the two. Finally, Foucault comes to appreciate that, far from the concept of truth implying domination and forcible unification, it is precisely contempt for the truth which characterizes the arbitrary use of political power: 'Nothing is more inconsistent than a political regime which is indifferent to truth; but nothing is more dangerous than a political system which claims to prescribe the truth . . . The task of speaking the truth is an infinite labour: to respect it in its complexity is an obligation which no power can pass over, except by imposing the silence of servitude.'[77] Characteristically, however, Foucault refuses to admit that there has been any genuine break in his outlook, blaming any appearance of discontinuity on the deficiencies of his readers, while simultaneously claiming that the right to change one's mind is a matter of intellectual integrity. Even more characteristically, he fails to observe how closely his own development has followed the contours of philosophical fashion in France.

Similarly, in the lesser known of the two books which he published in 1979, *Just Gaming*, Lyotard made major concessions to the emerging critics of the Nietzschean position. During the mid 1970s, he had held onto the possibility of a libidinal politics, but now he is obliged to agree with the objection of his interlocutor, Jean-Loup Thébaud, that 'Any philosophy of the will . . . inevitably gets into matters of velocity (slowdowns, acceleration, sedimentation), since ultimately, it is a monistic philosophy.'[78] Within a purely libidinal economy, in other words, there can be no distinctions of principle between forces, and consequently Lyotard admits that 'it is not true that the search for intensities or things of that type can ground politics, because there is the problem of injustice.'[79] Furthermore, even if a libidinal economy were politically desirable, we have no reason to believe that the need to provide grounds for its acceptance could be circumvented by rhetorical strategies. Thus, in *Just Gaming*, Lyotard states that, rather than the question of truth and falsehood concealing the power of the philosophical text, it is this power, in the sense of rhetorical force, which strives to conceal the problem of truth and falsehood. The intention of *Économie Libidinale* is theoretical, it is not simply a literary or poetical work, and – to this extent – there remains a 'gap between the *lexis*, that is, the mode of presentation on the one hand, and the *logos*, that is, the content, on the other, [and] this gap does violence: the theses are not up for discussion. But in reality they can be . . . This presupposes that the reader does not allow himself or herself to be intimidated, so to speak.'[80] This admission on Lyotard's part represents a crucial break with the Nietzscheanism of the 1970s, and indeed, in its insistence on the irreducibility of reason, *logos*, to force or style, can be said to sound the death-knell of post-structuralism.

Conclusion: Intersubjectivity and the Logic of Disintegration

We have seen that, around the turn of the decade, Foucault and Lyotard begin to relinquish the Nietzschean conception, according to which the notion of truth necessarily implies domination and unification, in favour of a distinction between the contingent, historically and socially conditioned features of language, and the implicit universality of claims to truth which are raised by linguistic utterances. Indeed, in *Just Gaming*, Lyotard hints that there is an internal relation between the raising of a claim to truth and willingness to enter into discussion, a commitment to the provision of grounds, should the validity of the claim be challenged; it is precisely the internality of this relation which explains why the gap between *logos* and *lexis* can be experienced as violence and intimidation. Foucault, at the very end of his life, adopted a similar view in an account of the logic of dialogue: 'The person asking the questions is merely exercising the right that has been given him: to remain unconvinced, to perceive a contradiction, to require more information, to emphasize different postulates, to point out faulty reasoning, etc. As for the person answering the questions, he too exercises a right that does not go beyond the discussion itself; by the logic of his own discourse he is tied to what he said earlier, and by the acceptance of dialogue he is tied to the questioning of the other.'[1] As in the case of Lyotard, Foucault suggests that it is not the quest for truth, but rather the violation of these rights that will tend to take the form of coercion and intimidation.[2]

It is difficult not to read these statements as a somewhat belated endorsement of Habermas's attempt – an attempt which is in continuity with the tradition of Critical Theory – to accommodate the

powerful arguments of the anti-foundationalists, while nevertheless avoiding the slide into relativism. Habermas seeks to achieve
this through the development of a 'universal pragmatics' – a
reconstruction of the assumptions and procedures to which we are
necessarily committed when involved in linguistic communication. His argument is that, in making an assertion, in assuming the
right to perform a particular speech-act, and in expressing our
feelings and intentions, we implicitly but unavoidably engage to
provide grounds, should the validity of the utterance be challenged with respect to its truth, its rightness, or its sincerity. We
undertake, in other words, to shift if necessary into the intersubjective medium which he terms '*Diskurs*', a form of discussion
oriented towards the consensual resolution of contested validity-
claims by no other means than the force of the better argument.
For Habermas, truth cannot be established by an appeal to ultimate evidence. Rather, it is 'a validity-claim which we connect
with statements when we assert them', and, like the other validity-
claims, it has as its ultimate horizon of resolution a universal and
argumentatively attained consensus.[3]

It is important for the political content of Habermas's position
that it should not be taken to imply that truth, or rightness, can be
defined in terms of any factually existing consensus. Speakers of a
langauge are conscious of the fact that the actual existence of a
consensus does not guarantee truth – if they were not, the abandonment of a hitherto universally accepted belief would be incom-
prehensible. But such a consciousness presupposes an ability to
distinguish between true and false consensus. In order to do this,
Habermas argues, speakers must possess an implicit awareness of
the conditions under which a consensus would guarantee truth.
Habermas attempts to spell out this awareness in terms of the features of what he calls an 'ideal speech situation': a situation of
dialogue free of external pressures and internal distortions, in
which participants would respond to the force of the better argument alone. It is important to note that this anticipation of unconstrained consensus is not merely an impotent ideal, but rather
embodies what Habermas terms the 'factual force of the counterfactual'. This is because, in order to engage in *Diskurs*, to attempt
to resolve a difference of opinion through argument, we must presuppose the ideal conditions of dialogue to be already realized,
even though we know simultaneously that this cannot be the case.
Thus, Habermas argues that 'As a matter of fact we can in no way
always (or even often) fulfil those improbable pragmatic preconditions, from which we nevertheless begin in communicative

everyday practice, and indeed, in the sense of a transcendental necessity, *must* begin. For this reason sociocultural life-forms stand under the structural limitations of a communicative reason which is *simultaneously denied and laid claim to*.'[4]

Habermas's account of the rational structure of dialogue makes clear the error of the central post-structuralist equation of truth and reason with limitation and constraint. For the post-structuralists, the universality implicit in the concept of truth appears as a threat. Since no conception of truth could ever justify the universal validity which it claims, such a claim can only mask a desire for power, the wish to unify coercively a multiplicity of standpoints. Truth becomes 'the weapon of paranoia and power, the claw of unity-totality in the space of words'.[5] What this argument overlooks, however, is that it is the very *universality* of truth-claims which makes for their vulnerability: it is only because assertions make demands on the assent of others, and cannot – as much modern philosophy has supposed – be validated by a method aimed at securing certainty for a monadic subject, that they are open to challenge. And it is precisely when assent cannot be elicited through argument that the use of force becomes a temptation. Hence it is not truth itself which is intrinsically linked to power, but rather truth-*claims* which could not be upheld if they were not shielded from critical probing by coercion and manipulation. Furthermore, although Habermas provides an account of truth, he does not fall victim to post-structuralist criticism of criterial theories of truth and of their circularity, since he does not aim to provide a *method* for sifting true from false statements. Habermas's position is fallibilistic – far more fallibilistic than a position based upon an a priori conception of discourse as an expression of desire or power – since, although we can discover, by revealing forces which formerly distorted the structure of communication, that we *were not* in a situation of unconstrained *Diskurs*, we can never be certain that we *are* in such a situation. Accepted truths can be problematized in *Diskurs*, but we cannot simultaneously enter into and question the validity of *Diskurs* itself: there is no metadiscursive level.[6]

However, even though Habermas's account of truth reveals the shallowness of post-structuralist equations of truth and coercion, it might still be considered philosophically vulnerable, rather than politically suspect, for reasons which are close to the heart of post-structuralist sensibility. Ironically, these anti-Habermasian arguments have recently been developed, in a far more convincing form than can be found in the perfunctory ripostes of Foucault and Lyotard, in a series of essays by Albrecht Wellmer, himself an influential representative of the Critical Theory tradition. In his book *Ethik und Dialog*, Wellmer raises a number of crucial questions about the connections between truth, rationality and consensus, which constitute an important probing of Habermas's assumptions. Wellmer denies that the rationality of a consensus can be formally characterized, since 'the concept of a consensus brought about by means of reasons, presupposes that of a conviction brought about by means of reasons.'[7] In other words, an assessment of rationality depends on an assessment of the substantive cogency of arguments, and cannot be achieved through a set of formal yardsticks. But if this is the case, Wellmer argues, the rationality of a consensus cannot function as a guarantee of truth: even under ideal conditions, the *fact* of consensus cannot be taken as an additional *ground* for the truth of what is agreed upon, since our view of the cogency of arguments can never be immune from revision. More broadly, Wellmer contests the meaningfulness of the conception of a 'future locus of final and absolute truth' which is built into Habermas's account of the pragmatic anticipation of an 'ideal speech situation'. In a close echo of post-structuralist arguments, Wellmer suggests that the notion of an ultimate consensus simply projects into the framework of a pragmatic philosophy of language the objectivist illusions of logical empiricism: 'The ideal communication community would be beyond error, dissent, non-understanding and conflict, but only at the cost of bringing language to a halt, of a dying-out of its productive energies, and this means at the cost of a cancellation of the linguistic-historical life-form of human beings.'[8]

But although Wellmer's criticisms successfully highlight the brittle points of Habermas's rationalism, his position is not as widely separated from that of Habermas as may at first appear. For while Wellmer argues that the supposition of an ideal speech situation, far from being the guiding anticipation of a possible form of life, is merely a 'dialectical illusion', he nevertheless admits that 'norms of argumentation are not the rules of a game which we can engage in or not engage in, as we see fit'.[9] Consequently, formal structures of rationality must be admitted as necessary, although not sufficient, conditions for an emancipated social life.[10] In his more recent work, Habermas has made reciprocal concessions in Wellmer's direction, abandoning his claims for the ideal speech situation as the anticipation of a concrete form of life, and stressing that the resolution of normative questions in the narrow sense, questions of justice, still leaves open the evaluative question of the 'good life'.[11] Furthermore, Wellmer's argument that the concept of an ideal community of communication cancels the constitutive plurality of sign-users 'in favour of a transcendental subject which now also understands itself in a practical-hermeneutical sense',[12] although perhaps telling against Karl-Otto Apel, whose work has has always been more directly connected to the tradition of transcendental philosophy, is scarcely applicable to Habermas. This is because Habermas, from the beginnings of his work, has stressed what he terms the 'broken intersubjectivity' of communication. Communication is not simply a matter of the transferral of identical meanings from one consciousness to another, but involves the simultaneous maintenance of the distinct identities of – in other words: the non-identity between – the partners in communication. This non-identity cannot fail to enter into the interpretation of meaning. Thus, Habermas argues that 'An unbroken intersubjectivity of the grammar in force would certainly make possible the identity of meanings and thereby constant relations of understanding, but would simultaneously annihilate the identity of the I in the communication with others.'[13] Accordingly, only in 'the sustained non-identity of a successful communication can the individual construct a precarious ego-identity, and protect against the risks both of reification and of formlessness.'[14] Ultimately, this position does not seem so far from Wellmer's stress on the ineliminability of misunderstanding and dissent in discourse: even in the absence of structural inequalities of power, the constitutive tensions of linguistic intersubjectivity will always remain.

The Logic of Disintegration

The development of the theory of intersubjectivity, in the work of the second generation Frankfurt School, is the central component of a strategy for overcoming what came to be seen as the impasse of the subject-based philosophy of the first generation. This impasse can perhaps best be explored through a consideration of Adorno's notion of a 'logic of disintegration' (*Logik des Zerfalls*), which he describes – in the afterword to the German edition of *Negative Dialectics* – as the oldest of his philosophical conceptions. At the most fundamental level, this conception embodies Adorno's critical inversion of the major systems of German Idealism, and in particular that of Hegel. In opposition to interpretations of reality as a temporal movement towards ever more complex and

226

differentiated forms of integration and reconciliation, Adorno
argues that the historical process must be understood as advancing
both towards less and less mediated forms of unity, and towards
increasing antagonism and incoherence, because of the abstraction built into the instrumental use of concepts, which idealist
philosophy overlooks. The more society becomes integrated
through the abstract principle of identity, which structures both
conceptual thought and an economy based upon market exchange,
the more intense becomes the conflict between the individuals of
whom this society is composed and the functioning of society as a
whole. The culmination of this process is a social world of which
every aspect has become inherently contradictory, and therefore
resistant to univocal interpretation. It is this conception of historical development which forms the background to Adorno's fundamental conviction that: 'Whoever chooses philosophical work as
a vocation today, must from the beginning renounce the illusion
with which philosophical systems formerly began: that it is possible to grasp the totality of the real through the power of
thought.'[15]

At the psychological level, the process of disintegration is
manifested in the decline of the bourgeois individual, the breaking
down of the autonomous ego. During the liberal phase of capitalism, Adorno argues, the mediating power of the ego in the process
of social reproduction reached a historical apogee. Although he
does not underestimate the extent to which capitalist society has
always rested on a framework of coercion he suggests that, during
the high bourgeois epoch, individuals were at least able to experience themselves as constituting their own society through the
market-mediated pursuit of private interest. However, through
the continuing process of instrumentalization, the significance of
individual initiative has been reduced almost to zero. Society now
confronts the individual as something cold and inhuman, as a system to which one is obliged to adapt in order to survive. The
implications of these developments are best comprehended if one
considers that, for the thinkers of the first generation of the Frankfurt School, the self is essentially constituted through a dialectic
of struggle and submission. It is this dialectic which is explored in
the Odysseus chapter of *Dialectic of Enlightenment*, and is redis-
covered in Freud's account of the Oedipus complex, which is seen
as involving both resistance to, and internalization of, the authority of the father. In the administered world, however, the antagonistic relation between the individual and society which Freud
theorized, and which – in its very difficulty and painfulness –

testified to a measure of autonomy, is replaced by a direct incorporation by socializing agencies such as the mass media. Obliged to conform to an overwhelming social reality in order to survive, the individual retreats into narcissism, into illusions of total self-containment or total fusion, which are the compensation for an actual powerlessness. The libidinal cathexis of the ego, the breaking down of the barrier between ego and id, which this narcissism implies, is of course far from signalling a genuine dissolution of compulsion, in favour of the pursuit of individual gratification. For to pursue one's own pleasure against society requires precisely a strong ego. Rather, the id and the socialized superego enter into collaboration, the result being what Adorno – in a haunting phrase – terms a 'subjectless subject', lacking the reflective coherence and continuity which make possible genuine experience, and reacting in a purely passive and disconnected way to every new stimulus and social demand.[16]

The Move to Intersubjectivity

From the standpoint of a theory of intersubjectivity, however, the fundamental premiss of Adorno's argument appears vulnerable. Adorno believes that 'the appearance of identity is inherent in thought itself, in its pure form. To think is to identify. Self-satisfied, conceptual order sets itself in front of that which thought seeks to comprehend. The illusion and the truth of thought entwine.'[17] Yet, as Albrecht Wellmer has pointed out, to assume an intrinsic indifference of the concept to the particulars which it subsumes, in this way, is to neglect how linguistic meanings are modulated and inflected by specific communicative situations: 'To say of something which is each time entirely different that it is a tool or a theory, to say in quite different situations, "I am sad" or "the weather is changing", does of course imply that linguistic expressions do not reflect what is different in the situation of their use; but they are the linguistic expressions which they are only by virtue of the fact that, in their singular use, a horizon of other uses – past and possible – is present.'[18] In other words, Adorno's position is based on the tacit assumption that language functions primarily as a means of rendering the disparate and diffuse homogeneous and manipulable for an isolated subject. Trapped within the philosophy of consciousness, Adorno sees language as directly dissecting and deforming reality, rather than as being the means whereby subjects communicate to each other *about* a reality which is nevertheless preserved in its non-identity.

As Wellmer suggests, once this shift of perspective is accepted, then objectification and reification, the harming of the non-identical, cease to be problems *of* language as such, and rather become problems *within* language, the signs of specific pathologies and disruptions of social communication and practice. As an example of this, Wellmer discusses the psychiatric use of labels such as 'manic' or 'depressive'. The adoption of a technical language can be a means of classifying individuals for easier control and manipulation; but it may also serve as a means of guiding the imagination and sensitivity of the therapist in a particular direction, thereby initiating a process concerned with the patient's *own* understanding of his or her particular history. We cannot assume that specialized terminologies, and, *a fortiori*, the everyday language of social life, are characcterized by a rigidity of classification and deduction which, as recently philosophy of science has demonstrated, is not even exemplified by the natural sciences themselves. Imagination and reason, in a non-instrumental sense, are built into communicative practice, and are not only to be attained through a strenuous turning of language against itself, by using concepts to go beyond concepts, in Adorno's sense. [19]

From this conception of communicative practice there follows, among contemporary representatives of Critical Theory, a set of objections to Adorno's conception of a 'totally administered society'. As we have seen, Adorno assumes that instrumental reason annexes more and more of nature, society, and – eventually – inner nature, until it becomes apparently self-grounding, freed from any goal which it would be instrumental in achieving, and rather now an end in itself. However, this assumption is only possible if one ignores the fact that all instrumental activity must be embedded in a network of intersubjective relations, and that this network of relations is therefore as essential to the continued existence of society as the material interchange with nature. In Habermas's recent social theory, this two-dimensional account of agency, formerly stated in terms of the contrast between 'labour' and 'interaction', is developed into the duality of system and life-world. Habermas wishes to take account of the argument that modern societies are necessarily characterized by a high degree of differentiation, and by the development of quasi-autonomous systems of administration and economy, without accepting that society could be totally functionalized, or that such autonomy can only be interpreted as reification. Opposition to this functionalization is located not simply in a repressed and deformed nature, which is pushed to the extreme margins of the social system, and whose very resistance, such as it is, tends to be operationalized, but rather in the structures of the life-world which cannot be bureaucratized and commodified without generating solidaristic countermovements. Habermas, therefore, rejects the philosophical conception of society as a potentially self-reflecting and self-determining subject, which has underpinned much Hegelian Marxism. He now prefers to articulate democratic aspirations in terms of a conception of condensed centres of communication, rooted in the life-world, which can bring the dynamic of systems under democratic control, without constituting the locus of a totalizing self-knowledge, which could only take the form of self-objectification: 'The polycentric outlines of totalities, which forestall each other, mutually surpass and incorporate each other, generate competing centres. Even collective identities bob up and down on the flow of interpretations, and are better pictured as a fragile network than as a stable centre of self-reflection.'[20]

The explicit introduction of a theory of intersubjectivity also makes possible, at the psychological level, an escape from the dynamic of disintegration built into an autonomy which can only be acquired at the cost of submission to a repressive authority. For, as Axel Honneth has argued, in the original Frankfurt School appropriation of psychoanalysis, no adequate distinction is drawn between the instrumental control of outer nature, and the moral control of inner nature. Since the father is not considered as a partner in interaction, but rather as the model which must be internalized in order to acquire both these forms of control, a decline of paternal authority is inevitably seen as bringing with it both a collapse of the individual conscience, which is replaced by the direct manipulation of social agencies, and a breakdown of the individual's ability to acquire knowledge of and act upon the external world.[21] However, if moral self-control is no longer seen as simply the internalized continuation of the social compulsion required for the control of nature, but is rather acquired through a process of interactive identification with a variety of other subjects in the immediate environment, a process which has an independent dynamic, then this conclusion can no longer be drawn. Rather, as Jessica Benjamin has suggested, the Oedipal model of individuation can be seen as merely *one* model, which institutionalizes an isolating and manipulative independence, at the cost of the values of co-operation and reciprocity.[22]

The Position of Post-structuralism

This debate between the first and the second generation of Critical Theory provides an extremely useful set of co-ordinates for mapping the central features of post-structuralist thought. For it is clear that post-structuralism is no less directed against the constraints of the paradigm of *Subjektphilosophie*, than is the recent work of Habermas or Wellmer. Thus, Jacques Derrida's thought revolves around the insight that the disseminative process of language cannot be accounted for in terms of the intentional and interpretive acts of a solitary consciousness. Similarly, one of Michel Foucault's main preoccupations was a theorization of historical and social processes which would not reduce them to the alienated activity of a macro-subject, but would respect their diverse and multidimensional nature, while Lyotard explores the incompatibility between the model of the monadic subject and the emancipation of 'desire'. All these approaches, in which the very concept of subjectivity is eliminated as redundant, or at the very least considered as derivative, and in which a concerted effort is made to move beyond the subject-object relation as the fundamental axis of philosophy, clearly contrast with Adorno's dogged meditations on the dialectic of subject and object. Yet, in another sense, post-structuralist thought can be seen to be more closely tied to the philosophy of consciousness than is the thought of Adorno, since it lacks any sense of the *interdependence* of identity and non-identity. Adorno refuses to take the self-understanding of the philosophy of consciousness at face value: in accordance with the logic of disintegration, the claim to absolute identity, to the extent that it is realized, can only take the form of unprecedented fragmentation, and this contradiction points towards the possibility of another form of subjectivity, however difficult to conceptualize. By contrast, post-structuralist thought takes the repressive self-enclosure of consciousness to be definitive of subjectivity as such, with the consequence that 'emancipation' can only take the form of a breaking open of the coercive unity of the subject in order to release the diffuseness and heterogeneity of the repressed.

The problem with this solution of course is that – far from providing an image of emancipation – such a dispersion of the self merely enacts what Adorno takes to be the central features of the contemporary social process: the overcoming of the compulsion of self-consciousness is only achieved through a return to a more primitive form of totalizing coercion. The dissolution of the reflective unity of the self can only mean the triumph of a unifying process at the pre-subjective level, since the oppositions between truth and illusion, essence and appearance, freedom and necessity, which structure and differentiate reality are themselves established through reflection – the activity of a subject, or rather of a community of subjects. The fundamental logic of this process perhaps appears most clearly in the work of Derrida, where, as we have seen, the attempt to move beyond the enclosure of transcendental consciousness through the thought of *différance* simply reproduces the cancellation of differences characteristic of Schelling's *Identitätsphilosophie*. As Richard Kearney has cogently enquired, 'If deconstruction prevents us from asserting or stating or identifying anything, then surely one ends up, not with "differance", but with indifference, where nothing is anything, and everything is everything else?'[23] Similarly, Foucault's stress on the complexity and multiplicity of forms of power and discourse tends, during the 1970s at least, to collapse into a vision of an omnipresent and homogeneous power, since he is obliged to eschew any discrimination of forms of domination and resistance in terms of the differing aims and intentions of human subjects. Finally, Lyotard's libidinal economy, far from preserving the singularity of each moment of experience, a preservation which could only be achieved within a discriminating continuity of experience, ends by embracing the punctuality, anonymity and indifference of the commodity form.

One of the central ironies of post-structuralist thought, in other words, is that it fails to comprehend the internal relation between subjective disintegration and the restoration of a featureless pre-subjective totality. For in order to comprehend this relation, rather than merely becoming caught up in it, it would be necessary to reflect on the dynamic of identifying reason from the standpoint of reconciliation – the interplay of identity and non-identity. Instead, post-structuralism tends to oscillate between totalizing ontological postulates and a more or less explicit perspectivism. In this respect, it embodies that freezing of the dialectic of universal and particular which Adorno detects in contemporary social development. Thus, in a reply to Gadamer, Derrida argues that 'Whether one begins from understanding or from misunderstanding (Schleiermacher), one must always ask oneself whether the condition of understanding, far from being a continually unfolding relation . . . is not rather the breaking of the relation, the break as relation, so to speak, a cancellation of all mediation?'[24] The 'break as relation', in Derrida's work, results, on the one hand, in a hypostatized textuality, which is considered to function outside of any mediation by an interpreting subject, and on the other hand, in an explanation of the 'axiom of incompleteness in the structure of the scene of writing' in terms of the 'position of the speculator as an interested observer', although this position cannot be explicitly accounted for as that of an interpreting subject.[25] Similar dichotomies have also appeared in our consideration of Foucault's and Lyotard's Nietzschean attempts to outflank the concept of truth. Throughout much of post-structuralist thought one finds the disjunction between endless, objectified process, whether theorized in terms of a 'play of the text', or of a metaphysics of power or desire, and a subjectivism which is paradoxically subjectless, since it abolishes the relation to the other which is constitutive of subjectivity.

For Adorno, of course, this dichotomy is itself a central symptom of the logic of disintegration. The narcissistically weakened self ceases to be capable of sustaining the tension of a relation of critical reflection to the object, and retreats into asseverations of opinion which are haunted by a sense of their own inadequacy and powerlessness: 'To the subject which has no genuine relation to the thing; which recoils from its strangeness and coldness, everything which it says about it becomes, both for itself and in itself, mere opinion, something reproduced and registered, which could also be otherwise. The subjectivist reduction to the arbitrariness of individual consciousness fits in precisely with submissive respect for an objectivity which such consciousness leaves standing uncontested, and which it reveres even in the assertion that whatever it thinks is non-binding in the face of its power; according to its measure, reason is nothing.'[26] In the face of a social process which progressively collapses the distinctions between truth and illusion, reason and unreason, the mere attempt to hold on to these distinctions comes to suggest a quixotic self-importance. Indeed, Adorno is in sympathy with the post-structuralist view that to think in general categories is to enter into collusion with the compulsion of totality. Yet he rejects the magical assumption that the fragmentation of knowledge will somehow break the grip of the object of knowledge. While it is true that harmonious syntheses in philosophy or social science, whatever their ostensible intent, will tend to disguise the disintegration of society, a simple concentration on isolated facets, which forgets the social determination of this very isolation, plays into the hands of a compulsion which has become so all-pervasive as to be almost invisible. In this situation, Adorno's solution, already outlined in his inaugural lecture on 'The Actuality of Philosophy', is to decipher the contradictory nature of the totality in the breaks and incoherences of the individual case. As Wolfgang Bonss has commented, for Adorno philosophy 'must adapt itself to the splintering, and take on the form of a *negative detection of traces*, which begins from individual elements, and attempts to comprehend them as a contradictory unity of possible reason and actual unreason.'[27] In contemporary Critical Theory this deciphering is likely to be more systematic, and to be guided by a theory of communicative reason which restricts itself to the formal infrastructure of life-worlds. Yet, in both cases, what is attempted is a coherent account of historical and social processes which does not rely on the assumption of an ultimately rational totality – an assumption which is also the central target of the post-structuralist reaction to Hegelian Marxism. As Adorno writes: 'Totality is not an affirmative but rather a critical category. Dialectical critique seeks to salvage or help to establish what does not obey totality, what opposes it or what forms itself as the potential of a not yet existent individuation.'[28]

This formulation of Adorno's once again highlights one of the central theoretical deficiencies of post-structuralism: the lack of any concept of individuation as an identity which is developed and sustained through the awareness of non-identity. Post-structuralism does indeed seek for difference, but it does so through an immersion in fragments and perspectives, not perceiving that this splintering is itself the effect of an overbearing totality, rather than a means of escape from it. In other words, post-structuralism can be understood as the point at which the 'logic of disintegration' penetrates into the thought which attempts to comprehend it, resulting in a dispersal into a plurality of inconsistent logics. The results of this defensive mimetic adaptation can be seen not only in the internal incoherences of different post-structuralist positions, but also in their complementary onesidedness. It seems clear, for example, that the energy of Derrida's attack on the primacy and integrity of self-consciousness derives from sources deeper than a dissatisfaction with traditional structures of philosophical argument. Indeed, Derrida himself has sometimes hinted at the revolutionary consequences of an overcoming of logocentrism for Western history and society.[29] Yet, at the same time, he is unable to provide any coherent account of the emancipation which would be brought about through an ending of compulsive identity, the 'metaphysics of presence', because of the lack of any naturalistic component in his account of the formation of the self. At the other extreme, Lyotard's work, during the 1970s, focuses on the problem of inner nature, yet, failing to perceive that this problem can only be addressed through an exploration of the logical fissures of a supposedly self-contained subjectivity, ends by totalizing 'desire' into an affirmative libidinal economy.[30]

The pattern of Michel Foucault's work is in many respects more complex, since – at different stages of his career – Foucault has concentrated on very different concerns. During the mid 1960s, his attention was directed almost exclusively towards the history of discursive formations, with scant concern for their relation to desire or power. For most of the 1970s, however, the autonomy of discourse is entirely dissolved, and epistemic structures are seen as entirely moulded by proto-social forces. Finally, in Foucault's late work, the problem of the subject – which up until this point had been viewed as an effect or a construct – emerges, and Foucault becomes interested in the modalities of moral self-constitution, and in what he terms an 'aesthetics of existence'.[31] However, Foucault was never able to hold these different concerns simultaneously in focus: rather, he tended to organize the whole field of his theoretical activity in terms of his current preoccupation. At one stage, for example, a frustration with the confines of the philosophy of consciousness leads to an announcement of the 'death of man', while at another Foucault advocates the promotion of 'new forms of subjectivity through the refusal of the kind of individuality which has been imposed on us for several centuries'.[32] The shifting perspectives of Foucault's work do powerfully illuminate, but at the same time fall victim to, the contradictory processes which they address.

At this point it might be objected, of course, that to understand post-structuralist thought as itself a shattered mirror of the logic of disintegration is to adopt a perspective which contemporary Critical Theory is supposed to have invalidated. Yet such an objection would be based on a misunderstanding of the way in which Critical Theory is transformed and appropriated. For it is not primarily a matter of proving Adorno 'wrong', but rather – as Albrecht Wellmer has expressed it – of reading him 'stereoscopically', of inserting his insights into a framework which no longer screens out the intersubjective dimension. If this is done, then many of Adorno's analyses can be seen as pinpointing ambivalent tendencies and potentialities of contemporary social development, rather than as delineating an inevitable fate. It is striking that, in many contemporary accounts of 'post-modern' culture, central emphases of Adorno's work of forty years ago are reproduced. Thus, Jean Baudrillard's work often appears simply to recycle Adorno's vision of the totally administered society, but without any of the latter's sensitivity to its fissures and contradictions.[33] Similarly, Fredric Jameson, in a major essay on postmodernism, refers to a 'waning of affect', an 'abolition of critical distance', and a loss of any sense of historical continuity, which indicate that the alienation of the subject has been replaced by its fragmentation.[34] Jameson, however, is more sanguine than Adorno about the breakdown of the 'windowless solitude of the monad, buried alive and condemned to a prison cell without egress',[35] and in this respect he rejoins writers in the Critical Theory tradition such as Helmut Dubiel. Dubiel argues that contemporary capitalism, far from exemplifying a seamless integration of individuals into society, is marked by an increasing discrepancy between the personality structures fostered by the modern family, characterized by the rejection of asceticism, authoritarianism and competition, and the functional demands of the world of work and public activity.[36] A similar discrepancy has been identified, from a neo-conservative standpoint, by Daniel Bell, in his book *The Cultural Contradictions of Capitalism*. For Bell, contemporary bourgeois society is torn between a modernist culture which emphasizes 'anti-cognitive and anti-intellectual modes which look longingly toward a return to instinctual sources of expression' and the 'characteristic style of industrialism', which stresses 'functional rationality, technocratic decision-making and meritocratic rewards'.[37]

Thus, there is a fundamental debate around the political significance of the decline of the 'bourgeois' individual, and the emergence of a new narcissistic personality, a process which is reflected in the theoretical structures of post-structuralist thought. For some, the proliferation of narcissistic disorders is a sign of the penetration of commodification, and a calculating hedonism unwilling to accept the ties of long-term relationships and commitments, into the very heart of the family. Intensity of involvement is still supplied, but this is in a series of dyadic relations between child and adult, which perpetuate the narcissistic influence of the primary object, rather than in the context of an articulated and cohesive social environment.[38] For others, such as Jessica Benjamin, the culture of the nuclear family has not been hollowed out in this way. Rather, 'The capacity for reflection, for psychological truth, for caring, but also the need for intimacy and the interplay of self-expression and recognition, which such families produce, can nowhere be satisfied outside the family, since the poverty of the public sphere of productive cultural life disappoints every individuality.'[39] Building on a line of argument first expressed within the Critical Theory tradition by Herbert Marcuse, who, in *Eros and Civilization*, proposed Narcissus as the symbol of a participatory relation to nature,[40] Benjamin suggests that there is a 'healthy narcissisism', an antidote to instrumental reason, which is fostered by the post-patriarchal family. Thus, as Dubiel has suggested, the new 'post-bourgeois' subject can be seen to have an ambiguous potential. The plasticity of the narcissistic personality, the attendant erosion of traditional values, and the breakdown of the complementarity between instrumentalism and a cordoned-off aesthetic sphere, could lead to further advances in the control of consciousness and consumption of the kind which Adorno describes. But these developments could also point towards a 'non-repressive ego-autonomy, which would be constituted by expressive self-externalization, affective solidarity, and a hedonistic attitude to life.'[41] Undoubtedly, in its sensitivities, in many of its analyses, and in its implicit – often unacknowledgeable – values, post-structuralist thought also wishes to point in this latter direction. Yet, because it remains negatively bound to the philosophy of consciousness, and therefore lacks any ideal of communicative reciprocity, it can only do so in forms which threaten incorporation and regression.

Lacan and Habermas on Intersubjectivity

By this point, the entirely exceptional status of Lacan's work within the ambit of post-structuralism will once more have become apparent. Like his contemporaries, Lacan is centrally concerned with the constraining and illusory features of conscious self-identity, yet he does not oppose to this self-identity a concept of difference or disintegration: the phantasy of the fragmented body is itself an index of the strength of the ego. Furthermore, just as the phantasy of the fragmented body can only emerge against the background of the imaginary other, so the metonymic and metaphorical instability of language can only emerge within the formal horizon of totalization which is represented in Lacan's work by the phallus (the impossible 'Other of the Other'). Unlike the other post-structuralist thinkers, Lacan comprehends that the understanding of meaning and of the self is necessarily grounded in a presumption of integrity: the denial of the phallus, in the form of the denial of castration, leads not to an emancipation from negative desire and an oppressive quest for meaning, but rather to the imaginary totalizations of psychosis. His theoretical proximity to post-structuralist positions, on the other hand, is marked by his insistence that this integrity can never be realized, that the phallus must always remain 'veiled'. Consequently, in Lacan's work, the reified, monadic identity of the ego can never be entirely overcome; but, to the extent that it can be, such overcoming takes place through the interplay of identity and non-identity, of conscious ego and unconscious subject, which characterizes the field of intersubjectivity. Alone among the prominent French thinkers of the 1960s and 1970s, it is Lacan who explores the communicative formation – and deformations – of the self, and who appreciates the crucial philosophical implications of this approach.

Because, like contemporary Critical Theorists, Lacan abandons the paradigm of subject and object, he has little patience with the Nietzschean argument that there might be endless interpretations of interpretations, masks behind masks, without any presumption of truth: in 'The Freudian Thing' he refers contemptuously to the 'Nietzschean trumpery of the vital lie.'[42] In Lacan, the shift to intersubjectivity reveals, as it does in Habermas, a fundamental *asymmetry* between truth and falsehood, which becomes apparent in the transition from the forms of imaginary capture exemplified by lures and decoys, in both the animal and the human world, to the order of the signifier. This asymmetry consists in the fact that, if a statement considered true at any given time is a statement whose claim to truth has been accepted or validated, a lie is not in the same way a statement whose claim to falsehood has been endorsed, but rather one which raises an unjustified claim to truth. There must therefore be a convention that the primary function of language is to tell the truth. However, this convention cannot be an empirical one, since in order for such a convention to be established the truth-telling function of language would have already to be presupposed. It is precisely this transcendental argument, central to contemporary German accounts of truth as a communication-constitutive validity-claim, which is outlined by Lacan when he states that: 'Speech begins only with the passage from "pretence" to the order of the signifier, and . . . the signifier requires another locus – the locus of the Other, the Other witness, the witness Other than any of the partners – for the Speech that it supports to be capable of lying, that is to say, of presenting itself as Truth.'[43] Thus, in one of its functions, the concept of the Other in Lacan's work stands for the site of those normative presuppositions of communication whose necessity other post-structuralists deny.

However, Lacan's very closeness to Habermas, and to fellow thinkers such as Karl-Otto Apel, in this respect, raises a number of puzzling questions. For, although Lacan agrees that truth is an inherent imperative of speech, he by no means accepts the political conclusions which Habermas draws from this fact. Far from proposing that the normative structure of communication provides a means of detecting socially superfluous, and practically removable, alienations and repressions, Lacan argues that what social criticism describes as the alienation of the subject is essentially the result of the splitting of the subject occasioned by the entry into language.[44] Furthermore, he stresses that, in psychoanalysis, 'it is not a question of the relation of man to language as a social phenomenon.'[45] This is not to say that there is no dimension of social criticism in Lacan's own work. But, for Lacan, the fundamental problem consists in the rise of modern individualism, and the consequent 'increasing absence of all those saturations of the superego and ego ideal that are realized in all kinds of organic forms in traditional societies, forms that extend from the rituals of everyday intimacy to the periodical festivals in which the community manifests itself.'[46] Lacan, in continuity with the Durkheimian tradition, appears to believe that, without a strong symbolic order with substantive content, the modern individual is destined to oscillate between narcissistic rivalry and a correlative neurosis of self-punishment. The form of Lacan's criticisms of American ego-psychology show that he fully appreciates the relation between individualism, instrumentalism and technocratic consciousness, and indeed the fundamental shift of emphasis in his theory, compared with that of Freud, towards the dangers of the narcissistic ego, shows him to be sensitive to long-term transformations in personality structures. Yet Lacan does not believe there to be any political solution to these problems of modern society. He is fully aware of the impossibility of a return to substantive traditions, of the kind advocated by neo-conservatism, yet neither does he believe in the possibility of new forms of community. Only psychoanalysis, in the particular case, can 'open up to this being of nothingness [the modern individual] the way of his or her meaning in a discreet fraternity – a task for which we are always too inadequate.'[47]

This political divergence between Lacan and Habermas over the implications of the normative structure of communication suggest the need for a closer enquiry into how this structure is conceptualized in the two cases. For Habermas, as we have seen, linguistic intersubjectivity is the medium within which claims to truth, in the cognitive sense, as well as claims to rightness and authenticity, can be raised and arbitrated. We cannot 'jump out of' the language with which our subjectivity is interwoven, but the reflexive possibilities of language do enable us to take our distance from the various dimensions of the world. In *The Theory of Communicative Action*, Habermas describes this situation in the following way: 'The structures of the life-world establish the forms of the intersubjectivity of possible understanding. It is to them that the participants in communication owe their extramundane position in relation to the innerworldly, concerning which they can reach an agreement. The life-world is, as it were, the transcendental place where speaker and listener meet; where they can raise the claim to each other that their utterances fit the world (the objective, the social or the subjective world); and where these validity claims can be criticized and confirmed, their disagreements sorted out, and an agreement aimed for. In a word: participants cannot take the same distance *in actu* to language and culture as they do to the totality of facts, norms and experiences, concerning which understanding is possible.'[48]

By contrast, as we have seen in chapter three, Lacan fails to distinguish between the social order and the symbolic order. Even more importantly, he does not consider truth to be a validity-claim raised within the intersubjective arena, but rather *equates* it with the intersubjective relation itself. It is in this sense that Lacan, in an early essay, distinguishes between *le discours vrai* (the discourse of knowledge) and *la vraie parole* (intersubjective recognition): 'Speech thus appears all the more truly speech the less it is founded in adequation to the thing: true speech is thus paradoxically opposed to true discourse, their truth being distinguished by the fact that the first constitutes the recognition by subjects of their being, insofar as they are interested (*inter-essés*) in it, while the second is constituted by knowledge of the real, insofar as it is aimed at by the subject in its objects.'[49] In this essay, 'Variantes de la cure-type', Lacan suggests that these two forms of truth intersect with and disturb each other. *Le discours vrai* is able to detect the fluctuations and discrepancies of the self-representation which is implicit in *la vraie parole*, while *la vraie parole* reveals the semantic instability of *le discours vrai*. Nevertheless, it is already clear that, for Lacan, it is *la vraie parole* which is more fundamental, and, in his later writings, this view becomes consolidated in an account of the primary function of language. Thus in the first *Seminar*, Lacan argues that 'Speech is *essentially* the means of being recognized.'[50] However, if truth simply *is* intersubjective recognition, then there can be no institutionalized barriers to the attainment of truth. For Lacan the structure of symbolic exchange is identical with the institutional order of society, and however 'distorted' this order may be, in terms of the unequal locations and powers of individuals, there must be a structure of recognition in order for society to function at all. Consequently, for Lacan, truth is always already present, yet, at the same time, it can never be attained, since, by definition, intersubjectivity cannot be objectified. It is this conception which lies behind Lacan's celebrated formula: 'Moi, la vérité, je parle . . . '[51] For all speech is a revelation of truth, insofar as it is read symptomatically, in its performative dimension, regardless of the misrecognitions which it may convey. Truth, in other words, is for Lacan independent of any structural constraints on the consensual achievement of knowledge.

For Habermas, however, the intersubjective dimension of speech cannot be disconnected from the cognitive in this way. This is because it is a distinctive feature of articulated speech that, even when an utterance takes the form of, say, a command or a question, rather than of an assertion, it nevertheless possesses a content which can be put into propositional form. Even a request to close a door, for example, contains a reference to a state of affairs – that of the door being closed. Habermas therefore argues against Wittgenstein – but the argument could equally be applied to Lacan – that the meaning-constitutive aspect of language cannot be examined in separation from its knowledge-constitutive aspect. In Habermas's view, Wittgenstein overlooks the fact that the cognitive use of language reveals the dimensions to which *all* speech acts must be related. He argues that, 'In every elementary utterance there appears a dependent proposition which depends upon the dominant proposition, and which expresses the propositional content concerning which agreement is to be reached. This double-structure of the speech-act mirrors the structure of speech in general; an understanding cannot be reached when both partners do not simultaneously occupy both levels – (a) the level of intersubjectivity, at which Speaker/Hearer speak *with each other* and (b) the level of objects or states of affairs, *concerning* which they reach agreement . . . Without the propositional content which is thematized in the cognitive use of speech, the interactive use of speech would also be impossible.'[52] Significantly, in the context of comparison with Lacan, Habermas suggests that it is precisely the one-sided emphasis upon the interactive use of speech in Wittgenstein which lends his later philosophy its predominantly *therapeutic* cast.[53]

The preceding account will have made clear that Habermas is fully aware of the 'dual structure of speech' (*Doppelstruktur der Rede*) on which Lacan lays so much emphasis. Every act of speech, he argues, communicates simultaneously on two levels: it conveys a content which can, in principle, be cashed out in propositional form, but also established a metacommunication which specifies what he terms the 'sense of application' (*Verwendungssinn*) of the content. Habermas insists that this level of metacommunication, should not be confused with a metalanguage, since in metacommunication, statements cannot be made. Rather, the metacommunication consists in a system of reciprocal expectations on the part of the participants in dialogue. Habermas is accordingly also fully aware that metacommunication cannot be determined at the level of explicit knowledge. Metacommunication can, of course, be objectified in a further act of speech, but this act of speech will in turn possess its own metacommunicative level, so that dialogue is characterized by an intersubjective dimension which cannot be simultaneously established and objectified.[54]

Habermas, however, would not consider that this account of the dual structure of speech is all that is fundamentally required for a theory of the unconscious. It has been far too infrequently noted that the Lacanian equation, intersubjectivity = truth = the unconscious, in fact depends on a set of extremely fragile philosophical assumptions. These are clearly spelled out in the *Discours de Rome* when Lacan states: 'If there still remains something prophetic in Hegel's insistence on the fundamental identity of the particular and the universal, an insistence which reveals the measure of his genius, it is certainly psychoanalysis that provides it with its paradigm by revealing the structure in which that identity is realized as disjunctive of the subject, and without appeal to any tomorrow.'[55] For Lacan, as we have repeatedly seen, the unconscious is constituted by the impossibility, for the individual, of representing at the linguistic level his or her own unique position within the intersubjectivity of language. There is no intrinsic connection in Lacan between the concept of the unconscious and the concept of inner nature. Lacan does not deny the existence of such a nature, but deprives it of any force which could not be entirely absorbed by its symbolic mediations. Nor does Lacan connect the concept of repression with the concept of social power – primal repression is a function of the entry into language as such, and not into a particular symbolic order which, because it bears the stamp of a specific power structure, fails to provide adequate resources for an expressive articulation of the self.

Yet there is no reason to accept Lacan's account of the 'alienation of the subject in the signifier'. For to do so is merely to rule out philosophically what Habermas terms the 'paradoxical achievement of intersubjectivity': 'Subjects who reciprocally recognize each other as such, must consider each other as identical, insofar as they both take up the position of subjects; they must at all times subsume themselves and the other under the same category. At the same time, the relation of *reciprocity* of recognition demands the non-identity of the one and the other, both must also maintain their absolute difference, for to be a subject implies the claim to individuation.'[56]

Paradoxical as it may be, this achievement becomes more comprehensible, once we appreciate the manner in which universal determinations can be inflected by their individual use. There are only one or two passages in Habermas's work where he comments on this process, yet it is crucial for an understanding of his position: 'In the reflexive use of language we present inalienably individual aspects in unavoidably general categories in such a way that we metacommunicatively comment upon and sometimes even revoke direct information (and confirm it only with reservations). We do this for the purpose of an indirect representation of the non-identical aspects of the ego, aspects which are not sufficiently covered by the general determinations, and yet cannot be manifestly represented other than by just these determinations.'[57] Thus, Habermas, like Wellmer, argues that the 'utopian' reconciliation of identity and non-identity can take place in everyday discourse. Rigidities of conceptualization and of self-identity cannot be attributed to the nature of language as such, but betray the pressure of specific distorting forces.

It is at this point that the crucial importance of Lacan's essay on the 'Mirror Stage' once more becomes apparent, as the foundation of his entire subsequent theoretical development. For, in Lacan's thought, the mirror stage functions to establish the objectifying nature of *any* reflexive access to the self, *prior to* the entry into intersubjectivity. It constitutes the 'symbolic matrix in which the *I* is precipitated in a primordial form, before it is objectified in the dialectic of identification with the other, and before language restores to it, in the universal, its function as subject.'[58] On the basis of this argument, Lacan is able to construct an unresolvable antinomy between knowledge, which he continues to restrict to the subject-object dimension, and intersubjective truth. However, the simultaneous complicity and separation between an all-dominating and an objectified ego, between the transcendental and the empirical self, which Lacan so subtly diagnoses, ceases to be inevitable if an irremovable screen of objectification is not erected, on the very tenuous evidence, across the intersubjective dialectic. Thus Habermas can argue that 'This alternative [of the transcendental or the empirical] falls away, as soon as linguistically generated intersubjectivity is given pre-eminence. For ego stands in an interpersonal relationship, which allows him or her to relate to him- or herself as a participant in an interaction from the perspective of the other. And in fact this reflection which is undertaken from the standpoint of a participant, escapes from the type of objectification which is unavoidable from the reflexively employed perspective of an observer.'[59] It is in conformity with this insight that Donald Winnicott should suggest, explicitly against Lacan, that the first mirror is precisely the mother: for Winnicott, there is no impassable gulf between the 'other' and the 'Other'.[60]

These considerations suggest the inadequacy of Lacan's account of the unconscious, as consisting in the antinomy of objectivity and intersubjectivity, and the correctness of Lyotard's attempt, during the 1970s, to propose a conception of the unconscious as a more rudimentary, scenic 'language', which forcibly intrudes upon conscious discourse. Lyotard's assertion, in *Discours, Figure*, that 'there is no ego whose function it would be to lift, to reverse repression', suggests an awareness of the inherent limits of the philosophy of consciousness no less acute than that of Lacan. Yet Lyotard shows little sensitivity – as our comparison with Adorno made clear – to the internal incoherences of the monadic ego, and he is consequently led to hypostatize the opposition between self-reflection and a disruptively energetic unconscious, generating a theoretical impasse far worse than any in Lacan. For whatever one's assessment of the extent to which inner nature must remain intrinsically resistant to socialization, it is surely implausible to suggest that repression can be attributed purely to the nature of language as such, rather than largely resulting from the rigidification of language under specific institutional pressures. Unfortunately, Foucault's concern with the relation between power and discourse fails to fulfil its promise of providing a corrective to Lyotard's position in this respect, since Foucault, while rightly sceptical of any dogmatic conception of a kernel of resistant nature, also refuses to acknowledge the logical and epistemological incoherences which are generated by the operation of power.

These failures and inconsistences are not lightly incurred, but are rather the outcome of an entirely legitimate metacritique, most clearly articulated at the logical level by Derrida, which rejects any critical standpoint that would anticipate reconciliation in the form of a self-transparent subjectivity. Yet the inability to provide anything other than a repudiation of the philosophy of the subject, which continues to share its fundamental premises, ultimately leads to the collapse of the critical dimension of the metacritique. Lacan, by contrast, provides a genuine supersession of the standpoint of consciousness, but in a form which empties the concept of intersubjectivity of its political content. Thus, post-structuralist thought is not in any simple sense opposed to Critical Theory, but rather consists of a mosaic of theories which cover very similar ground. Together, these two traditions contain some of the finest philosophical explorations of the deep structures of modernity. Yet, at the same time, the rejection of the claims of an integrated critical standpoint in post-structuralism, in the mistaken belief that such a standpoint implies repressive totalization, is far from providing a more decisive liberation from the illusions of philosophy, and a more powerful illumination of the contemporary world. The fate of post-structuralism makes clear that critique is not a question of the arbitrary and coercive espousal of premises and precepts, but rather of a commitment to that coherence of thought which alone ensures its emancipatory power.

Notes

Introduction

1. See Claude Lefort, *The Political Forms of Modern Society*, Oxford 1986.
2. See, for example, Jean-Luc Nancy, *L'Impératif catégorique*, Paris 1983.
3. See, for example, Luc Ferry and Alain Renaut, 'Penser les droits de l'homme', *Esprit*, March 1983.
4. See François Ewald, 'Une expérience Foucauldienne: les principes généraux du droit', *Critique* 471-2, August-September 1986 (special issue on Michel Foucault).
5. Luc Ferry and Alain Renaut, *La Pensée 68*, Paris 1985.
6. See Luc Ferry, Alain Renaut et al., 'Qu'est-ce qu'une critique de la raison?', *Esprit*, April 1982, and *La Pensée 68*, pp. 217-24.
7. This conception of the independence of philosophy has become an important component of Lyotard's thought during the 1980s. It pervades *Le différend*, Paris 1983. See also his discussion with Jacques Derrida, 'Philosophie in der Diaspora', in Lyotard et al., *Immaterialität und Postmoderne*, Berlin 1985.
8. Jürgen Habermas, 'Modernity – An Incomplete Project' in Hal Foster, ed., *Postmodern Culture*, London 1985, p. 5.
9. Gerald Graff, 'Culture, Criticism and Unreality' in *Literature against Itself*, London 1979, p. 8.
10. See, for example, Terry Eagleton, 'Capitalism, Modernism and Postmodernism' in *Against the Grain: Selected Essays*, London 1986.
11. See Jürgen Habermas, *Der philosophische Diskurs der Moderne*, Frankfurt 1985; Axel Honneth, *Kritik der Macht*, Frankfurt 1985; and Albrecht Wellmer, *Zur Dialektik von Moderne und Postmoderne*, Frankfurt 1985. The extent of my intellectual debt to these authors will be evident throughout the present work; in particular to the conception, developed by Habermas in his own critique of poststructuralism, of philosophical paradigm-shift from consciousness to intersubjectivity.

245

12. See Michel Foucault, *The Use of Pleasure*, Harmondsworth 1986; and *Le souci de soi*, Paris 1984.

Chapter One

1. See Jacques Lacan, *Le séminaire Livre II: Le moi dans la théorie de Freud et dans la technique de la psychanalyse*, Paris 1978, chs 3-4.
2. See Paolo Caruso, *Conversazione con Lévi-Strauss, Foucault, Lacan*, Milan 1969, p. 117; and 'Structuralism and Post-Structuralism: an Interview with Michel Foucault', *Telos* 55, Spring 1983, pp. 203-4.
3. See Michel Foucault, *The Order of Things*, London 1974, p. 263.
4. This mid-sixties outlook is well exemplified in François Châtelet, 'Où en est le structuralisme?', *La Quinzaine Littéraire*, no. 31, 1 July 1967.
5. Behind Durkheim himself, of course, there stands the figure of Auguste Comte. As the originator both of the positivist tradition in French sociology and of the distinctive tradition of historical epistemology continued through Bachelard and Canguilhem, Comte's influence on French thought in the twentieth century has yet to be adequately evaluated.
6. Gerard Granel's review of *Of Grammatology*, reprinted in *Traditionis Traditio*, Paris 1972, welcomes Derrida's work as the rebirth of philosophical thought after a period of arid dogmatism.
7. Jacques Derrida, 'The Time of a Thesis', in Alan Montefiore, ed., *Philosophy in France Today*, London 1983, p. 41.
8. For an account of the intellectual background to Husserl's original project, see Karl-Otto Apel, 'Die beiden Phasen der Phänomenologie in ihrer Auswirkung auf das philosophische Vorverständnis der Gegenwart', in *Transformation der Philosophie*, Frankfurt 1976, vol. 1, pp. 79-86.
9. Jacques Derrida, ' "Genesis and Structure" and Phenomenology' in *Writing and Difference*, London 1978, p. 159.
10. *Writing and Difference*, p. 189n.
11. Ibid., p. 86.
12. Jacques Derrida, *Of Grammatology*, London 1976, p. 61.
13. Jacques Derrida, *Positions*, London 1981, pp. 104-5.
14. 'The Time of a Thesis', p. 39.
15. Ibid.
16. For a recent discussion of Husserl from this standpoint, see Bernhard Waldenfels, *In den Netzen der Lebenswelt*, Frankfurt 1985, chs 1-2.
17. Edmund Husserl, 'The Origin of Geometry', in *The Crisis of the European Sciences and Transcendental Phenomenology*, Evanston Ill. 1970, pp.357-8.
18. Ibid., p. 360.
19. Ibid.
20. Jacques Derrida, *Edmund Husserl's Origin of Geometry: An Introduction*, Stony Brook N.Y. 1978, p. 76.
21. Ibid., p. 88.
22. F.D.E. Schleiermacher, Heinz Kimmerle, ed., *Hermeneutik*, Heidelberg 1959, p. 38.
23. Ibid., p. 82.
24. Ibid., p. 81.
25. Hans-Georg Gadamer, *Truth and Method*, London 1975, p. 378.
26. Ibid., p. 361.
27. Jacques Derrida, 'The Double Session', in *Dissemination*, London 1981, p. 251.
28. *Positions*, p. 45.
29. Translated by Willis Domingo as *Against Epistemology: A Metacritique*, Oxford 1982.

30. *Against Epistemology*, p. 100.
31. Theodor Adorno, 'Die Aktualität der Philosophie', in *Gesammelte Schriften*, vol. 1, Frankfurt 1972, p. 333.
32. Ibid., p. 334.
33. Ibid.
34. Maurice Merleau-Ponty, 'The Philosopher and Sociology', in John O'Neill, ed., *Phenomenology, Language, Sociology*, London 1974, p. 104.
35. Maurice Merleau-Ponty, 'Phenomenology and the Sciences of Man', in *Phenomenology, Language, Sociology*, p. 276.
36. 'The Philosopher and Sociology', p. 102.
37. *Edmund Husserl's Origin of Geometry*, p. 112.
38. Ibid., p. 114.
39. Ibid., p. 116. In general, Derrida's interpretation of the development of Husserl's thought here seems rather one-sided. It would be more plausible to argue that Husserl is striving for an ever greater coincidence of the factual and the transcendental, precisely to avoid leaving anything 'outside'.
40. Ibid., p. 92.
41. Edmund Husserl, *Ideas: General Introduction to Pure Phenomenology*, New York 1962, p. 356.
42. *Against Epistemology*, p. 31.
43. 'The Origin of Geometry', p. 356.
44. *Edmund Husserl's Origin of Geometry*, p. 153.
45. Jacques Derrida, *Speech and Phenomena*, Evanston Ill. 1973, p. 81.
46. Ibid., p. 82.
47. Ibid., pp. 103, 86.
48. J.G. Fichte, 'First Introduction to the Science of Knowledge', in *The Science of Knowledge*, Cambridge 1982, p. 6.
49. See Hans Rademacher, *Fichtes Begriff des Absoluten*, Frankfurt 1970, ch. 1.
50. Here I follow Dieter Henrich's classic discussion of Fichte's engagement with the reflection theory of consciousness, 'Fichte's Original Insight', in Darrel E. Christiansen, ed., *Contemporary German Philosophy*, vol. 1, 1982.
51. J.G. Fichte, 'Second Introduction to the Science of Knowledge', in *The Science of Knowledge*, p. 38.
52. See Manfred Frank, *Eine Einführung in Schellings Philosophie*, Frankfurt 1985, ch. 3. My discussion of Fichte and Schelling and their relation to Derrida is greatly indebted to Frank's work. See also Andrew Bowie, 'Individuality and Différance', *Oxford Literary Review*, Vol. 7, no. 1-2, 1985.
53. F.W.J. Schelling, 'Of the I as Principle of Philosophy', in Fritz Marti trans. and commentary, *The Unconditional in Human Knowledge*, Lewisburg Pa 1980, p. 84.
54. F.W.J. Schelling, 'Zur Geschichte der neueren Philosophie', in Manfred Schröter, ed., *Werke*, Munich 1927, vol. 5, p. 163.
55. See Hans Michael Baumgartner, 'Das Unbedingte im Wissen: Ich-Identität-Freiheit', in Baumgartner, ed., *Schelling*, Freiburg/Munich 1975; and *Eine Einführung in Schellings Philosophie*, chs. 4-5.
56. See 'Of the I as Principle of Philosophy', pp. 73-4, 77.
57. *Positions*, p. 29.
58. *Of Grammatology*, p. 65.
59. Ibid., p. 61.
60. Ibid.
61. 'Of the I as Principle of Philosophy', pp. 71-2.
62. *Of Grammatology*, p. 63.
63. 'Of the I as Principle of Philosophy', p. 75.
64. On this aspect of Schelling, see Wolfgang Wieland, 'Die Anfänge der Philosophie Schellings und die Frage nach der Natur', in Manfred Frank and Gerhard Kurz, eds,

Materialien zu Schellings philosophischen Anfängen, Frankfurt 1974, pp. 250-254.

65. This difficulty of Derrida's position was noted at an early date by François Wahl: '. . . un concept nu de *différance* est contradiction, car la différence ne peut manquer d'être specifiée (*Qu'est-ce que le structuralisme?: philosophie*, Paris 1973, p. 186. Originally published 1968.)

66. *Speech and Phenomena*, p. 68; 'The Double Session', p. 209.

67. Jacques Derrida, 'Différance', in *Margins of Philosophy*, Brighton 1982, p. 17.

68. Jacques Derrida, 'The Ends of Man', in *Margins of Philosophy*, p. 134.

69. See Manfred Frank, *Was ist Neostrukturalismus?*, Frankfurt 1984, pp. 551-2.

70. J.G. Fichte, *Versuch einer neuen Darstellung der Wissenschaftslehre*, Hamburg 1975, p. 106.

71. Ibid., p. 107. For a discussion of this argument see Walter Benjamin, *Der Begriff der Kunstkritik in der deutschen Romantik*, Frankfurt 1978, pp. 14-21.

72. 'Dissemination', in *Dissemination*, pp. 333-4.

73. Thus, David Wood argues that 'differance is a condensation of a theory of the impossibility not of everyday presences in the empirical sense, but of a certain philosophical/metaphysical *value* of presence: *meaning* is never completely fulfilled.' ('Differance and the Problem of Strategy', in Robert Bernasconi and David Wood, eds, *Derrida and Differance*, Coventry 1985.) Yet the distinction between the 'empirical' and the 'metaphysical' is untenable in Derridean terms. The insistence on infinite regress – if it were coherent – would ruin *any* possibility of presence or meaning.

74. *Speech and Phenomena*, p. 92.

75. J.G. Fichte, *The Vocation of Man*, La Salle Ill. 1965, p. 89.

76. 'Of the I as Principle of Philosophy', pp. 83, 71.

77. Maurice Merleau-Ponty, *The Prose of the World*, Evanston 1973, p. 148.

78. Ibid., p. 103.

79. Maurice Merleau-Ponty, *The Visible and the Invisible*, Evanston 1968, p. 126.

80. *The Prose of the World*, p. 36.

81. Ibid., p. 22.

82. Jacques Derrida, 'Structure, Sign and Play in the Human Sciences', in *Writing and Difference*, p. 289.

83. Maurice Merleau-Ponty, *The Phenomenology of Perception*, London 1962, p. 85.

84. 'Structure, Sign and Play in the Human Sciences', p. 292.

85. Jacques Derrida, 'Du Tout', in *La carte postale de Socrate à Freud et au-delà*, Paris 1980, p. 536.

86. Jacques Derrida, 'Ja, ou le faux-bond', *Digraphe* 11, 1977, p. 117.

87. Jacques Derrida, 'Où commence et comment finit un corps enseignant', in Dominique Grisoni, ed., *Politiques de la philosophie*, Paris 1976, p. 67.

88. 'Dissemination', in *Dissemination*, p. 328.

89. See, for example, Jacques Derrida, 'The Principle of Reason: The University in the Eyes of its Pupils', *Diacritics*, Fall 1983.

90. *Positions*, p. 86.

91. *Speech and Phenomena*, p. 99.

92. 'Dialogue with Emmanuel Levinas', in Richard Kearney, *Dialogues with Contemporary Continental Thinkers*, Manchester 1984, p. 69.

93. Jacques Derrida, 'Ousia et Grammē', in *Margins of Philosophy*, p. 51; *Of Grammatology*, p. 46. It is true that, on one or two occasions, Derrida notes an anti-metaphysical potential of science. But, in general, his tendency is to portray the concept of science as inherently riveted to the concept of presence.

94. Theodor W. Adorno, *Philosophische Terminologie*, Frankfurt 1974, vol. 2, p. 286.

95. Theodor W. Adorno, *Negative Dialectics*, London 1973, pp. 22-3.

96. Ibid., pp. 176-7.
97. *Philosophische Terminologie*, vol. 2, p. 23.
98. *Negative Dialectics*, p. 197.
99. Ibid., p. 183.
100. Ibid., p. 186.
101. Ibid., p. 181.
102. *Positions*, p. 42.
103. *Against Epistemology*, p. 14.
104. *Negative Dialectics*, p. 103.
105. *Against Epistemology*, p. 183.
106. *Negative Dialectics*, p. 5.
107. Jacques Derrida, in the discussion following 'Structure, Sign and Play', in Richard Macksey and Eugenio Donato, eds, *The Structuralist Controversy*, Baltimore 1975, p. 272.
108. *Was ist Neostrukturalismus?*, p. 550.
109. See *Speech and Phenomena*, pp. 60-9.
110. See Martin Heidegger, 'Der Satz der Identität', in *Identität und Differenz*, Pfullingen 1957.
111. 'Freud and the Scene of Writing', in *Writing and Difference*, p. 229.
112. *Negative Dialectics*, p. 6.

Chapter Two

1. Three examples, from distinct philosophical traditions, are A.C. MacIntyre, *The Unconscious*, London 1958; Paul Ricoeur, *Freud and Philosophy*, London 1970; Jürgen Habermas, *Knowledge and Human Interests*, London 1972, chs 10-11.
2. *The Standard Edition of the Complete Psychological Works of Sigmund Freud*, J. Strachey, ed., London 1953-74, vol. 1, p. 295.
3. *Standard Edition*, vol. 5, p. 510.
4. For Reich's view of Freud, and his critique of other currents in psychoanalysis, see Wilhelm Reich, *Reich Speaks of Freud*, Harmondsworth, 1975, pp. 21-114.
5. For an account of Reich's intellectual itinerary, see Charles Rycroft, *Reich*, London 1971.
6. The founding document of this school is Heinz Hartmann, *Ego Psychology and the Problem of Adaptation*, New York, 1958. This work was first presented as a paper to the Vienna Psychoanalytic Society in 1937.
7. See Jacques Lacan, *Écrits: A Selection* (ES), London 1977, pp. 114-17.
8. Jacques Lacan, *Écrits* (E), Paris 1966, p. 329. This edition will be employed for those writings not available in the English selection.
9. E, p. 438.
10. Ibid.
11. Ibid.
12. Jacques Lacan, *De la psychose paranoïaque dans ses rapports avec la person-nalité*, collection 'Points' edition, Paris, 1974, p. 13.
13. See Jacques Lacan, 'Motifs du crime paranoïaque; le crime des soeurs Papin', reprinted in the full edition of *De la psychose paranoïaque*, Paris 1975. References will be to the 'Points' edition.
14. *De la psychose paranoïaque*, p.247.
15. Ibid., p. 337.
16. Jacques Lacan, 'Le problème du style', in *Le problème du style, suivi de Merleau-Ponty*, pirate edition, Paris (no date), pp. 4-5.
17. *De la psychose paranoïaque*, p.320.
18. Ibid., p. 319.

19. Ibid., p. 248.
20. E, p. 65.
21. E, p. 88.
22. E, p. 89.
23. See ibid.
24. ES, p. 8.
25. See E, p. 178.
26. While England and Italy had thriving schools of Hegelian thought during the 19th century, Hegel made no direct impact on French philosophy until the 1930s. Jean Wahl's *Le malheur de la conscience dans la philosophie de Hegel* (Paris 1929) marked the turning point, and it is significant that the Hegel to which the French educated public was introduced was the 'existentialist' rather than the 'systematic' Hegel. Kojève's courses, which interweave Hegel with Marx and Heidegger, began in 1933. Jean Hyppolite published the first part of his translation of the *Phenomenology* in 1939, and the second in 1941. His thesis on Hegel, *Genèse et structure de la Phénoménologie de l'Esprit*, appeared in 1946, and Kojève's courses were published a year later. In the *Écrits* Lacan pays tribute to Kojève and Hyppolite (p. 172n.). For more detail on the reception of Hegel in France see Hyppolite, 'La *Phénoménologie* de Hegel et la pensée française contemporaine', in *Figures de la pensée philosophique*, Paris 1971, vol. 1.
27. See Alexandre Kojève, *Introduction to the Reading of Hegel*, London 1980, pp. 3-30, and G.W.F. Hegel, *Phenomenology of Spirit*, A.V. Miller trans., Oxford 1977, pp. 104-111.
28. Ibid., p. 112.
29. Ibid., pp. 112-3.
30. Ibid., p. 112.
31. Ibid., p. 110.
32. ES, p. 4.
33. Ibid.
34. Freud, 'On Narcissism: An Introduction', *Standard Edition*, vol. 14, p. 98.
35. Freud, *The Ego and the Id*, *Standard Edition*, vol. 19, p. 29.
36. Ibid., pp. 55-56.
37. Ibid., p. 56.
38. For a helpful commentary on the origins of Lacan's view of the ego, see Sergio Benvenuto, 'Note a "Della psicosi paranoica" di J. Lacan', *Aut-Aut* 182, March-June 1981.
39. *De la psychose paranoïaque*, p. 324.
40. E, p. 69.
41. E, p. 374.
42. See Jacques Lacan, *Le séminaire Livre I: Les écrits techniques de Freud*, Paris 1975, pp. 240-2.
43. See ES, p. 6.
44. *Séminaire I*, p. 242.
45. *Phenomenology of Spirit*, p. 395; *Introduction to the Reading of Hegel*, p. 43.
46. *Introduction to the Reading of Hegel*, p. 6.
47. ES, p. 17.
48. Jacques Lacan, *Le séminaire Livre III: Les psychoses*, Paris, 1981, p. 50; ES, p. 17.
49. Jacques Lacan, *Le séminaire Livre II: Le moi dans la théorie de Freud et dans la technique de la psychanalyse*, p. 198.
50. *Séminaire III*, p. 50.
51. Ibid.
52. E, p. 375.
53. E, p. 166.

54. Jacques Lacan, 'Merleau-Ponty', in *Le problème du style suivi de Merleau-Ponty*, p. 13.
55. ES, p. 126.
56. Ibid.
57. *Séminaire I*, p. 126.
58. Ibid., p. 264.
59. E, p. 82.
60. ES, p. 87.
61. ES, p. 83.
62. ES, p. 85.
63. ES, p. 77.
64. See Paul Ricoeur, *Freud and Philosophy*, pp. 461-82; Jürgen Habermas, *Knowledge and Human Interests*, pp. 271-2; Jean Hyppolite, '*Phénoménologie de Hegel et psychanalyse*', in *Figures de la pensée philosophique*, vol. 1.
65. *Phenomenology of Spirit*, p. 491.
66. *Séminaire I*, p. 20.
67. Ibid.
68. Ibid., p. 46.
69. E, p. 144.
70. ES, p. 54.
71. ES, p. 52.
72. Ibid.
73. ES, p. 53.
74. Jacques Lacan, *The Four Fundamental Concepts of Psychoanalysis*, trans. by Alan Sherican of *Le séminaire Livre XI*, Harmondsworth 1979, p. 180.
75. E, p. 875.
76. ES, p. 51.
77. *Séminaire I*, p. 294.
78. *Séminaire II*, p. 58.
79. This conception of analysis, and the American 'ego-psychology' on which it is based, is one of Lacan's favourite targets.
80. E, p. 302.
81. See Martin Heidegger, *Being and Time*, Oxford 1962, pp. 434-9.
82. ES, p. 4.
83. Jacques Lacan, 'The Neurotic's Individual Myth', *Psychoanalytical Quarterly*, vol. 48, 1979, p. 423.
84. See ES, pp. 47-48.
85. E, p. 86.
86. See E, p. 172.
87. ES, p. 80.
88. E, p. 373.
89. Jean-Paul Sartre, *Being and Nothingness*, trans. Hazel Barnes, London 1958, pp. 53-4.
90. Maurice Merleau-Ponty, *The Phenomenology of Perception*, London 1962, pp. 157-8.
91. Erich Fromm, 'Freud's Model of Man and its Social Determinants', in *The Crisis of Psychoanalysis*, Harmondsworth 1973, p. 47.
92. R.D. Laing, *The Divided Self*, Harmondsworth 1973, p. 19.
93. ES, p. 76.
94. 'The Neurotic's Individual Myth', p. 406.
95. *Séminaire I*, p. 82.
96. Ibid., p. 178.
97. Ibid., pp. 32, 20.
98. E, p. 381.

99. The '*Discours de Rome*' is the common name for the longest *écrit*, 'The function and field of speech and language in psychoanalysis' (ES, pp. 30-113). Due to be delivered to an official congress in Rome, in September 1953, it was delivered to an alternative gathering of analysts in the same city, because of a split in the Paris Psychoanalytic Society centred on Lacan.
100. *Séminaire II*, p. 386.
101. 'Hegel is at the limits of anthropology. Freud went beyond them. His discovery is that man is not completely in man. Freud is not a humanist': *Séminaire II*, p. 92.
102. See, for example, E, pp. 867-8.
103. Jacques Lacan, 'Of Structure as an Inmixing of an Otherness Prerequisite to any Subject Whatever', in *The Structuralist Controversy*, p. 188.
104. *De la psychose paranoïaque*, p. 309.
105. Ibid., p. 38.
106. Ibid., p. 309.
107. Ibid., p. 314.
108. Ibid.
109. *Séminaire I*, p. 7.
110. ES, p. 281.
111. ES, p. 149.
112. See ES, pp. 84-5, for Lacan's demonstration that the 'language of the bees' is not a language in the human sense.
113. 'Of Structure as an Inmixing', p. 194.
114. ES, p. 150.
115. See *Séminaire III*, ch. 14.
116. Ibid., p. 223.
117. Ibid., p. 216.
118. Claude Lévi-Strauss, 'Introduction à l'oeuvre de Marcel Mauss', in Marcel Mauss, *Sociologie et Anthropologie*, Paris 1950, p. xix.
119. Claude Lévi-Strauss, 'A Confrontation', *New Left Review* 62, July-August 1970, p. 64.
120. Claude Lévi-Strauss, *L'Homme nu*, Paris 1971, p. 562.
121. 'Introduction à l'oeuvre de Marcel Mauss', p. xxxii.
122. Claude Lévi-Strauss, *Totemism*, London 1964, p. 68.
123. Ibid., p. 77.
124. ES, p. 66.
125. ES, p. 46.
126. ES, p. 48.
127. ES, p. 307.
128. E, p. 857.
129. *Séminaire II*, p. 96.
130. ES, p. 301.
131. *Séminaire II*, p. 96.
132. Lacan's discovery that linguistic meaning cannot be grounded in intention may be compared with almost contemporary developments in analytical philosophy, where the attempt to theorize meaning in terms of communicative intention ran aground on the realization that communicative intention, in order to succeed, requires a higher-level intention to secure the recognition of the intention to communicate (see P.F. Strawson, 'Intention and Convention in Speech Acts', in J.R. Searle, ed., *The Philosophy of Language*, Oxford 1971). But once this is appreciated, an indefinitely escalating series of intentions can be seen to be required, a mirror-play of intention and recognition which corresponds to Lacan's realization that *all* intersubjectivity is imaginary.
133. *Séminaire II*, p. 43.

134. E, p. 346.
135. *Séminaire III*, p. 47.
136. *Séminaire II*, p. 286.
137. Ibid., p. 48.
138. ES, p. 126.
139. ES, p. 172.
140. *Séminaire II*, p. 286.
141. ES, p. 304.
142. ES, p. 101.
143. E, p. 23.
144. E, p. 25. Lacan's phrasing neatly condenses his distinction between the predictability of a code-determined reaction, and the unpredictability of a human reply.
145. E, p. 30.
146. Jacques Lacan, 'Introduction à l'édition allemande d'un premier volume des *Écrits*', *Scilicet* 5, 1975, p. 11.
147. ES, p. 288.
148. ES, p. 287.
149. E, p. 709.
150. E, p. 830.
151. E, p. 834.
152. 'The unconscious is that part of the concrete discourse, in so far as it is transindividual, that is not at the disposal of the individual in re-establishing the continuity of his conscious discourse': ES, p. 49; 'The unconscious is the sum of the effects of speech on a subject, at that level where the subject constitutes itself from the effects of the signifier': *The Four Fundamental Concepts*, p. 126.
153. E, p. 469.
154. Jacques Lacan, 'Psychanalyse et médicine'. Cited in Moustafa Safouan, *Le structuralisme en psychanalyse*, Paris, 1973, p. 32.
155. *Séminaire I*, p. 79.
156. E, p. 469.
157. *Séminaire I*, p. 79.
158. *The Four Fundamental Concepts*, p. 25.
159. 'Psychanalyse et médicine'. Cited in Safouan, p. 32.
160. *Séminaire II*, p. 150.
161. Freud, 'Inhibitions, Symptoms, Anxiety', *Standard Edition*, vol. 20, p. 139.
162. ES, p. 285.
163. Jacques Lacan, 'La relation d'objet et les structures freudiennes' (*compte rendu* of the fourth *Seminar*), *Bulletin de Psychologie*, vol. 11, 1957-8, p. 852.
164. Ibid., p. 851.
165. *Séminaire III*, p. 329.
166. Freud, 'Analysis Terminable and Interminable', *Standard Edition*, vol. 23, p. 225.
167. Jacques Lacan, 'Ou Pire', in *Scilicet* 5, p. 9.
168. See, for example, 'The Freudian Thing', in E, p. 128-9.
169. E, p. 158.

Chapter Three

1. ES, p. 165.
2. ES, p. 138. For a comparison of Schelling's critique of Descartes with that of Lacan, see Manfred Frank, *Was ist Neostrukturalismus?*, pp. 376-81.
3. See *Was ist Neostrukturalismus?*, ch. 19.

4. Maurice Merleau-Ponty, 'On the Phenomenology of Language', in *Phenomenology, Language and Sociology*, p.85.
5. ES, p. 285.
6. For Lacan's connection of the object *a* with the question of style, see E, p. 10.
7. *The Four Fundamental Concepts*, p. 103.
8. Jacques Lacan, 'La relation d'objet et les structures freudiennes', resumé of *Séminaire IV, Bulletin de Psychologie*, vol. 10, 1956-7, p. 269.
9. *Was ist Neostrukturalismus?*, p. 376.
10. Jacques Lacan, 'Desire and Interpretation in Hamlet, in *Yale French Studies*, no. 55/56, 1977, p. 29. For further discussion of the connections between Lacan's and Fichte's theories of the self, see Jacques-Alain Miller, 'Action de la structure', in *Cahiers pour l'analyse*, no. 9, Summer 1968, pp. 103-5.
11. ES, p. 315.
12. *Speech and Phenomena*, p.82.
13. ES, p. 307.
14. See 'Radiophonie', pp. 55-6; *Positions*, p. 90.
15. See 'Plato's Drugstore', in *Dissemination*, pp. 142-55, and ES, p. 199.
16. E, p. 470.
17. For example Roland Barthes's *S/Z* (Paris 1970), based on courses given at the Ecole Pratique des Hautes Etudes in 1968 and '69, both inveighs against the difference-suppressing 'system of closure of the West' and employs a Lacanian account of the relation between the symbolic and castration. Much of the work of the *Tel Quel* group from around the same period also bears the mark of both thinkers. In his *Psychanalyser*, Paris 1968, Serge Leclaire, a close follower of Lacan, refers favourably to Derrida (p. 69). Lacan's adherents were subsequently forbidden to follow Derrida's teaching.
18. GREPH was founded in 1974 as an organization of philosophy teachers in secondary and tertiary education, and of philosophy students, to research critically into the history of philosophy teaching and to combat the government's proposed cutbacks in this area. See the collective volume *Qui a peur de la philosophie?*, Paris 1977.
19. Collected in Jacques Derrida, *La carte postale: de Socrate à Freud et au-delà*. Translated as 'The Purveyor of Truth', *Yale French Studies* 52, 1975.
20. See Philippe Lacoue-Labarthe and Jean-Luc Nancy, eds, *Les fins de l'homme*, Paris 1981.
21. See 'Discussion' following Jacques Derrida, 'Structure, Sign and Play in the Human Sciences', in Richard Macksey and Eugenio Donato, eds, *The Structuralist Controversy*, London 1970, pp.271-2.
22. *Positions*, p. 28.
23. 'Différance', in *Margins of Philosophy*, p. 15.
24. Ibid., p. 12.
25. Ibid.
26. 'Structure, Sign and Play', in *Writing and Difference*, p. 280.
27. *Positions*, p. 90.
28. E, p. 840.
29. Jacques Lacan, *Le séminaire Livre XX: Encore*, Paris 1975, p. 10.
30. Edmund Husserl, *Logical Investigations*, trans. J.N. Findlay, London 1970, vol. 1, p. 276.
31. 'Le Désir et Son Interpretation' (*compte rendu* of sixth *Seminar*) *Bulletin de Psychologie*, vol. 13, 1959-60, p.264.
32. ES, p. 304.
33. ES, p. 306.
34. Ibid.
35. ES, pp. 665-6.
36. *The Four Fundamental Concepts*, p. 199.

37. ES, p. 300.
38. Jacques Derrida, 'The Purveyor of Truth', *Yale French Studies* 52, p. 65.
39. Ibid., p. 84.
40. E, p. 24.
41. 'An Interview with Derrida', in David Wood and Robert Bernasconi, eds, *Derrida and Differance*, Coventry 1985, p. 111.
42. Jacques Derrida, *Schibboleth pour Paul Celan*, Paris 1986, pp. 30-31.
43. 'Dialogue with Jacques Derrida', in Richard Kearney, *Dialogues with Contemporary Continental Thinkers*, p. 123.
44. 'Dissemination' in *Dissemination*, p. 328.
45. *Séminaire III*, p. 18.
46. *Séminaire XX*, p. 23.
47. E, p. 388.
48. *The Four Fundamental Concepts*, p. 167. As with so many elements of his theory, Lacan is directly indebted to Kojève for this argument. In his celebrated lectures on Hegel, Kojève states that, 'I do not believe that one can define the *Real* in the strict sense in any other way than Maine de Biran (among others) has done: the real is that which *resists*. One is completely wrong to think that the real resists thought. In fact it does not resist it . . . The Real resists Action, and not thought.' (*Introduction à la lecture de Hegel*, collection TEL edn, Paris 1979, pp. 432-33.)
49. Dan Sperber, *Le structuralisme en anthropologie*, Paris 1973, pp.81-2.
50. See Pierre Bourdieu, 'Symbolic Power', in *Critique of Anthropology* 13/14, Summer 1979, pp. 78-85.
51. Jacques Lacan, 'Actes du Congrès de Rome', cited in Vincent Descombes, 'L'Equivoque du symbolique', *Modern Language Notes*, vol. 94, no. 4, May 1979, p. 657-8.
52. ES, p. 308.
53. *Séminaire II*, p. 236.
54. Ibid.
55. Jacques Lacan, *Télévision*, Paris 1973, p. 51. For further discussion of the status of the Oedipus complex in Lacan's thought, see Alain Juranville, *Lacan et la philosophie*, Paris 1984, pp. 199-207.
56. E, p. 782.
57. *Séminaire I*, p. 51.
58. ES, p. 119.
59. E, p. 709.
60. E, p. 834.
61. ES, p. 269.

Chapter Four

1. See Claude Lévi-Strauss, *L'Homme nu*, pp. 563, 570.
2. Jean François Lyotard, *Dérive à partir de Marx et Freud*, Paris 1973, p. 11.
3. *Dérive*, p. 311.
4. Jean-François Lyotard, *La phénoménologie*, Paris, 1954.
5. Ibid., p. 43.
6. Ibid., p. 44.
7. 'Structure, Sign and Play', p. 292.
8. 'Dissemination', p. 328.
9. *La phénoménologie*, p. 43.
10. Ibid., p. 43.
11. Ibid., p. 5.
12. Jean-François Lyotard, *Discours, Figure* (DF), Paris 1971, p. 9.

13. DF, p. 11.
14. DF, p. 14.
15. DF, p. 33.
16. DF, p. 34.
17. DF, p. 32.
18. DF, p. 31.
19. DF, p. 118.
20. DF, p. 109.
21. *Positions*, p. 90.
22. Ibid.
23. Ibid., p. 40.
24. In the discussion following his 'Structure, Sign and Play in the Human Sciences', in Macksey and Donato, eds, *The Structuralist Controversy*, Baltimore 1972, p. 272.
25. DF, p. 38.
26. DF, p. 52.
27. DF, p. 129.
28. DF, p. 211.
29. DF, p. 218.
30. *Dérive*, p. 229.
31. *The Visible and the Invisible*, p. 38.
32. See, for example, ibid., pp. 107-8.
33. Ibid., p. 58.
34. Ibid., p. 230.
35. DF, p. 56.
36. Ibid.
37. Cited in DF, p. 108n.
38. DF, p. 59.
39. DF, p. 271.
40. Freud, *The Interpretation of Dreams*, *Standard Edition*, vol. 4, p. 278.
41. ES, p. 159.
42. Ibid.
43. ES, p. 164.
44. Ibid.
45. Ibid.
46. DF, p. 129.
47. DF, p. 238.
48. DF, p. 244.
49. *Standard Edition* vol. 4, pp. 296, 169-76.
50. Cf. ES, p. 157 and DF, p. 259.
51. *Standard Edition*, vol. 4, p. 306.
52. *Dérive*, p. 225.
53. *Standard Edition*, vol. 5, p. 546.
54. Ibid., p. 534.
55. ES, p. 161.
56. ES, p. 259.
57. Jacques Lacan, 'Radiophonie', in *Scilicet*, vol. 2/3, 1970, p. 69.
58. *Standard Edition*, vol. 5, p. 667.
59. DF, p. 270.
60. DF, p. 349.
61. *Dérive*, p. 240.
62. DF, p. 360.
63. DF, p. 384.
64. *Dérive*, p. 174.

65. Jean-François Lyotard, 'Presentations', in Alan Montefiore, ed., *Philosophy in France Today*, p. 128.
66. DF, p. 19.
67. *Dérive*, p. 104.
68. Ibid., p. 306.
69. Ibid., p. 208.
70. Epistémon (pseudonym of Didier Anzieu), *Ces idées qui ont ebranlé la France*, Paris 1968, p. 17.
71. *Dérive*, p. 226.
72. Ibid., p. 226.
73. Ibid., p. 225.
74. DF, p. 246.
75. Jean-François Lyotard, *Des dispositifs pulsionnels*, Paris 1973, p. 281.
76. See Gilles Deleuze and Félix Guattari, *Anti-Oedipus*, London 1984.
77. Phillipe Lacoue-Labarthe, 'Theatrum Analyticum', in *Glyph* 2, 1977, p. 123.
78. Nietzsche, Walter Kaufman, ed., *The Will to Power*, New York 1968, p. 550.
79. *The Will to Power*, p. 36.
80. Jean-François Lyotard, *Économie Libidinale*, Paris, 1974, back cover.
81. *Économie Libidinale*, p. 64.
82. *Des dispositifs pulsionnels*, p. 63.
83. *Économie Libidinale*, p. 11.
84. Jean-François Lyotard, 'Contributions des tableaux de Jacques Monore', in Gerald Gassiot-Talabot et al., *Figurations 1960-1973*, Paris, 1973, p. 154.
85. 'Contributions des tableaux de Jacques Monory', p. 158.
86. Ibid., p. 156.
87. Ibid., p. 155.
88. *Économie Libidinale*, p. 36.
89. Freud, 'Beyond the Pleasure Principle', *Standard Edition*, vol. 17, p. 36.
90. Freud, 'An Outline of Psychoanalysis', *Standard Edition*, vol. 23, p. 149.
91. *Économie Libidinale*, p. 311.
92. Ibid., p. 309.
93. *Des dispositifs pulsionnels*, p. 18.
94. *Economie Libidinale*, p. 257.
95. *Des dispositifs pulsionnels*, pp. 308-9.
96. *Économie Libidinale*, p. 311.
97. For the critique of Deleuze and Guattari's position, see *Économie Libidinale*, pp. 54-5.
98. See Jean-François Lyotard and Jean Loup Thébaud, *Just Gaming*, Manchester 1986, pp. 89-90.
99. *Negative Dialectics*, p. 146.
100. Friedrich Nietzsche, *The Twilight of the Idols*, in *The Twilight of the Idols/The Anti-Christ*, trans. R.J. Hollingdale, Harmondsworth 1968, p. 37.
101. *Économie Libidinale*, p. 294.
102. See, for example, Jean-François Lyotard (with J. Monory), *Récits Tremblants*, Paris 1977, pp.53-7.
103. DF, p. 357.
104. Theodor Adorno, *Negative Dialectics*, p. 317.
105. Theodor Adorno, 'Theorie der Halbbildung', in *Gesammelte Schriften*, vol. 8, p. 115.
106. Theodor Adorno, 'Psychology and Sociology', *New Left Review* 47, January-February 1967, p. 88.
107. Jean-François Lyotard, *Des dispositifs pulsionnels*, p. 315.
108. 'Adorno come Diavolo', in *Des dispositifs pulsionnels*, pp. 122-3.
109. See 'Psychology and Sociology', pp. 86-91.

Chapter Five

1. Jean-François Lyotard, *Discours, Figure*, p. 213.
2. The phrase is employed by Lyotard in *Dérive à partir de Marx et Freud*, p. 311.
3. Lyotard's *Économie Libidinale* differs from Gilles Deleuze and Félix Guattari's *Anti-Oedipus*, in explicitly embracing this consequence.
4. See Michel Foucault, 'Omnes et Singulatim: Towards a Criticism of "Political Reason"', in S.M. McMurrin, ed., *The Tanner Lectures on Human Values*, Cambridge 1981.
5. Michel Foucault, *Madness and Civilization*, New York 1973, p. 61.
6. Ibid., p. 278.
7. Michel Foucault, *The Birth of the Clinic*, London 1973, p. 28.
8. *The Birth of the Clinic*, p. 79.
9. Ibid., p. xix. The word 'structural' is omitted from more recent French editions.
10. This reworking can be observed in an interview of the early seventies, where Foucault states: 'What I am trying to do is grasp the implicit systems which determine our most familiar behaviour without our knowing it. I am trying to find their origin, to show their formation, the constraint they impose upon us. I am therefore trying to place myself at a distance from them and to show how one could escape': 'Interview with J.K. Simon', *Partisan Review*, vol. 38, no. 2, 1971.
11. Michel Foucault, *Discipline and Punish*, Harmondsworth 1977, p. 192.
12. Michel Foucault, Colin Gordon, ed., *Power/Knowledge*, Brighton 1980, p. 151.
13. Ibid., pp. 151-2.
14. *Discipline and Punish*, p. 206.
15. Ibid., p. 301.
16. See 'Structuralism and Post-Structuralism: An Interview with Michel Foucault', *Telos* 55, p. 200.
17. *Discipline and Punish*, p. 174.
18. In a discussion of the Soviet prison system, for example, Foucault describes a form of modern power which is 'authoritarian', 'cynical', and 'fear-instilling': 'The Politics of Crime', *Partisan Review*, vol. 43, no. 3, 1976. Foucault argues that the systems of surveillance and control employed by the Soviet state are simply an enlarged and perfected version of those developed by the nineteenth-century bourgeoisie.
19. *Power/Knowledge*, p. 156.
20. Theodor Adorno and Max Horkheimer, *Dialectic of Enlightenment*, London 1979, p. 36.
21. *Negative Dialectics*, p. 180.
22. Theodor Adorno, 'Subject and Object', in Andrew Arato and Eike Gebhardt, eds, *The Essential Frankfurt School Reader*, Oxford 1978, p. 499.
23. See Jürgen Habermas, *The Theory of Communicative Action*, vol. 1, trans. Thomas McCarthy, Boston, 1984, p. 387.
24. See ibid., pp. 10-15.
25. See Jürgen Habermas, 'What is Universal Pragmatics?', in *Communication and the Evolution of Society*, London 1979.
26. Jürgen Habermas, *Theorie des kommunikativen Handelns*, Frankfurt 1981, vol. 2, pp. 489-91.
27. *Negative Dialectics*, p. 160.
28. Max Horkheimer, *Eclipse of Reason*, New York 1974, p. 138.
29. *Negative Dialectics*, p. 277.
30. See Jürgen Habermas, 'Moral Development and Ego-Identity', in *Communication and the Evolution of Society*.

31. Friedrich Nietzsche, *The Genealogy of Morals*, in *The Birth of Tragedy/The Genealogy of Morals*, trans. Francis Golffing, New York 1956, p. 190.
32. Ibid., p. 217.
33. Ibid., p. 220.
34. *Madness and Civilization*, pp. 115, 83.
35. Ibid., p. 248.
36. Ibid., pp. 267, 247.
37. Ibid., p. 265.
38. Ibid., p. 369.
39. Ibid., p. 250.
40. Ibid.
41. *The Birth of the Clinic*, p. 38.
42. Ibid., p. 52.
43. Ibid., p. 39.
44. *Discipline and Punish*, p. 29.
45. Ibid., pp. 202-3.
46. Ibid., p. 193.
47. *Theorie des kommunikativen Handelns*, vol. 2, pp. 115-7.
48. Michel Foucault, *The History of Sexuality: Volume 1: An Introduction*, Harmondsworth 1981, p. 58. The title of the French original, *La volonté de savoir*, gives a much more informative clue to Foucault's intentions. Throughout this work, '*The History of Sexuality*' refers to vol. 1.
49. *The History of Sexuality*, p. 64.
50. Ibid., p. 59.
51. Ibid., p. 60.
52. *Power/Knowledge*, p. 103.
53. *Discipline and Punish*, p. 222.
54. Ibid. (my emphasis).
55. *Negative Dialectics*, p. 171.
56. Michel Foucault, 'Revolutionary Action: "Until Now"', in Donald Bouchard, ed., *Language, Counter-Memory, Practice*, Oxford 1977, p. 222.
57. *Discipline and Punish*, p. 30.
58. *Power/Knowledge*, p. 98.
59. See the 'Preface' to Michel Foucault, *Folie et déraison: histoire de la folie à l'âge classique*, Paris 1961.
60. *Madness and Civilization*, p. 250.
61. Ibid., p. 281.
62. See Paolo Caruso, *Conversazioni con Lévi-Strauss, Foucault, Lacan*, pp. 98-100.
63. *Discipline and Punish*, pp. 29, 30.
64. Ibid., pp. 137, 145.
65. *Language, Counter-Memory, Practice*, pp. 222, 208.
66. *Power/Knowledge*, pp. 8-9.
67. Ibid., p. 164.
68. 'Non au sexe roi' (interview with Michel Foucault), *Le Nouvel Observateur*, no. 644, 12-21 March 1977, p. 113.
69. *The History of Sexuality*, p. 22.
70. Ibid., p. 155.
71. See *Dérive à partir de Marx et Freud*, p. 145.
72. See Jean-François Lyotard, Contribution des tableaux de Jacques Monory', in *Figurations 1960-1973*, pp. 154-238.
73. *The History of Sexuality*, p. 93.
74. Ibid., p. 103.
75. Ibid., p. 53.

76. Ibid., p. 57.
77. Ibid., pp. 152-3.
78. Michel Foucault, 'Introduction' to *Herculine Barbin: Being the Recently Discovered Memoirs of a Nineteenth-Century French Hermaphrodite*, Brighton 1980, pp. xiii, vii.
79. *The History of Sexuality*, p. 4.
80. *Power/Knowledge*, p. 191.
81. Ibid., p. 190.

Chapter Six

1. Max Weber, Talcott Parsons ed., *The Theory of Social and Economic Organization* (Part I of *Economy and Society*), Toronto 1964, p. 339.
2. See *Language, Counter-Memory, Practice*, p. 225.
3. Alain Schapp and Pierre Vidal-Naquet, eds, *The French Student Uprising November 1967-June 1968*, Boston 1971, p. 117.
4. *Eclipse of Reason*, p. 62.
5. *Discipline and Punish*, p. 249.
6. Ibid., pp. 220-1.
7. Ibid., p. 27.
8. See *Histoire de la folie à l'âge classique*, collection 'Tel' edition, Paris, 1976, pp. 56-9. This edition will be used for those sections not translated in the condensed English edition. The full 'Préface' appears only in the original French edition, Paris 1961.
9. Ibid., p. 481.
10. Ibid., p. 480.
11. *The Birth of the Clinic*, p. 16.
12. Ibid., p. 16.
13. Ibid., p. 42.
14. *The Archaeology of Knowledge*, London 1972, p. 45.
15. *Discipline and Punish*, p. 27.
16. *Power/Knowledge*, p. 59.
17. Ibid., p. 61.
18. *Discipline and Punish*, p. 193.
19. Ibid., p. 28.
20. Georges Canguilhem, 'L'Objet de l'histoire des sciences', in *Études de l'histoire et de la philosophie des sciences*, Paris 1968, p. 18.
21. It is for this reason that Canguilhem can attack Thomas Kuhn for allowing normal science only 'an empirical mode of existence as a fact of culture': Georges Canguilhem, *Idéologie et rationalité dans l'histoire des sciences de la vie*, Paris 1977, p. 23. By contrast, Foucault persistently reads Canguilhem as a relativist. See Michel Foucault, 'Georges Canguilhem: philosopher of error', *Ideology and Consciousness*, No. 7, Autumn 1980.
22. Nietzsche, *The Birth of Tragedy*, in *The Birth of Tragedy/The Genealogy of Morals*, p. 93.
23. *The Will to Power*, p. 263.
24. Ibid., pp. 272, 281.
25. See, for example, Eugen Fink, *Nietzsches Philosophie*, Stuttgart 1960.
26. *The Will to Power*, p. 263.
27. *The Birth of Tragedy*, pp. 53.
28. *The Will to Power*, p. 330.
29. Ibid., p. 305.
30. Ibid., p. 307.
31. Ibid., p. 280.

32. Ibid., p. 550.
33. *Power/Knowledge*, p. 133.
34. Michel Foucault, *Maladie mentale et psychologie*, Paris 1966, p. 7.
35. 'Préface', in *Histoire de la folie à l'âge classique*, p. iv.
36. *Madness and Civilization*, p. 84.
37. *Histoire de la folie à l'âge classique*, p. 462.
38. Ibid., p. 330.
39. *Madness and Civilization*, p. 117.
40. Ibid., p. 176.
41. Ibid., p. 177.
42. Ibid., p. 276.
43. 'Preface', in *Histoire de la folie à l'âge classique*, p. vii.
44. Ibid.
45. Ibid.
46. See, for example, Henri Lefebvre, *L'idéologie structuraliste*, Paris, 1971.
47. Caruso, p. 126.
48. Michel Foucault, 'Interview with M. Chapsai', *La Quinzaine Littéraire*, no. 5, 16 May 1966, p. 15.
49. Michel Foucault, 'La folie, l'absence d'oeuvre', *La Table Ronde*, May 1964, p. 18.
50. Michel Foucault, 'Preface', in *The Order of Things*, London 1970, p. xxiv.
51. Ibid.
52. *The Archaeology of Knowledge*, p. 47.
53. Ibid.
54. Caruso, pp. 94-5.
55. Ibid., p. 56.
56. Ibid.
57. *Madness and Civilization*, p. 250.
58. *Discipline and Punish*, p. 18.
59. Ibid., p. 198.
60. 'Introduction' to *Herculine Barbin*, p. viii.
61. *The Archaeology of Knowledge*, p. 13.
62. *The History of Sexuality*, pp. 94-5.
63. *The Will to Power*, p. 326.
64. This tendency is also prominent, perhaps even more so than in Foucault himself, in work produced under the Foucauldian aegis. See, for example, Pasquale Pasquino, 'Theatricum Politicum. The genealogy of capital – police and the state of prosperity', and Giovanna Procacci, 'Social economy and the government of poverty', in *Ideology and Consciousness*, no. 4, Autumn 1978. See also Jacques Donzelot, *La police des familles*, Paris 1977.
65. Jacques Léonard, 'L'historien et le philosophe', in Michelle Perrot, ed., *L'impossible prison*, Paris 1970, p. 12.
66. Gianna Pomata, 'Storie di "police" e storie di vita: note sulla storiographia foucaultiana', in *Aut-Aut* 170-1, March-June 1979, p. 62.
67. Michel Foucault, 'Table ronde du 20 mai 1978', in *L'impossible prison*, p. 55.
68. *Madness and Civilization*, p. 271.
69. *Power/Knowledge*, p. 47.
70. Ibid., p. 118.
71. *Discipline and Punish*, p. 296.
72. *Power/Knowledge*, p. 82.
73. *Discipline and Punish*, p. 27.
74. *Power/Knowledge*, p. 83.
75. Ibid., p. 84.
76. *Discipline and Punish*, p. 27.

77. *Negative Dialectics*, p. 10.
78. See 'Questions on Geography', in *Power/Knowledge*, p. 66, where Foucault presents his aims as being to trace the 'hazardous career of truth'.
79. Jürgen Habermas, *Knowledge and Human Interests*, London 1972, p. 191.
80. Ibid., p. 196.
81. Jürgen Habermas, 'Technology and Science as Ideology', in *Towards a Rational Society*, London 1971, p. 111.
82. Jürgen Habermas, 'Eine psychoanalytische Konstruktion des Fortschritts', in *Kultur und Kritik: Verstreute Aufsätze*, Frankfurt 1977, p. 114.
83. 'Technology and Science as Ideology', pp. 105-6.
84. See Jürgen Habermas, 'Die Krise des Wohlfahrtsstaates und die Erschöpfung utopischer Energien', in *Die neue Unübersichtlichkeit: Kleine Politische Schriften V*, Frankfurt 1985, esp. pp. 151-2.
85. *Discipline and Punish*, p. 184-5.
86. Michel Foucault, 'The Subject and Power', *Critical Inquiry* 8, Summer 1982, p. 777.
87. *Histoire de la folie à l'âge classique*, p. 465.
88. Ibid., pp. 56-9.
89. In his book on Foucault and the Frankfurt School, *Kritik der Macht*, Frankfurt 1985, Axel Honneth argues that, during the 1970s, Foucault develops a *strategic* concept of power, which can be seen as a corrective to the Adorno/Horkheimer conception of totalized instrumental reason, although he also admits that Foucault's concept ultimately lapses into functionalism, since he can give no account of how relations of power are intersubjectively sustained. Against this, I would suggest that the conception of the social domain as the battlefield of social forces is very much a secondary theme in Foucault's later work. Honneth himself stresses that one of Foucault's crucial mistakes is to counter the metasubject of the philosophy of history with an abolition of the subject, rather than moving to the 'more plausible model of a plurality of historical actors' (p. 136). But without any adequate conception of the plurality of social actors, Foucault's theory of power is bound to remain predominantly functional and institutional.
90. *Madness and Civilization*, p. 248.
91. *Discipline and Punish*, p. 61.
92. Ibid., pp. 63, 249.
93. Ibid., p. 200.
94. *Madness and Civilization*, p. 262.

Chapter Seven

1. Michel Foucault, 'Truth and Power', in *Power/Knowledge*, p. 114.
2. Michel Foucault, 'The Eye of Power', in ibid., p. 154.
3. Michel Foucault, 'Revolutionary Action: "Until Now"', in *Language, Counter-Memory, Practice*, p. 233.
4. Michel Foucault, 'Two Lectures', in *Power/Knowledge*, p. 83.
5. See Jean-François Lyotard, 'La place de l'aliénation dans le retournement marxiste', in *Dérive à partir de Marx et Freud*.
6. Jean-François Lyotard, 'Dérives', in ibid., pp. 14-15.
7. Ibid., p. 13.
8. Caruso, p. 117.
9. Jean-François Lyotard, 'Leçon d'impouvoir', in *Dérive*, p. 275.
10. Friedrich Nietzsche, *Human, All too Human*, trans. R.J. Hollingdale, Cambridge 1986, p. 302.
11. Ibid., p. 13.
12. Friedrich Nietzsche, *Beyond Good and Evil*, trans. R.J. Hollingdale, Harmondsworth 1973, p. 143.

13. Friedrich Nietzsche, *The Gay Science*, trans. with a commentary by Walter Kaufmann, New York, 1974, p. 334.
14. Daniel Breazeale, ed., *Philosophy and Truth, Selections from Nietzsche's Notebooks of the early 1870s*, Sussex 1979, p. 40. The '*Philosophenbuch*' is the name often given to a central section of these notebooks.
15. Ibid., p. 23.
16. *The Gay Science*, p. 336.
17. *Beyond Good and Evil*, p. 47.
18. *The Genealogy of Morals*, p. 255.
19. *Philosophy and Truth*, p. 96.
20. *Beyond Good and Evil*, p. 123.
21. Michel Foucault, 'Nietzsche, Freud, Marx', in *Nietzsche* (Cahiers de Royaumont), Paris, 1967, p. 189.
22. Ibid., p. 192.
23. Ibid., p. 192.
24. Gilles Deleuze, *Nietzsche and Philosophy*, London 1983, p. 158.
25. 'Nietzsche, Freud, Marx', p. 192.
26. *Language, Counter-Memory, Practice*, p. 151.
27. Ibid., p. 146, 148.
28. Ibid., p. 153.
29. Ibid., p. 151.
30. Ibid., p. 154.
31. Ibid., p. 156-7.
32. Michel Foucault, 'Réponse au cercle d'épistémologie', *Cahiers pour l'analyse*, No. 9, Summer 1968, p. 16.
33. *Power/Knowledge*, pp. 81-2.
34. Ibid., p. 85.
35. Ibid., p. 80-81.
36. Michel Foucault, 'The Order of Discourse' in Robert Young, ed., *Untying the Text: a Post-Structuralist Reader*, London 1981, p. 54.
37. Ibid.
38. Ibid.
39. *Power/Knowledge*, p. 133.
40. 'En attendant Guiffrey', in *Des dispositifs pulsionnels*, p. 226.
41. 'The Order of Discourse', p. 56.
42. *Économie Libidinale*, p. 289.
43. Ibid., p. 294.
44. Ibid., p. 291.
45. Ibid., p. 295.
46. Ibid., p. 296.
47. Ibid.
48. Ibid.
49. Ibid., p. 305.
50. *Language, Counter-Memory, Practice*, p. 161.
51. Jean-François Lyotard, 'Futilité en revolution', in *Rudiments païens*, Paris 1977, p. 160.
52. See Daniel Guérin, *Class Struggle in the First French Republic*, London 1977, pp. 137-54.
53. See 'Futilité en revolution', p. 180.
54. Ibid., p. 164.
55. Friedrich Nietzsche, *Thus Spoke Zarathustra*, trans. R.J. Hollingdale, Harmondsworth 1969, p. 131.
56. Jean-François Lyotard, 'Sur la force des faibles', in *L'Arc* 64, 1976 (special issue on Lyotard), p. 5.

57. *Rudiments païens*, pp. 229-30.
58. Nietzsche, *Human, All Too Human*, p. 12.
59. See *The Archaelogy of Knowledge*, p. 205.
60. Ibid., p. 207.
61. *Power/Knowledge*, p. 87.
62. Ibid., p. 83.
63. Ibid., p. 126.
64. *Language, Counter-Memory, Practice*, p. 208.
65. *Power/Knowledge*, p. 87.
66. Ibid., p. 64.
67. 'It seems to me that the possibility exists for fiction to function in truth, for a fictional discourse to induce effects of truth, and for bringing it about that a true discourse engenders or "manufactures" something that does not as yet exist, that it "fictions" it. One "fictions" history on the basis of a political reality that makes it true, one "fictions" a politics not yet in existence on the basis of historical truth.' *Power/Knowledge*, p. 193.
68. 'Apathie dans la théorie', in *Rudiments païens*, p. 23.
69. Ibid., p. 9.
70. Ibid., p. 29.
71. *Économie Libidinale*, p. 54; *Des dispositifs pulsionnels*, p. 227.
72. *Rudiments païens*, p. 116.
73. *Beyond Good and Evil*, p. 175.
74. *The Will to Power*, p. 267.
75. One of the earliest and clearest statements of this reversal of perspective was Guy Lardreau, 'L'Universel et la différence', in *La Nef*, vol. 38, no. 4, 1981.
76. Michel Foucault, 'Le souci de la vérité' (interview with François Ewald), in *Magazine Littéraire*, no. 207, May 1984, p. 18.
77. Ibid., p. 23.
78. Jean-François Lyotard and Jean-Loup Thébaud, *Just Gaming*, Manchester 1986, p. 90.
79. Ibid.
80. Ibid., p. 5.

Conclusion

1. 'Polemics, Politics and Problematizations: an Interview with Michel Foucault', in Paul Rabinow, ed., *The Foucault Reader*, Harmondsworth 1986, p. 381.
2. See ibid., p. 382-3.
3. See Jürgen Habermas, 'Wahrheitstheorien', in *Vorstudien und Ergänzungen zur Theorie des kommunikativen Handelns*, Frankfurt 1984, pp. 137-49, and 184-83.
4. Jürgen Habermas, *Der philosophische Diskurs der Moderne*, Frankfurt 1985, p. 378.
5. *Économie Libidinale*, p. 287.
6. See Jürgen Habermas, 'Vorbereitende Bemerkungen zu einer Theorie der kommunikativen Kompetenz', in Habermas and Niklas Luhmann, *Theorie der Gesellschaft oder Sozialtechnologie. Was leistet die Systemforschung?*, Frankfurt 1971, p. 135.
7. Albrecht Wellmer, 'Zur Kritik der Diskursethik', in *Ethik und Dialog*, Frankfurt 1986, p. 70.
8. Ibid., p. 93.
9. Ibid., p. 107.
10. See Albrecht Wellmer, 'Über Vernunft, Emanzipation und Utopie. Zur kommunikationstheoretischen Begründung einer kritischen Gesellschaftstheorie', in *Ethik und Dialog*, p. 208.

11. See Jürgen Habermas, 'Über Moralität und Sittlichkeit – Was macht eine Lebensform "rational"?', in Herbert Schnädelbach, ed., *Rationalität*, Frankfurt 1985, pp. 218-235; also my discussion in the 'Introduction' to Peter Dews, ed., *Habermas: Autonomy and Solidarity*, London 1986, pp. 17-22.

12. 'Zur Kritik der Diskursethik', p. 91.

13. Jürgen Habermas, *Zur Logik der Sozialwissenschaften*, Frankfurt 1970, p. 260.

14. Ibid.

15. Die Aktualität der Philosophie', p. 325.

16. See Theodor Adorno, 'Sociology and Psychology', *New Left Review* 47, p. 85. For a useful commentary on this process, see J.F. Schmucker, *Adorno – Logik des Zerfalls*, Stuttgart 1977, pp. 76-108.

17. *Negative Dialectics*, p. 5.

18. Albrecht Wellmer, 'Adorno, Anwalt des Nicht-Identischen', in *Zur Dialektik von Moderne und Postmoderne*, p. 156.

19. See Albrecht Wellmer, 'Zur Dialektik von Moderne und Postmoderne', in ibid., pp. 85-100. This section of the essay ('Zur Mteakritik der Kritik cer identitätslogischen Vernunft') is almost entirely omitted from the English translation: 'On the Dialectics of Modernism and Postmodernism', *Praxis International*, vol. 4, no. 4, 1985.

20. *Der philosophische Diskurs der Moderne*, p. 417.

21. See *Kritik der Macht*, pp. 97-111.

22. See Jessica Benjamin, 'Die Antinomien des patriarchalischen Denkens', in Wolfgang Bonss and Axel Honneth, eds., *Sozialforschung als Kritik*, Frankfurt 1982, pp. 426-55.

23. Richard Kearney, 'Dialogue with Jacques Derrida', in *Dialogues with Contemporary Continental Thinkers*, p. 114.

24. Jacques Derrida, 'Guter Wille zur Macht (I): Drei Fragen an Hans-Georg Gadamer', in Philippe Forget, ed., *Text und Interpretation*, Munich 1984, p. 58.

25. Jacques Derrida, 'Speculer – sur "Freud" ' in *La carte postale: de Socrate à Freud et au-delà*, p. 334.

26. Theodor Adorno, 'Meinung, Wahn, Gesellschaft', in *Eingriffe: Neun kritische Modelle*, Frankfurt 1963, p. 169.

27. Wolfgang Bonss, 'Empirie und Dechiffrierung von Wirklichkeit. Zur Methodologie bei Adorno', in Ludwig von Friedeburg and Jürgen Habermas, eds, *Adorno-Konferenz 1983*, Frankfurt 1983, p. 204.

28. Theodor Adorno, 'Introduction', in Adorno et al., *The Positivist Dispute in German Sociology*, London 1976, p. 12.

29. See, for example, 'The Ends of Man', in *Margins of Philosophy*, pp. 134-6.

30. I have discussed these complementary failings of Derrida and Lyotard in more detail in 'Adorno, Post-Structuralism, and the Critique of Identity', *New Left Review* 157, May-June 1986.

31. See Michel Foucault, 'On the Geneaology of Ethics: An Overview of Work in Progress', in *The Foucault Reader*.

32. Michel Foucault, 'The Subject and Power', *Critical Enquiry* 8, p. 785.

33. See, for example, Jean Baudrillard, *Simulacres et simulation*, Paris 1981.

34. See Frederic Jameson, 'Postmodernism, or the Cultural Logic of Late Capitalism', *New Left Review* 146, July-August 1984.

35. Ibid., p. 64.

36. See Helmut Dubiel, 'Die Aktualität der Gesellschaftstheorie Adornos', in *Adorno-Konferenz 1983*, pp. 303-5.

37. Daniel Bell, *The Cultural Contradictions of Capitalism*, London 1976, p. 84.

38. Joel Kovel, 'Narcissism and the Family' (contribution to a symposium on narcissism), *Telos* 44, Summer 1980, p. 86.

39. 'Die Antinomien des patriarchalischen Denkens', p. 448.

40.   See Herbert Marcuse, *Eros and Civilization*, London 1972, pp. 119-25.
41.   'Die Aktualität der Gesellschaftstheorie Adornos', p. 305.
42.   ES, p. 118.
43.   ES, p. 305.
44.   See, for example, E, p. 70.
45.   E, p. 688.
46.   ES, p. 26.
47.   ES, p. 29.
48.   Jürgen Habermas, *Theorie des kommunikativen Handelns*, vol. 2, p. 192.
49.   E, p. 351.
50.   *Séminaire I*, p. 264 (my emphasis).
51.   E, p. 409.
52.   Jürgen Habermas, 'Sprachspiel, Intention und Bedeutung. Zu Motiven bei Sellars und Wittgenstein', in R.W. Wiggershaus, ed., *Sprachanalyse und Soziologie*, Frankfurt 1971, p. 336-7.
53.   See ibid., p. 337.
54.   See Jürgen Habermas, 'Was heisst Universalpragmatik?', in *Vorstudien und Ergänzungen zur Theorie des kommunikativen Handelns*, pp. 407-8.
55.   ES, p. 80.
56.   'Sprachspiel, Intention und Bedeutung', p. 334.
57.   Jürgen Habermas, 'On Systematically Distorted Communication', in Paul Connerton, ed., *Critical Sociology: Selected Readings*, Harmondsworth 1976, p. 355.
58.   ES, p. 2. In the next paragraph Lacan repeats the point: the mirror stage 'situates the agency of the ego, *before its social determination*, in a fictional direction . . . ' (my emphasis).
59.   *Der philosophische Diskurs der Moderne*, p. 347.
60.   See D.W. Winnicott, 'Mirror-role of Mother and Family in Child Development', in *Playing and Reality*, Harmondsworth 1980.

Index

NOTE: Emboldened page references indicate chapters on subject